FUSANG

FUSANG

THE CHINESE

WHO BUILT AMERICA

By STAN STEINER

HARPER COLOPHON BOOKS

HARPER & ROW, PUBLISHERS

NEW YORK, CAMBRIDGE, HAGERSTOWN, PHILADELPHIA, SAN FRANCISCO

LONDON, MEXICO CITY, SÃO PAULO, SYDNEY

"The Ancient Mariners" has appeared in *Natural History Magazine.*

A hardcover edition of this book is published by Harper & Row, Publishers.

First HARPER COLOPHON edition published 1980.

ISBN: 0-06-090750-9

80 81 82 83 84 10 9 8 7 6 5 4 3 2 1

CONTENTS

BOOK THREE

The Chinese Who Became America

*Dedicated to my longtime editor
and longtime friend, Jeannette Hopkins*

PROLOGUE

THE RULER of the Southernand the Ruler of the Northern (Sudden) and the Ruler of the Center was Chaos. Shu and Hu often visited the land of Chaos, where they were treated very well. They wished to repay this kindness, and they said: "Men have seven orifices for the purposes of seeing, hearing, eating, breathing, and necessary things, but the Ruler of Chaos has only one orifice. Let us make seven orifices for him." And so every day they dug an orifice in him, and at the end of seven days, he died. . . .

It is said this story was written by Chang Tsu, who lived from the year 660 to 740 in the Sung dynasty. But it was written long before he had written it. Some say it comes from the Han dynasty, or even before the beginnings of written history.

For it is an old, old story with an old, old moral:

No one can say what another human should be. If one human being tries to make other human beings into his own image, he shall surely kill them. This is true even of gods.

And it is true, as well, of people in a book, who are made of paper and words. Maybe more so. When a writer describes people and tells their story, if that writer re-creates them in his or her own image, the story may be successful, but the people may not survive, except as shadows of the writer's ego.

Many books about the Chinese people seem to have been written in this way. The authors "dug holes" in the people, presumably to see inside them and make them understandable to the Western reader by their own, not by the people's, images and expressions.

These writers seem to suffer a "bitter disappointment that the Chinese do not turn out to be as we thought and indeed intended them to be," as Nancy and David Milton, compilers of the *Chinese Reader*, Volume VI, have said.

And that is why I have attempted to write this book from the thoughts and words of the people themselves, as they have seen themselves. These feelings and emotions, as expressed in the songs, in the dress, in the art, in the manners, in the myths of the people, have guided me. Whenever possible. Not that this book attempts to speak for the Chinese people—it does not. It does not have to. They can speak brilliantly and eloquently for themselves, whenever and however they wish to.

Fusang is a book about the Chinese who discovered America, who built America, and who became America. It is a book about heroes. Those bold, adventurous, undaunted, strong-willed, ingenuous, tough, persevering, and crazy men and women were the founding fathers and mothers of the American West, and their sacrifice and daring created much of the physical wealth and the noble ideas upon which the nation's strengths have rested ever since. Many of the historic feats that we celebrate owe an unacknowledged debt to the pioneers and frontiersmen and -women from China that neither this book nor any other can begin to repay.

So this is a book about heroes, old-fashioned heroes. It is not a book about a "minority" or an "ethnic" group. Nor is it about their "contribution" to the "mainstream" of American life. For one thing, in the beginning of the West the "minorities" were the majority. And for another, the Chinese *were* the "mainstream" of American life.

If the stories in this book seem strange to the reader, it is only because they have not been known. The mysteries of history are mysterious only to those who are ignorant of them. Even so, it is not the readers who are at fault here; it is history's ignorance that has denied to our country its own founding fathers and mothers.

Long ago, in the days of the Gold Rush, a venomous newspaper in California, the *Post*, prophesied; "The silence of the grave would be all that would tell of the Chinamen's existence here."

One of the reasons I have written this book is to break that silence—to tell the untold tales of hidden history because it is time to tell them and because they are wondrous to tell. Maybe I can better explain why I have written this book by telling one more old story, a story so old that it has no beginning and an end that has been modernized.

It was told by Chang Shih-chieh in the *Journal of Folk Literature*, published in Peking in December 1959. And it goes like this:

An old fisherman earns his living by fishing at the Dragon River. One day he sees in the rolling waves a white jade fish jar, which he procures at the risk of his life. An engraving on the jar shows a tiny fisher boy. This fisher boy comes to life and grows; with his fishing rod, he hooks the fish engraved on the bottom of the jar, which also becomes alive. As the fisher boy lifts up the rod, the fish splashes on the water. The splash scatters water in all directions, and the water falls in golden drops. When the fisher boy stops angling and returns onto the jar, a spray of gold beans lies all around.

The old fisherman picks up a handful of the gold beans and heads for the market. Just as he takes out the gold beans to make a purchase, a foreign missionary swaggers by, sees the beans, and questions him. The honest old fisherman tells the missionary all that has happened. Next day the fisherman is brought to the courthouse and accused of having stolen a fish jar from the missionary. After questioning the fisherman, the mandarin decides that the missionary should possess the jar. The old man is so incensed that he falls into a faint and breaks the jar. The fisher boy comes back to life, hooks the upper jaw of the missionary, and tosses him up in the air. The mandarin dies of fright. . . .

Sometimes I think that I am that old fisherman. But sometimes I think I am the fisher boy. One thing is certain. This book is that jade jar.

BOOK ONE

The Chinese

Who Discovered

America

I

THE VOYAGE TO THE LAND
OF FUSANG IN 441 A.D.

Where the sun rises
In the land of Fu Sang
There is my home.
Seeking fame and riches
I came to the land
Of the eternal flowers.   —ANONYMOUS

And this Fu Sang, the Oriental garden of the Hesperides, this
Atlantis of the East, the home of fairies, is our own fair California.
                                                —LOS ANGELES *Times*

ON A BOLD VOYAGE in the fifth century, several Buddhist missionaries may have landed on the shores of America by mistake.

"In the year of Yung yuan during the Ch'i dynasty [in 499
A.D.] a priest by the name of Hui shen came to Ching chou.
He told of the Kingdom of Fusang [America?] that was 20,000
li [about 7,000 miles] to the east of Tahan. And that country
was to the east of China." So it was written in the Forty-first
Book of Chüan, in the two hundred and thirtieth volume of
the *Great Chinese Encyclopedia,* compiled by court historians
of the Liang emperors from 502 to 556 A.D.

Fusang was a strange land, said Hui shen. But it was not
barbarian; he talked of the people there as being remarkably
human and civilized, considering that they were not Chinese.

"They have neither arms, nor armor," said the priest. "Nor
do they make war." Since they were peaceful, for the most part,

"they have no walled towns," as in China, but seemed to live in harmony with one another.

"They possess a mode of writing and make paper from the bark of the Fusang [tree]," he said. And from the bark they also made their clothing. Surely an industrious people.

In this land of Fusang, he said, the people had domesticated a breed of cattle "with very long horns"—most likely deer. They used these cattle, or deer, as beasts of burden, and they milked them to make "a food drink from their milk"—possibly yogurt.

Still, they did have a few uncivilized customs. One of these, Hui shen said, was the power given to the women of Fusang. In marriage it was the bride who chose the husband: "If the woman does not accept him, he is sent away, but if he pleases her the marriage is consummated," the perplexed priest observed.

No wonder in later chronicles the kingdom of Fusang was sometimes confused with the land disparagingly known as "The Country of Women." The modern Chinese man of the fifth century knew there could be no land where women "chose" men.

In spite of this dubious feminism, the men of Fusang seemed happy. For it was a land of abundant liberty and freedom, said Hui shen, where there were not only no wars, but, unbelievably, "there are no taxes."

More than one thousand years were to pass before Europeans heard of the Chinese discovery of this paradisiacal place. Even then, few believed it.

In 1716, a French scholar by the name of M. de Guignes announced that he had found and translated an ancient document telling of the voyage of Hui shen. His revelations were published by the Académie de Belles Lettres in Paris, under the title: *"Recherches sur les navigations des Chinois du côte de l'Amérique."* And they startled Europe. They still do.

"America discovered nine hundred years before Columbus, and by *Chinese!*" an unbelieving scholar was later to exclaim. "It surpassed all belief." The world "of science was stupefied," proclaimed another.

Few believed it possible. And fewer could imagine that the Chinese had a knowledge of the sea and ships, or a science of navigation, sufficient to enable them to sail so far into the unknown.

There were some scholars who were believers, but they were laughed at as romantics. One of these was a celebrated sinologist of Germany, Karl Frederick Neumann, who traced the voyage of Hui shen in his imagination and decided the kingdom of Fusang not only existed but was in Mexico, somewhere near Acapulco. And that was also the conclusion of the iconoclastic parochial scholar Edward Payson Vining, in his Jules Verneian history of Hui shen's adventure, *The Inglorious Columbus.*

And yet the scholarly encyclopedia of the voyage compiled by Vining in 1885 did little to resolve the debate. If anything, it offered scholars more things to debate about.

The magnificently esoteric and obtuse work by Vining was a study of not one, but eight translations of Hui shen's texts and of those related to it, no matter how vaguely, in which every note, reference, phrase, and word was subjected to detailed analysis for nearly eight hundred pages. The scholarship of Vining has been compared to that of cabalists who devote a lifetime to understanding the meanings of the commas in the Scriptures.

Envisioning the voyage as realistically as he could, Vining declared that Hui shen had sailed or drifted across the Pacific on the sweeping currents of the northern seas. He came by way of the Kurile and Aleutian islands, then down the coasts of Alaska and aboriginal America, landing at last on the shores of Mexico. For millennia boats have sailed or drifted across the seas in this way. The great current is relentless. Even now it flows inexplicably on, its course unaltered by time.

To many scholars in Europe and America, the stories of Chinese explorers are nonetheless not history. Rather, they are fairy tales of fantastical voyages that took place in the dreams of Hui shen. He was a Chinese Don Quixote, at best, and at worst his story was "erroneous" and mere "exaggeration," a historian has said. He was, that is, no more than a splendid liar.

In reality, this fabulous kingdom of Fusang was most probably a barren, primitive island off the coast of Japan, and the people Hui shen described of the Ainu tribe, whose way of life was remarkably like the supposed people of Fusang. No! no! intoned still other scholars; Fusang was really the island of Sakhalin, off Siberia—a belief held by the renowned Professor Gustave Schlegel of the University of Leiden. Ridiculous! retorted some less adventurous scholars; it was an island merely a few miles off the coast of China; a Chinese Columbus, indeed!

From time to time in recent years the debates have been revived. It seems as if each time the kingdom of Fusang recedes further into obscurity and the voyage of Hui shen becomes more mythological. One historian, writing in the *California Historical Quarterly* ("Did the Chinese Discover America?" by D. C. Watson, 1936), flatly declared "authorities are almost unanimous" in denying any Chinese discoveries. Such tall tales, he said, are now met with a "smile of derision."

Poor Hui shen!

Still, the account of Hui shen's voyage remains inscribed in the *Great Chinese Encyclopedia*. The doubts of the scholars have not erased his fascinating descriptions of the kingdom of Fusang, nor have they dimmed the sense of wonder his words still evoke.

One of the few modern historians who has sought to record

the voyages of these fantastic seamen was Charles Chapman, who devoted a fascinating chapter in *A History of California* to "The Chinese Along The Pacific Coast in Ancient Times." The early explorers from China, he wrote, not only crossed the ocean, as did Hui shen, but left their mark on the native American cultures. And so, there are similarities between "the old Mexican religion [and] early Buddhism [that] are many and striking." There are similarities as well in rituals, in sculpture, and in language which Chapman attributed to the adventurous voyages of the seafarers from South China, who reached the Americas long before the Europeans.

These Chinese explorers may have been here to greet the Spanish Conquistadores, thought the maritime historian, Maurice Holmes, a retired Marine Corps general who was not enamored of romantic tales of the sea. In the archives of the Naval Museum in Madrid he discovered documents of the Coleccion Navarrette, a *California historia y viajes*, that told of exotic ships with figureheads of golden pelicans which were sighted by a company of Coronado's expedition at the mouth of the Colorado River in 1540. These men, thought Holmes, were most likely Chinese, and what "lured the Orientals" into the Gulf of California may have been the mines that the Spaniards found them working in along the coast.

Not only that, but in 1573 the Spanish archives told of a Franciscan friar, Juan de Luco, who sighted "eight sail" of strange ships off the western coasts of Mexico, at Tepic. These, too, it was believed, may have been signs of the familiarity of the explorers from China with the waters of the Americas.

In modern times, as the world converged on China and China withdrew from the world, there were fewer sightings of real or imaginary ships from the Orient. But, though these seafarers were confined to waters nearer to the shores of China, their skills and seamanship did not necessarily atrophy. When the Yankee Clippers opened trade with China in the nineteenth century, the practical New England captains soon learned that the seamen of China had lost none of their daring and expertise. And by the late nineteenth century most of the sailors on American ships in the Pacific were Chinese. On the largest ships that were the pride of the American merchant fleet from 1876 to 1906 there were 80,523 Chinese seamen, and, typically, on the renowned *Oceanic*, two thirds of the crew was Chinese.

No one was more capable in seamanship than the Chinese, said a famed Yankee captain. They were "a race of seamen" declared an English maritime historian, G. R. Worchester, in his *Sail and Sampan in China;* their "skill and resourcefulness is second to none in the world."

If the Chinese coming to America was a fantasy, it was a realistic fantasy. The life that Hui shen told of was as vivid and human as any tale of the European explorers, with their wild stories of native men with blue skins and long tails, and native women who were virgin as Eve and as evil as witches. The paradise of the Chinese travelers was not only more realistic, it existed—somewhere.

As a Buddhist priest, Hui shen was content with his perfect kingdom. He talked admiringly of the peaceful lands he had discovered, where the people lived so morally and so purely that, he noted with awe, "neither gold nor silver is esteemed" in Fusang.

There was only one thing wrong with these people. "They know not the laws of the Buddha," he said.

So it was that "in the second year of the dynasty of the Sung [458 A.D.] five *bhikshu* [mendicant monks] came to this country from the land of Chi' Pin [Kabul or Cophene]," said Hui shen, and they "spread the sacred books and images of Buddha to instruct the people in the holy ascetic life." And this "made a change in the customs of the people." The people became Buddhists.

On reading these words of Hui shen I remembered something that the Navajo tribal matriarch Anne Wauneka once said to me years ago. "If those Chinese discovered America," she said, "we Indians would go to Buddhist temples instead of Christian churches." And then she laughed in that special way she laughed.

And I wondered then, as I wonder now, why she said that.

II

WHEN CHINA DISCOVERED THE WEST

> . . . We did not discover China; on the contrary, China discovered us . . . —JOSEPH NEEDHAM, Cambridge University

> The Westerners have shriveled the history of the world when they grouped around the Hebrews, Greeks, and Romans the little they knew of the exploration of the human race, being completely ignorant of those voyagers who plowed the China Sea and traveled the ancient caravan routes.
> —HENRI CORDIER, *Historie General de la China*

IN THE SECOND CENTURY B.C., the Emperor Wu Ti sent an ambassador, Chang ch'ien, on a mission of peace into the wilderness of the West to subdue those barbarians who, it was said, had large noses and mated with wild monkeys. Chang ch'ien discovered these strange people were not as primitive as was first thought.

The emperor of the Han dynasty had been troubled by the warriors of the tribes of the Hsiung-hu, the ancestors of the Huns. These tribes had been pillaging the caravans of the traders from the courts of the emperor. The diplomatic mission of Chang ch'ien was to seek out friendly tribes to defeat the Hsiung-hu so that the flow of commerce, the nectar of court civilization, might be restored.

On this journey of exploration Chang ch'ien was gone for twelve years. Some historians have said that he may have traveled twenty thousand miles or more. Chang ch'ien, to be honest, lost his way—and thereby discovered a new world, as have so many explorers before him and after. He wandered into the empire of Alexander the Great. And so he found that exotic and mysterious land known in China as the West.

Many centuries before, the nomadic traders of the steppes had told of the long-nosed people. The caravan drivers and merchants of the deserts, who had sold the silk of China to the long-noses, spoke of them too. None of the nomads were, however, ambassadors of the emperor, and so the tales they told were not to be wholly believed. Thus it was that the official honor of discovering Europe was to be given to Chang ch'ien.

The discovery of Chang ch'ien was, however, not recognized in Europe. For there seems to have been no mention of it in any of the Greek or Roman texts of the time. And for two thousand years after, Europe seemed ignorant of this momentous event in its history.

Not until recently, as the distinguished English historian of Chinese science Joseph Needham has observed, was it recognized that "Europe was discovered by the Chinese, and not China by Europe, as we like to think." There had been a geographic gap between East and West. And "the bridging of this gap was accomplished not from the west, but from the east . . . by the Chinese," affirmed Oxford University's G. F. Hudson: "It was the Chinese who, first by exploring diplomacy and then by force of arms, broke through."

Once begun, the Chinese explorations of the West increased, year after year. When ancient Europe began to decline and had plunged feudally into "what are generally known as the Dark Ages," Needham said, "there were no Dark Ages in China." So the Chinese explorers who traveled to the West were impressed by European wealth but were dismayed by European barbarism and backwardness, even as Chang ch'ien had been in the second century B.C.

It was a splendorous and rich world he came to, Chang ch'ien wrote of his travels to the borders of the Greek, Persian, and Indian empires, but the people were barbarians!

There were great cities of untold wealth and vast marketplaces, beyond any rationality. And yet the people often lacked the simplest necessities of civilization. Some of the barbarians of the West did not even have a written language. Nor did they know how to raise and weave silk. Instead they wore clothes unfit for horses. And they were content to eat from dishes and bowls made of earth and mud, knowing little of porcelain, or of jade, or of lacquer. Strangest of all, they seemed to live without human harmony or celestial order. There were some who were so uncivilized they had no rulers.

One thing these barbarians did have that Chang ch'ien thought would please the emperor were their miraculous horses "that sweat blood," a breed so powerful that the warriors who rode them seemed to "shoot from horseback." Surely these were the "heavenly horses" mentioned in the Book of Changes, the *I Ching*, as the "divine horses due to appear from the west." As Chang ch'ien had thought, the emperor became determined to possess these horses.

Ssu-ma chien, the historian of antiquity, was later to write disdainfully of the emperor's equestrian view of history. The imperial trade with the West was largely begun, he said, because "the Son of Heaven greatly loved horses."

In any event, on his return from the borders of Europe, Chang ch'ien advised the emperor to forget about war and think of commerce. Barbarians of the West were ignorant of so many of the necessities of civilization they would become excellent customers for whatever they were sent.

The emperor was delighted. He sent forth many caravans of missionaries and traders to educate the barbarians, not by teaching the Chinese ways, but by selling them Chinese merchandise.

In spite of his conquest of the Hsiung-hu, the emperor's aim was not the conquest of the Hsiung-hu; he could see far beyond, across the steppes and mountains of Asia, to the marketplaces of the Mediterranean and Caspian seas, and he wished "to keep in touch with the lands to the west," thought Ssu-ma chien. For "this reason embassies set out, one after another, on the road to that country."

Some of these "embassies" were composed of caravans of several hundred men—traders and diplomats, poets and soldiers. As many as ten caravans were sent west every year. They traveled so far from China that some did not return for "eight to nine years," and some never returned.

And this, it has been said, was the beginning of the "Silk Road" on which China emerged from its isolation. But it was not so. The envoy of the Emperor Wu ti was not the first traveler on these trade routes to the West. He was not even the pioneer. He was like a Chinese Columbus, who, like his European counterpart, was celebrated for the wrong reason and for going to the wrong place.

In the footsteps of Chang ch'ien there came many travelers. There was Fa hsien, a Buddhist monk, who in the last year of the fourth century A.D. set out across the Gobi deserts and the Hindu Kush to bring sacred Buddhist prayers back to China. He traveled for fourteen years through countries not "originally inhabited by human beings, but only by devils and dragons with whom the merchants of neighboring countries traded by bartering." There was Hsuan tsang, an equally adventurous monk, who in the sixth century went west "to ask the wise men on points that were troubling his mind." He learned, among many things, that the "moon has many names."

These men traveled the same paths and trails that nomads and traders had for thousands of years before them. And they differed from their tribal predecessors mainly in that they wrote of their travels. It was their words, not their deeds, that distinguished them. It was with wonder and naiveté that Chang chien told of meeting the caravans of tribesmen and women whom he described as barbarians; but it was they, not he, who knew the ancient trade routes and knew the civilizations of both east and west. And it was they who taught him the way.

From the nomads of Stone Age Asia he learned not one, but three distinct trade routes to the West. He was shown the swiftest and safest road so that he was able to advise others, much as the explorers Lewis and Clark were guided by the native tribes of America and so could mark the trail for the pioneers who came after.

The shepherds and the hunters of the nomadic tribes had been traveling across the continents for more years than anyone knew. And they had, for millennia, been exploring and developing these trails and trade roads through mountain passes and impassable deserts. It was they who forged the path out of the wilderness upon which humans escaped from their narrow, self-centered caves. The older civilizations of the ancient worlds were, the bolder were their explorations of discovery. And the civilization of China was one of the oldest and boldest.

In the Paleolithic era the evidence of Chinese tools and seashells that traveled halfway around the world has just begun to be unearthed. One such shell, a sacred cowrie, from either China or India, has been discovered in a Stone Age cave on the Côte d'Azur in France, near Cannes.

Even before these beginnings of known history, as long as one hundred thousand years ago, whole families of Neanderthal men and women were known to have ranged over many thousands of square miles. The caves of these earliest explorers, studied by archaeologists such as the famous Carlton Coon, and Joseph Birdsell (in his *Man, The Hunter*), have revealed the vast distances these worldly ancients traveled. The archaeologist James Skinner once estimated that one Neanderthal group he studied ranged over fourteen thousand square miles.

The antiquity of these ancient trails is beyond contemporary vision. Perhaps our vision is limited by our modern myths about the past. And yet there ought to be little surprise at the finding of Chinese tools in a cave in the mountains of Siberia, near the borders of European Russia. These mountains were six thousand miles from China; the tools were five thousand years old.

On the Orkhon River, in Mongolia, lie the ruins of the old capital of Karakorum, the site of the fabled pleasure domes of the great khan Ugedei, son of Chingis (Genghis). Not too far from there is a paleolithic burial and camp site said to be perhaps as old as the Peking man. Here the Soviet archaeologist A. P. Okladnikov discovered stone tools that he mused "you could slip onto a shelf in a museum in France, and the curator would not be able to swear they were not local finds."

The Soviet archaeologist would not speculate on whether the similarity of stone tools in France and Mongolia, was due to contact between these faraway people or simply meant that the toolmakers had developed similar skills. But the sinologist Owen Lattimore, who visited this site, was less hesitant. "Primitive man," said Lattimore, "ranged the whole world." And of all the Paleolithic world travelers, "the Chinese of pre-history were among the earliest explorers of Asia." They "spread from their home in the great valley of the Yellow River to discover and occupy territories to the south and west, and to discover others, to the west and north, through wars and trade.

"From the archaeological record it is clear that other men of Asia also began to 'discover Asia' very early," Lattimore said. "There was movement not only of trade goods, but of the people themselves."

Though much has been written of the migrations of the ancient people, little has been written of their explorations. And few have given much thought to how these travels may have changed people, opened their minds to new worlds, forced the learning of new skills necessary for survival in unfamiliar territory and, perhaps, even marked the beginnings of modern science and technologies. For the world of exploration was necessarily the world of experience and knowledge.

These Marco Polos of China in prehistory, C. G. F. Simkin wrote in his *The Traditional Trade of Asia,* became "partners and connecting links" between ancient civilizations. "Nomads, so far from being barbarians, had an economic organization of some complexity," he said; for they "bartered with one another, especially in gold, copper and tin, during the Bronze Age, and in iron, later." They had to be knowledgeable in the earth sciences. They had to be knowledgeable as well in astronomy and geography to build caravan routes "developed over considerable distances, linking urban civilizations not only with adjoining pastoral tribes, but with far distant urban civilizations."

The nomadic tribes, because of the need for beasts of burden on the caravan trails they developed, became experts in the domestication of wild cattle and oxen, camels and horses. In this sense those dashing horsemen of Chingis (Genghis) Khan did not ride forth out of myth, but rode forth out of millennia of horsemanship learned on weary, monotonous, arduous, endless caravans of wise-eyed traders.

No one will ever know how many thousands of years before the mythic dynasty of the Shang, beginning in 1523 B.C., these nomads first traded the exquisite works of tribal Chinese artistry across the steppes of Asia. The silk, lacquers, ceramics, jades, and bronzes of ancestral China were sought by merchants in every neighboring land. And so many caravans came to China that it is said the legendary emperors believed that it was merely necessary to keep the trade routes open and the entire world would come to them.

And yet trade is never a one-way traffic. The culture of China benefited greatly from the ideas and products it obtained in trade. From the Persian empire, under the reign of Darius, came the seeds of wheat, and from India came the water buffalo and domesticated fowl, while from Southeast Asia came grains of rice, unknown in China until then as a cultivated crop.

Many of the historians of the West have long found it difficult to contemplate, much less to encompass, the vast panorama of exploration and commerce that was created in early China. The ancients' history was too full of myth and legend. And these tales were so vague that even those who knew them did not know their meaning. Nor were the bone markings and cave scratches that the archaeologists were so fond of much more precise. Even the written history was suspect.

In despair, the historian C. P. Fitzgerald, in *The History of China*, lamented that it was too difficult "to distinguish between the full and authentic history of the last two thousand years and the sketchy and purely imaginary 'records' of an earlier age." From the depth of his quandary, he concluded ". . . there is little evidence that the Chinese had any contact with distant foreign people or knew of their existence before the second century B.C."

The ancient historians of Babylon, Egypt, and Greece knew better. In the geographers' works of that time, it is true, there was often confusion and uncertainty concerning the exact nature and location of China. But its wonders were known as myth and accepted as magic.

If anything, the mysteries that clothed China in ancient writing may have been a way of guarding oneself against its miraculous power.

The Romans, whose imperial trade with China was well established, guardedly called it the Unknown Land; as if the Caesars had never sent envoys and merchants to the court of the Celestial Emperor of the Middle Kingdom. In the East, where the sun rose, there had to be a land of sacred mystery. It may be that the historians preferred to keep it that way. The Babylonian and Egyptian writings that it is thought may refer to China seem to be deliberately vague and abstract, as if discussing a holy subject that is not to be discussed.

The historians of Greece were more precise, but no more exact. Some say that Herodotus, in the fifth century B.C. during his travels to southern Russia amongst the traders of the Asian steppes, heard firsthand tales of the Chinese, whom he called Hyberboreans. But even Herodotus, in that mannerism of modesty that historians have imitated ever since, cited as a reference for his own opinions a historian, Aristeas, who lived several centuries before he did and whose works had been conveniently lost.

By the era of the Caesars, the knowledge of China was too widespread for fears. Ptolemy, in his *Geography,* had enough information so that he could attempt an exact, though not quite accurate, description of China's location on the map.

Pliny, the Elder, in his *Natural History*, writing in the first century A.D., had already spoken of these Seres "who dwell beyond the mountains of Edodus [Himalayas]." In Rome the Latin word for silks, *seres,* became synonymous with the word for China; and this was so noted in the writings of Virgil and Horace. They became "known to us by the commerce that is carried on with them," Pliny explained. By then the Chinese were well enough known to the Romans for Pliny to describe the voices of their merchants. They had "hoarse voices," he said.

The Roman desire to be realistic in describing China was a practical necessity born of the silk trade. A merchant could not afford to be romantic about commerce.

Still, the Europeans' myths persisted. Late into the fourth century A.D., the historian Ammianus Marcellinus insisted that China was paradise, a land of heavenly bliss. He portrayed the Chinese as a people of "sedate and peaceful temper" who "trouble none of their neighbors." They had no weapons. They fought no wars. And more wonderous still, their sublime climate was so perfect that there were no clouds in the Chinese skies. Not only that, but the blessings of Chinese luxuries clothed the Romans. "The use of silk, which was once confined to the nobility, is now spread to all classes, without distinction, even to the lowest," Marcellinus rhapsodized.

Not all of the Romans were enamored with the silks of China. Some thought of them as obscene, a hedonistic fabric that was immoral and un-Roman.

Seneca lamented: "I see silken clothes, if you can call them clothes at all, that in no degree afford protection either to the body or the modesty of the wearer. And clad in this silk no woman could honestly say she is not naked." He seemed especially upset by Romans who had begun to wear silk lingerie under their togas. If Pliny believed the silk trade was based upon "lust for gain," then Seneca believed it was based on lust, alone.

On one thing the Romans seemed agreed: These Chinese were remarkable traders and merchants. They bargained "by their eyes alone," said Marcellinus, so they finished a deal before the Roman could begin. "And so free are they from wants that, though ready to sell their own merchandise, they need purchase none from abroad."

So great was this Roman trade with China and so one-sided that it soon became a "drain on our empire," complained Pliny. The cost, he estimated, equaled "one hundred million sesterces a year," in a deficit balance of trade.

"That is the price that our luxuries and our womankind cost us!" he raged.

And while the Roman men fumed about the decadent extravagances of their women, the Chinese congratulated their merchants on their business acumen. The royal treasuries of the emperors filled with gold—so much so that Chang ch'ien, the Marco Polo of China who traveled to the West more than fifteen hundred years before the Marco Polo of Europe traveled to the East, became famous not for his discovery of the barbarians of the West, but for making it possible for these barbarians to discover China.

In the *Shih Chi* of the historian Ssu-ma chien it was written that after the journey of Chang ch'ien to the lands of the barbarians the world changed: "All the barbarians of the West stretched their necks to catch a glimpse of China."

III

THE ANCIENT MARINERS

And how did the rivers and streams come by their kingship over the lesser streams? It was by being lower than the streams that they came by their kingship.

—TAI TI CHING, *Canon of Virtue of the Tao*

. . . the sea comes to an end somewhere in China . . .

—ANONYMOUS ROMAN AUTHOR, 100 A.D.

There was a father who had two sons. He was a merchant. So were they. Whenever he sailed across the seas to trade in far-off countries, he would ask his sons to accompany him. On one of these voyages their ship was engulfed in a terrible storm; it was tossed so violently by the waves that the father and his sons feared that they soon would be drowned.

But the youngest daughter of the family rescued them.

She was merely seven years old, but she already possessed supernatural powers. The little girl sensed her father and brothers were in frightening danger. And so her soul left her body and flew over the turbulent waves to the sinking ship. Her soul flew like a bird, sweeping down from the sky, and with a single thrust she grasped her brothers, one in each fist, and her father in her mouth, and flew away to safety.

When the little girl's soul had left her body in her father's house, her physical being became empty and limp. Her mother, on seeing this, began to comfort and fondle her child's cold limbs.

"Are you all right?" her mother asked.

"Yes," the little girl said.

But when she opened her mouth to say yes to her mother, her father fell out of her mouth. His body dropped into the stormy seas, and he drowned.

"You," the little girl angrily told her mother, "are to blame for the death of my father!"

In sorrow, she told her mother how her soul had flown out to sea to rescue her father and her brothers on the sinking ship, and how she had saved their lives. But because her mother had been so worried about her physical being, the little girl had opened her mouth to comfort her, and by doing that her father had fallen from her lips into the seas and died.

"Is it really true?" her mother asked her.

"Look, my hair is still moist from the sea," the little girl said. And seeing this, the mother wept.

Compassion filled the heart of the little girl. In a moment, her anger left her; for she grieved for the sorrow of her widowed mother. She took an oath never to marry. And until her mother died, the youngest daughter cared for her. She was as selfless as a daughter should be.

She became an immortal. She was known by the name T'ien hou, the goddess of the sea, protector of ships and seamen on all the oceans of the earth and the rivers of China.

And, it was said, she even became an Empress of Heaven.

THAT IS WHY all along the Fukien coast of China one of the sacred and most popular of deities has been T'ien hou. Her cult spread throughout southern China. Her worshipers carried her image across the Pacific onto the shores of America. And they built temples for T'ien hou in many of the Chinatowns of California.

Some of the writings celebrating the powers of the goddess of the sea are known to date from the tenth century A.D. There are some writers who trace her origin to the third century B.C., to the river goddess of Wushan, as did Sung yu. In *Fu of the*

Goddess, he told of the dreams of the Emperor Hsiang of the Chao dynasty (298–64 B.C.), in which she is described as the source of the rain and mist. It is likely that her deification is much older. The antiquity of her worship is most probably as old as the earliest fishermen and seamen of tribal China, who sailed the rivers and seas before the beginning of written history.

And if so, who was T'ien hou? Where did she come from? Why was she so powerful?

On a sacred tablet in the Temple of T'ien hou in the village of Foshan, the seamen's pragmatic faith in the divine goddess is put in this way: "As the ancients said: In the age of perfect government, the spirits become unnecessary." But at sea "when the Way of Man fails to do right, the spirits and the gods come into the light."

It may be that she was a mythic sister of the great goddess of the seafaring Pelasgians of pre-Grecian tribalism, or the daughter of the mother goddess of the ancestors of Phoenician seamen whom the Egyptians called People of the Sea, known to the Roman Apuleius in the *Golden Ass* as having "risen from the midst of the sea" to guide "the seas' winds," and whose "true name" was Isis. The worship of these goddesses may be as ageless as the fears of the first tribal seamen and seawomen who needed guidance upon the unknown seas.

Even older, her lineage may be in the darker beginnings of the sea, going back to the earliest worship of water. In the Shang dynasty there was believed to be a god of Ho, or the Yellow River, who lived like a drowned man beneath the water. At every time of flood and storm, he was calmed by the gift of a young girl, who upon a raft for a bridal bed was given in marriage to the water god. In his palace of fish scales and cowrie shells, she became goddess of the river, while on the shore, 3,500 years ago, the people sang her wedding song:

> Oh, you mount a white turtle!
>   Your robe is a stripped fish!
> Oh, I wander at your side
>   in the corridors of Ho!
> Oh, we combine our hands
>   as we travel to the East!
> Oh, waves in steady surges
>   come to welcome us!

The symbol of the dragon as a giver of life is common to many people, but vital to the Chinese. And what is a dragon but a great fish with feet—a serpent with wings? In China, this awesome and powerful creature was not a bringer of knowledge and evil, as it was in the Garden of Eden in the West; it brought fertility and abundance, which were knowledge and wealth. It was a magical fish that created human progeny: the legendary father of Heaven of the legendary emperors.

In the oldest of the older legends, the heavenly dragon was often said to be a woman, a young woman. She at times was seen as an innocent girl, the forsaken virgin, or the abandoned bride at the altar who went forth, as a dragon, to bring her lover back from the seas. It might be that T'ien hou, the goddess of the sea, was the daughter of that dragon.

The origin of Chinese civilization may owe more to the importance of fishing on its rivers and its seas than has been recognized. Fish were an essential food of the nuclear civilization of northern China, wrote Kwang Chin Chang in *The Archaeology of Ancient China*. Some authorities on early Chinese history have come to believe, he said, that "the birthplace of farmers and herders" in ancient China was in that cradle of land at the confluence of the northern rivers, the "habitat for the sedentary waterside fishermen" of neolithic times. Here was the origin of the "distinctive pattern," Kwang wrote, of the Chinese civilization's "independence and originality."

Fishing may well have provided an easier and more accessible source of food than hunting to ancient peoples. The long coasts and longer rivers of China offered a natural reservoir of fish that was self-renewing and inexhaustible. Both in the folklore of the ancient fishermen and in the scientific lore of modern archaeologists there is evidence of the importance of fishing not only for the survival of the people, but in the creation of their character.

Some of the caves of the Yang Shao civilization in Hunan province have been found filled with towering heaps of fishbones. These ceremonial and culinary mounds date to 3000 B.C., and before.

And on the banks of the Yellow River and its many tributaries, fishing was a highly skilled neolithic industry, the source of myth and food. The fish has a symbolic significance in early Chinese history that is extraordinary.

So it was from the beginning of history, and so it is.

"In subsequent centuries, down to the modern period, stories of the miracles of T'ien hou continued to be told by sailors returning from dangerous voyages up and down the China coast," C. K. Yang wrote in *Religion in Chinese Society*. The Chinese seamen were "among the most adventurous and self-confident" of explorers, said Yang; but their belief in the "magical practices" of their goddess of the sea was so old that it began long before the "dawn of history."

The scholar of ancient Chinese religions did not say when that was. Nor did he say how long before the dawn of history it was that the goddess of the sea may have appeared in tribal China. He did not know.

No one knew, or can ever know, how long ago the tribal fishermen and seamen of China set sail. There is no written history of their journeys, nor is there much archaeological evidence of their way of living, as there is of hunting tribes. On the seacoasts the boats and tools of seafaring peoples were vulnerable to waves and weather; they were not as well preserved as the fires and tools of hunters deep within their caves, where even the pollen of flowers has been preserved after a hundred thousand years. And the rafts of logs and boats of reeds, dugout canoes and primitive sails, have vanished as if they had evaporated.

The sea has never been gentle with the memory of its dead. It buries its conquerors and victims indiscriminately, with equal oblivion and grace.

Still, there is evidence of seamen in Asia who sailed forth on incredible voyages upon those glacial blue waters of the Ice Age, blown by stormy trade winds. They braved the turbulent waves as courageously as their tribal contemporaries walked across entire continents. They crossed the oceans, leaving stories of their voyages in legends and on stones, which their unimaginative descendants have just begun to decipher. We can hardly imagine the skill nor measure the daring of our ancestors. If the ancient seas were not filled by ancient mariners, still there may have been more of them than we have imagined.

On the islands of the Pacific there are still sailors who remember the near forgotten science of the ancient mariners. In seeking to record their dying science, the Australian anthropologist David Lewis has explored the ways that islanders "unaided by modern navigational equipment [traveled] great distances on the open sea." His journal, *We, the Navigators: The Ancient Art of Landfilling in the Pacific*, has been described by a fellow Australian anthropologist, Steven Harris, as listing the ways of ancient navigators, such as "the more obvious ones of sun and moon positions, positions of the zenith stars, land loom, cloud lore, homing birds, sea marks and wind direction, but also the less obvious features of swell orientation, wave refraction patterns, wave shapes, deep phosphoresence and current speed and direction."

The islanders, even today, would be able to sail for great distances using their sea and sky technology. One of these contemporary ancient seaman was said to know a "world of navigation [that] spanned an area of 2,600 miles wide." By using the sea and sky as navigational guides, there were no oceans they could not cross.

Chinese and Japanese mariners were surely no less—and perhaps more—skilled. The known, recorded voyages of the seamen of the Asian continent, seem remarkable in length and duration. But they were not. In the most distant times, seamen sailed the seas as far and as freely as those whose later voyages happened to be remembered on paper. And we have merely begun to read their legends and stones with a recognition and appreciation of their accomplishments.

In recent years, archaeologists have been startled by the discovery on the shores of the Americas a pottery of the Japanese Jomon design. Its resemblance to Japanese pottery was surprising because its prototype was created in 3000 B.C. The thought that Chinese or Japanese ships may have reached the coasts of Ecuador nearly five thousand years ago was baffling; it could not be. Maybe the pottery was traded from island to island across the Pacific; but that, too, would indicate the existence of neolithic trade routes of thousands of miles across the world's largest ocean.

In ancient Mexico, too, signs of oceanic contact between the Stone Age tribes of Asia and America have been unearthed. The evidence of a possible Chinese influence on the art and ritual of the Olmec culture has long been a source of wonder for Mexican archaeologists; as Miguel de Covarrubias demonstrated in *Mexico South,* even the spiritual use of jade was similar in both cultures. It was a riddle, commented the Chinese Historical Society of America, that seemed destined to remain unsolved.

China itself may have been subject to "disturbing influences [from] as far afield as the arctic coasts of north America, central and southern America, and the south Pacific, in late pre-historic times," declared William Willetts in *Chinese Art.* The effects of such influences on Chinese culture have long been debated and they still are; but to Willetts it seemed clear enough that the "findings of archaeology" supported a belief in Stone Age crossings of the Pacific Ocean. In any event, "the implications are evidently highly rewarding."

These surprising discoveries confirmed "possible transpacific contact" as long ago as 3000 B.C. or before, as cautious scholars have written in an issue of *Science.* In the nineteenth century, such historians of the West as H. H. Bancroft and Charles Walcott Brooks were less cautious. They boldly believed that early explorers had crossed the Pacific Ocean in "both directions."

In a speech before the California Academy of Sciences in May 1876, Brooks, as always, was extravagant and adventurous: "Great maritime empires existed in very remote times," he said. "And both Atlantic and Pacific oceans were crossed, and races and civilization widely extended in ages still called pre-historic. A knowledge of the western shores of the American continent has long existence in both China and Japan. That a restricted communication has existed by sea across the Pacific does not admit to question."

The seamanship needed to cross such vast and uncharted seas in a small boat of primitive design required a knowledge of geography and astronomy that could be acquired only by years of experience—perhaps by generations and centuries spent upon the sea. The fishing and seafaring tribes of China had to be practiced in the engineering and navigational sciences for as long as their goddesses and legends of the sea were old. These were rough and robust men, who were skillful and knowing in mastering the discontents of winds and waves.

More than that, these earliest of seamen had to learn the character of the sea. They had to become daring and bold, stoic and cautious, as people of the sea have been throughout history. For the character of the sea had to become their own.

And what of their shipbuilding skills? They sailed forth on seagoing canoes dug out of huge neolithic trees, on great rafts of reeds, and in flat-bottomed boats made of tied logs. Many of these boats of tribal people in our era are larger than the vessels of those European explorers who "discovered" America and Africa and Asia. Most likely those ancient boats of the Chinese were as large as, or larger than, the more famous ships of the Renaissance.

In classical times the Chinese were already building massive junks that could cross oceans. These heavy and ornate seagoing junks were known to have reached South Asia and India before the birth of Christ. "For upwards of twenty centuries the Chinese junks have been known to be large, fast and strong, their people skilled mariners, excellent carpenters and marine architects. They early possessed mechanical skill to build junks of comparatively great tonnage, capable of conveying large amounts of cargo and great numbers of passengers," wrote Charles Walcott Brooks.

So large were these early junks that they rivaled the ships of Arab caliphates. In the Tsin dynasty, in the fourth century A.D., sea voyages of thousands of miles were recorded, during which the crews survived at sea for months without reaching port. The mastery of the sea by these men "may account for [ancestral China's] skilled boatmen, who have lived upon the water from time immemorial, and for the enormous fleets of junks, generally of large dimensions," thought Brooks. "A taste [for the sea] early cultivated may have come down through many centuries."

One of the earliest emperors of the Ch'in dynasty, in 221 to 210 B.C. sent a fleet of seagoing junks to "the Isles of the Immortals" in the "Eastern Sea." It is now believed that these may have been the islands of Japan, but there is no one who can say they were not the Solomons, or the Hawaiian or Aleutian islands.

No one knows the islands of the Pacific by the names that the early Chinese seafarers knew them. So while the scholars argue about their geographic location, all that we can say for certain is that the sailors and traders of Ch'in simply sailed to them, and in celebration of their daring gave these islands names so poetic that no one will ever discover them upon our prosaic maps of exact science.

The sea flows many ways, and so do the ships that sail upon the sea. When the Roman Emperor Marcus Aurelius Antonius sought the silks of China, he sent a fleet of traders to buy them, and it is said these Roman merchants reached Asia in 166 A.D., "going around Arabia and across the Indian Ocean." It was evidence, wrote one historian, "that the sea route from the West to China was already in operation" at the time of the Caesars.

Recent discoveries of Roman lamps and trading goods in the seacoast cities of Thailand have confirmed the extent of the trade between Europe and Asia in the earliest years of the Christian era. The sea route was a well-traveled thoroughfare.

No Latin or Greek equivalents for the names the Chinese gave the envoys of the Roman emperor exist; but they were recorded by the historians of the Han dynasty. The Chinese were at first suspicious of the Roman merchants, doubting their credentials. And so the Roman emperor sent a second fleet of traders, who brought convincing credentials. The Han emperor diplomatically sent a Chinese envoy to Rome, but unfortunately he died during the long voyage to Europe.

It was not a sea expedition for the weak in mind or body. The ships were small and the sea unending. One Chinese traveler, Fa Hsien, who had journeyed to India in 399 A.D., described how he had sailed back to China from India by way of Java, and how the sea captain had lost his way in the China Seas. This ship sailed for seventy days before land was sighted, a voyage that was longer than that of the English pilgrims on the *Mayflower*, more than one thousand years later.

Even so, for centuries the sea trade to China was dominated by foreigners. Roman, Egyptian, Persian, Indian, Arabian, and Jewish merchants and seamen so crowded the harbor of Canton that by the sixth century it was one of the world's largest and most cosmopolitan ports. But a Tang history reported that in 727 the "Posse [Persians] sacked and burned the city of Kwangchou [Canton]," as the Arabs had done and would do again. At first, the Tang emperor was furious and banned foreigners from the city. But on second thought he launched a vast shipbuilding program that was to create China's greatest merchant and naval fleets.

In the Sung dynasty that followed the Tang, the first Chinese navy grew to hundreds of ships: an impressive armada that by 1237 was larger than the Renaissance navies of Spain and England. The fleet was manned by 52,000 sailors. And the gigantic seagoing junks of the emperors of Sung were built at this time, huge vessels that could hold six hundred people and "a year's supply of grain." Chou ch'u-fei described these junks as being "like houses," with sails "like great clouds in the sky."

On these seagoing junks, cargoes were listed in the *Annals of the Sung* that by the year 999 included exports and imports of all sorts, from rhinoceros horns to chain mail armor. The geographers of the emperors had learned enough, even by then, to describe faraway lands like Somaliland, Arabia, and Sicily; for these dragon-shaped ships were becoming known far into the western seas.

Enormous as the junks were, they must have seemed an apparition to the first Westerners who were to see them when the great Kublai Khan sent an entire fleet to bring a Mongol princess to her royal wedding in Iran. In some disbelief the Chinese junks were described as having four to six masts; fifty to sixty cabins, separated into watertight compartments for safety; as many as ten lifeboats on board and two or three boats in tow, full of supplies; and room on their decks for vegetable gardens for their hundreds and hundreds of passengers and crew.

In the memory of Europeans the Golden Horde of the great khans was the spectre of the horsemen who swept across the steppes of Asia to the banks of the Volga and the Danube. They were one of the most brilliant and victorious land armies in all of history. Less known were the maritime exploits of the great khans, for they were less triumphant.

Soon after the Mongols' conquest of the Sung empire, Kublai Khan commanded their Chinese fleets in an invasion of Japan. His naval force of nine hundred ships and 25,000 men tried in 1274, and tried again in 1281, with six hundred newer ships and 140,000 men. But the Kamakura shogunate and the god of weather, who unleashed a typhoon, combined to all but destroy the fleets of the great khan. Nor were the fleets sent to conquer Viet Nam and Java any more successful, or any less spectacular. On the sea, as on the land, the Great Khan wished to be second to none. Even his defeats were massive.

By the year Marco Polo arrived at the court of the great khan, the Mongol-commanded Chinese fleets on the Yangtze River alone were so numerous that the dumbfounded traveler from Venice wrote in amazement: "The amount of shipping it [the river] carries, and the total volume and value of its traffic, exceeds all the rivers of the Christians put together, and their seas into the bargain." On coming to the port of Sinju (I-ching), Polo described seeing five thousand ships "at once" in the harbor.

The seaports of China were "a marvel to behold," he wrote, most of all Zaiton (Ch'uan-chou), which another European traveler, Odoric of Pordenone, said was twice as big as Rome. The Arabian chronicler ibn Battutah, who visited Ch'uan-chou not long after, pronounced these Europeans too modest: "The harbor is one of the greatest in the world," he proclaimed. "No! I am wrong! It is the greatest!"

Of all the feats of Chinese seamanship, none surpassed the voyages of the admiral of the Ming dynasty. These "Seven Voyages of Cheng ho" equaled the fantasies of Sinbad.

The Emperor Hung-wu, founder of the Ming dynasty, had decided to extend Chinese mastery of the sea as far west as his fleets could sail. His successor, Emperor Yung-lo, chose the "Three-Jeweled Eunuch" of the court, Cheng ho, as the commander of the imperial fleets to go into the western seas. And though Cheng ho had come from the inland province of Yunnan, his seamanship was so exemplary and so skilled, he will be remembered with Odysseus, Leif Erikson, Magellan, and Pedro Alonso Nino, the black African pilot of Columbus, as one of the great captains of the sea.

In 1405, Chengo ho set sail from Foochow at the head of a fleet of sixty-three junks and 27,870 seamen. His flagship measured 444 by 180 feet, as large as a modern ocean liner. And the fleet explored Java, Ceylon, Malacca, and the coast of India, sweeping the sea of enemies throughout the Indian Ocean before returning in triumph to China. From 1405 to 1433 seven of these royal fleets, really armadas, sailed into the western seas. One of the greatest was the third fleet of thirty thousand men and forty-eight junks, the largest carrying a crew of about one thousand, the average holding six hundred men. These fleets not only reached the Persian Gulf and the Red Sea (at Aden, they captured a giraffe for the emperor's gardens), but the sixth fleet explored the coast of East Africa, perhaps as far as Kenya.

Of his voyages Cheng ho wrote, with no immodesty: "The Imperial Ming dynasty, in unifying the seas and continents, surpassing the three dynasties, even goes beyond the Han and Tang. The countries beyond the horizon and at the ends of the earth have all become our subjects." The ships sailed 100,000 li, he said, more than the now known circumference of the earth. "Our sails, loftily unfurled like the clouds, day and night continued on their course, rapid as a star, traversing the savage waves as if we were treading a public thoroughfare," Cheng ho declared to the emperor.

The last of the fleets had barely returned when the mandarins of the court began to decry the extravagance of sailing so far away—as so often is the opinion of those who stay at home. No sooner had the emperor begun to doubt the wisdom of the sea voyages than Japanese piracy swept across the sea like a scourge; it had been provoked by the invasions of Kublai Khan and the civil war raging between the warlords of feudal Japan. One after another the ports of China were sacked by these Japanese pirates, who attacked not singly, but in roving packs, year after year.

And the emperors of the Ming enacted a decree prohibiting sea voyages. The explorations of the vast fleets ended ingloriously, an era of Chinese seamanship died stillborn, for within one century it was too late. European ships commanded the seas.

Since that time historians have wondered what might have happened to the course of history if the emperors of the Ming dynasty had not withdrawn their fleets from the seas. And if they had sailed down the coasts of East Africa and around the Cape Horn? And if, in doing so, they had met the ships of the Dutch and the Portuguese, so much smaller and lighter, head on? And if they had gone farther, into the Atlantic, to the shores of Europe?

One thing is certain: The seamanship of these ancient mariners of China refuted the myth that the Chinese were a withdrawn, backward, landlocked nation, living in a self-imposed isolation. The mystique of the mysterious Orientals, inscrutable and secretive, hidden behind the veil of a great wall of silence, has little foundation in the robust and raucous history of the seas. If anything, these seamen of China seem to have opened many of the trade routes to the West upon which the West reached China.

"No race [on earth] can compare with the Chinese in their capacity as traders, colonists, and pioneers," wrote Sir John Pratt in his history of the China trade.

"As far back as we can discern the sea-borne trade between the countries bordering on the Indian Ocean and the China Seas exceeded many times in volume the petty traffic of the Mediterranean world," wrote Pratt. "If their vessels never sailed the Atlantic or the Mediterranean it was because, as Ch'ien lung pointed out, China had no [need to] import manufactures of outside [namely, European] barbarians."

"The Chinese, like the British, are a seafaring race," Sir John Pratt said; and no Englishman could say any more than that.

IV

THE VISIONS OF CATHAY

> No one can deny that this nation is the most beautiful in the world, and the most flourishing kingdom known. Such an Empire as that of China equals what all of Europe would be if the latter were united under a single sovereign.
>
> —FRANÇOISE QUESNAY, 1676

> You, O King, from afar have yearned after the blessing of our civilization, and in your eagerness to come within the touch of our civilizing influence have sent an Embassy across the seas . . . I have taken note of your respectful spirit of submission.
>
> —CH'IEN LUNG EMPEROR TO KING GEORGE III OF ENGLAND

ON HIS LONG JOURNEY across the steppes of Asia, those waves of sands that form a stony sea, the Venetian merchant Marco Polo never really reached China. Instead, he came to the mythical land of Cathay; but then, he was not really seeking China. In the year of 1271, the merchants of Italy had no great need for the goods of China, but they, and all Europe, greatly needed the myths of Cathay, the richest kingdom of their dreams.

The splendors of the courts of the great khan, Kublai, were well known to the young Polo. His father and his uncle, who had traveled to Asia before him, had excited the young man's fantasies with tales of the grandeur and wonders of the wealth of the emperor who had conquered so much of the Old World. And so Polo's sense of anticipation preceded him, and he was greeted by his expectations; his vision of Cathay was eveything that he had imagined it to be.

But what of China? It was wonderful how much of China he saw but did not see.

In the palace of the great khan one of the sights that did impress Polo was a peculiar custom: "No one dares spit on the floor." Everyone had a "handsome little vessel to spit into"; "when he hath spitten he covers it up and puts it aside." Not only that, but there was "no noise of shrill voices, or loud talk" in the palace.

That the gentleman from Venice, one of the wealthiest and most cultured of feudal Europe's cities, would be impressed by the lack of spitting may seem somewhat odd. But in the palaces of the doge in Venice, such refinement was not known. And so he was almost as bemused by the manners of the Chinese as he was enthused by their wealth. Of course he was impressed by "the wealthy among these people [who] dress in cloth of gold and silk," and by the "fine marble palace" of the great khan, "the rooms of which are [gold] gilt." For like most travelers, he most clearly described the things he knew.

And China to Marco Polo may have seemed an oriental Venice of his dreams, so that he seemed to be singularly uninterested in the Chinese achievement of printing, of which he had no knowledge—though, as a merchant, he did notice the printing of paper money, which he decided was "alchemy." The magnetic compass, unknown in Europe, escaped his notice. So did the existence of sulphur matches. Nor was he interested in the religious freedom of the Mongol Empire, where the great khan celebrated Buddhist, Muslim, Christian, and Jewish ceremonies. It may have been beyond the comprehension of a man who came from a country where religion was devoted to Holy Crusades and unholy heresies. Those aspects of Chinese life that did intrigue him, Polo wrote about with more enthusiasm than realism. One was his erotic fantasy of men in China who "keep six, eight, or ten women" for their enjoyment. In his bedchamber the great khan himself sanctioned this custom by enjoying the nightly "services" of the "most beautiful young women," he wrote; these beauties satiated the khan's desires in amorous teams of five. And "he does with them what he likes," Polo fantasized.

And so the European fantasy of Chinese voluptuousness was born. The gentlemen of feudal Europe, where love was sacred, and sex was sinful, were forever after seduced by their own images of the sensuality of *l'Orient* as they imagined it and desired it.

Of the things that he actually had seen, Polo wrote with an extraordinary accuracy, but he seemed more fascinated, at times, with what he imagined. It was perhaps fitting, therefore, that the book of his travels was written by one Rustichello of Pisa, a poor gentleman whom he met one day in the Genoese prison where both of them were imprisoned. Rustichello was a writer of popular romances.

The courts of Europe during feudal times were most often parochial and boorish. Although they had a vitality, a rough and aggressive spirit, they knew little of science and too much of superstition. By comparison, the civilization of China may have seemed a paragon of wealth and wisdom; it was a celestial kingdom known by the mythic name of Cathay, a land that did not exist. And Europe viewed it with awe.

Scientists of the Sung dynasty, which ruled China from the tenth to the thirteenth century, had perfected three inventions that Sir Francis Bacon said "changed the whole face and state of things throughout the world." These three "miraculous" inventions were Pi sheng's movable type for printing, the magnetic "south-pointing compass" for seagoing junks that Shen kua described in his *Dream Stream Writing* in 1088, and the gunpowder that Taoist monks developed to "ward off evil spirits" in their temples. Many of the Sung dynasty inventions were scientifically detailed in the *Chinese Military Handbook* of 1042; but in medieval Europe they were viewed less as evidence of scientific knowledge than as magic and alchemy. And the popes and kings of the Dark Ages of Europe sent many missionaries to witness these miracles.

None of these travelers from Europe, before or after Marco Polo, dissuaded their countrymen from imagining that China was the land of their most feudal fantasies. They tried to outdo each other, and they did. In the visions of European rulers and intellectuals, for hundreds of years, Cathay was to be synonymous with China, so that the desire became the reality.

One of the most joyous of these mythmakers was the monk Blessed Odoric of Pordenone in Italy, a Franciscan of sorts who possessed the ecstacies but little of the humility of the saint of Assisi. To Blessed Odoric, who sailed to China early in the fourteenth century, it was a land that consisted entirely of superlatives. He said he saw more ships in Canton harbor than in "all Italy." In Hangchow, he marveled at the "greatest city in the whole world." In Peking, he described the great khan riding about in a chariot made of gold and precious jewels, "drawn by four elephants, *and* also four horses."

"And, as for the women, they are the most beautiful in the world!" enthused the wayward Franciscan, echoing Polo. The monk titillated himself with a description of one Chinese merchant who was waited on by "fifty virgin damsels" who "fed him as though he were a sparrow. And thus he leadeth his daily life," sighed Odoric, "until he shall have lived it out."

On coming home, Blessed Odoric visited the pope in Avignon, then took to his bed and died. His romantic reputation was so well known that "female devotees" came in throngs to his funeral to kiss his face, but a religious frenzy seized them and they attempted to tear the robe from his corpse and to clip his hair for sacred relics. A too ardent worshiper sought to cut off his ear, but "miraculously her scissors did not close."

In time, Blessed Odoric was offered beatification. He was canonized a saint, though not for his experiences in China.

Not as self-infatuated, though as self-deceptive, were the tales of China told by those emissaries of the popes Friar John Pian de Carpini and the Sicilian Archbishop John of Montecorvino, who saw what they had been sent to see, a country eager for Christianity. That illusion was no doubt created by the great khans themselves, by encouraging the heresy of the Nestorian Christians for political reasons. Had not Blessed Odoric seen the khan kiss the cross? After all, the mother of Kublai Khan was a Nestorian Christian, and the khan had invited missionaries. So it was that a papal bull was issued in Avignon, ordering that John of Montecorvino take "full charge and care of all souls living in the whole dominion of the Tartars." The year was 1308.

Of all these fantasies of medieval Europe, however, none was as popular as the gothic romance *The Travels of Sir John Mandeville*, said to be the "medieval best-seller." More manuscripts of this book survive than of any other of its kind.

In his memoir, Sir John, a knight of King Louis IX, told of a land so sublime that its sensual pleasures and material wealth were undoubtedly divine. The Celestial Kingdom bordered on paradise, he said; for it was a place where the palaces were built of solid gold. Where the ordinary drinking cups were carved from single emeralds. Where dishes were made of sapphires. Where a miraculous light as "bright as the day" illuminated night in the boudoirs of the concubines of the great khan. Where the walls were covered with the skins of "red panthers." Where the sidewalks and streets of the cities were paved with silver.

Sir John Mandeville, need it be said, never existed. Nor did his China. He was most likely Jean d'Outremeuse, a writer of French romances, who had not only never been to China, but had never left France. He was a literary ancestor of Don Quixote. Nonetheless, or perhaps because of this, for hundreds of years his book was thought to be the authoritative work on Chinese life, though it is now remembered ungenerously as "the most successful fraud in world literature."

And yet, is it a fraud or is it a fable? It was what Europe wished to believe, and did. The creator of heroic Sir John Mandeville had merely taken the descriptions of China, from Pliny to Blessed Odoric, and transformed their fact into fiction.

There was one European who was foolish enough to attempt to write a realistic narrative of his journey to the court of the great khans. He was the friar William of Rubruck, who had been sent to Karakorum in 1253 by King Louis IX. Saint Louis, whose Crusades to the Holy Land had ended in ignoble defeat, conceived a brilliant but unlikely military strategy: He proposed an alliance with the Mongols in which the Golden Horde would attack the infidels in Jerusalum from the rear as the Crusaders attacked from the sea. Friar William was entrusted with this impossible dream.

After the foreseeable failure of his mission, Friar William returned to Europe weary and wiser. In the calm that typified him, he wrote what was by all accounts the most detailed and descriptive of journals, a worldly and witty book full of sensitive and subtle comment and human compassion, but much too down to earth to please the phantasmania of Europe. The palace of the great khan, he said, was no larger than a village church. And the khan himself was "not a Christian, but a Mongol." More than that, though they had "divided among themselves the land from the Danube to the rising sun," the people were nomads, living in a city on wheels, and they even built their

houses on carts drawn by oxen "so they go slowly as sheep."
This could not be a true description of the fearful Golden Horde
of the great khan. Friar William was not to be believed.

*The Journey of William of Rubruck to the Eastern Parts of
the World* was written in 1255. It was seldom to be heard of
again until the middle of the nineteenth century. Europeans
desired and needed fantasies that reflected their medieval lives.
Reality, as always, was a heresy.

Monks and merchants who set off on foot and on horseback
across those steppes of Asis, with neither maps nor compasses
to guide them, were inspired by visions no less farsighted than
the holy religions that had sustained the knights in the Holy
land. If they had foreseen the reality of their journey they might
never have undertaken such hardships. So it was that in 1340,
in a *Merchants' Handbook* on the trade routes to China, Francesco Balducci Pegolotti had written that travel to Asia, whether
"by day or by night," was *sichurissmo*—"perfectly safe."

No matter what lay before them, at the end of the road was
paradise. The mythical land of Cathay was surely heavenly: Was
it not named the Celestial Kingdom, ruled by the Son of Heaven?
Sir John Mandeville himself had assured his readers that paradise
lay just off the coast of China, beyond the "Island of the Hermaphrodites." With unexpected modesty, he wrote: "Of Paradise
I cannot speak properly for I was not there. It is far beyond;
and I repent not going there, but I was not worthy." Friar William of Rubruck, as well, in his wanderings had heard of these
enchanting lands, but he did not go there for less modest reasons.
"They told me as a fact [which I do not believe] that there
was a province of Cathay [where] at whatever age a man enters
it, that age he keeps," wrote the friar, unconvinced.

Europeans were for centuries to seek, but never find, this
paradise of eternal life. So they had to be contented with its

myth. It was a mythical land they created in their minds but in China, where it was known as the place where the "Peach of Immortality" grew, they never found it, for it did not exist, except in myth.

The dawn of enlightened reason in Renaissance Europe did not greatly affect these myths of the medieval mind nor the quest for the perfect life, in a fabled utopia of China. It merely enlarged and reshaped the feudal fable into more philosophical and scientific fantasies. But the myths were as potent as ever. In the palaces of Peking the dynasty of the great khans was replaced by the Ming and Ching dynasties, and the European belief in the miracles of the Celestial Kingdom was replaced by a belief in the scholarly and rational wisdom of the mandarin bureaucrats of the new emperors, who were renamed the philosopher-kings.

In all the ages of man there is a man who articulates what his own age needs to hear. So it was that the "Age of Reason" in Europe found a voice to proclaim a new vision of a rationalist Cathay, which was perhaps its new image of itself, in the writings of that most brilliant of Jesuit missionaries Father Matteo Ricci.

Son of a poor nobleman from the desolate eastern coast of Italy, Ricci seemed destined by a childhood Jesuit schooling to seek the newest vision of Cathay. In his heart he may have wished to fulfill the mission of the founder of his order, St. Francis Xavier, who died in the year of Matteo Ricci's birth— who died within sight, but without ever reaching the shore, of the land he so longingly described: "China, an immense empire, enjoying profound peace, and which the Portuguese merchants tell us is superior to all Christian states in the practice of justice and equity." It was as though the sensual "heathens" of feudal myth has ceased to exist.

Father Ricci was to see in China what St. Francis had envisioned: a land of "justice and equity, peace and order." In the provincial town of Chao ch'ing, where he began his sojourn, he had scoffed with a comfortable conceit at the ideas of the local Confucian scholars: "It is amazing how little they know, for they are concerned entirely with moralizing," Ricci wrote. "All of this makes me laugh."

On coming to the royal academies of the emperor's court in Peking, he changed his mind. The entire kingdom seemed to be governed by philosophers, he said. Philosophers even ruled the military: "The wisdom of those who excel in the profession of ethics is held in such high esteem" that they decided who among the generals shall be "doctors of philosophy"; surely, a curious country.

"The sect of the Literati . . . is the most ancient in the kingdom," Father Ricci explained. And so "they rule the country." If this last comment was meant for the pope, he did not say so.

Confucius, the more Ricci learned of his thought, seemed indeed to be the "Prince of Philosophers." Not merely did Ricci translate the works of this master of the Literati, K'ung Fu-tzu, into Latin, but he gave him his Latin name of Confucius. The concepts of the Confucians, he now decided, were "quite in conformity with the light of conscience and with Christian truth." That Europe might learn this wisdom he had learned, Ricci compiled one of the first Chinese-European dictionaries— in Italian and Portuguese. And, in turn, he translated Euclid into Chinese; he was a one-man cultural exchange.

In the end the governor of Kweichow province said of him: "Ricci has been so long in China that he is no longer a foreigner, but a Chinese." On his grave in Peking, where he died in 1610, the tombstone erected in his honor by the royal governor simply stated his Chinese name, Li Ma-tou.

Though the Jesuit had sought to "convert" the Chinese, the Chinese had "converted" him. In Europe, his writing was spreading the belief that China was a land of infinite wisdom, ruled by "moral philosophy," and those Europeans who read his translation of Confucius and his *Journals* would soon indulge in an infatuation with the newest of pseudo-Chinese fantasies.

In 1644, when the Dutch government sent forth ambassadors to establish trade relations with the boy emperor, Shin Chih, the chronicler of the voyage, John Nieuhoff, described China mostly from shipboard in coastal ports, rarely going ashore, and faithfully recorded the prevailing myth: "The whole of the kingdom is swayed by [the] Philosophers, to whom not only the people, but the grandees of the court yield an awful reverence."

The philosophers ruled "with so much quietness," said Nieuhoff, that "it is most incredible for anyone to believe unless they have seen it."

On that kind of breathless naiveté the French philosopher Voltaire usually fed his skepticism, but not even he could resist the unlikely tale of a land where philosophy reigned: "One need not be obsessed with the merits of the Chinese to recognize at least that the organization of their empire is, in truth, the best the world has seen." Addressing the kings of Europe who gazed longingly upon the best of all possible worlds of the Chinese, Voltaire admonished with a sardonic pleasure: "Admire and blush—but above all imitate."

In Germany, that master of mathematics and philosopher of early European sciences Wilhelm Leibniz was unreservedly ecstatic. The dour scientist had read the translation of Confucius, whom he called king of philosophers. "It is not possible to describe the wisdom with which the Chinese order everything concerned with public order and the relations between men . . . it is incomparably better done than among other people," he proclaimed. Even as he wrote that, the Ming dynasty had fallen, and China was embroiled in another of many bloody civil wars.

So "far superior" in philosophy was China to Europe that Leibniz hoped that "the inordinate lengths which corruption of morals had advanced" within European thought would be corrected by Chinese wisdom. He sought unsuccessfully to convince the Royal Academy in England and the *Académie Française*, both of which he belonged to, to emulate the Chinese. They would not. Undaunted, he set up his own scientific societies to study Chinese wisdom, in Berlin and Moscow. More incongruously still, he sought to convince the tsar to study the Chinese government as a model for Russia, an endeavor in which he was about as successful as Voltaire had been in seeking to interest Louis XV in Confucian philosophy.

Men of that "Age of Reason" had rediscovered China in their scientific mind's eye. The utopia of philosophers born of Plato's *Republic* was reincarnated in the imperial courts of eunuchs and mandarins of the emperors who sat upon the Dragon Throne. And Plato was reincarnated as Confucius.

None, or very little, of all this had much to do with China, for as a perceptive French writer, Grimm, had written in 1776: "The Chinese empire has become in our time the object of special attention and special study . . . to serve as a model for all nations." In the beginning, "the missionaries first fascinated public opinion by rose-colored reports from that distant land, too distant to be able to contradict their falsehoods. Then the philosophers took it up, and drew from [China] whatever could be of use in denouncing and removing the evils they observed in their own country." And China became the philosophers' alter ego "house of wisdom."

But the rulers of Europe seemed less fascinated by the wisdom than the wealth of China. Not wealth of gold, but wealth of luxury and extravagance, subtlety and beauty; for European royalty was lacking not in treasure, but in refinements. The courts of Europe from Spain to Russia became obsessed with a *"façon de la Chine,"* by *"à la chinois"* morals and pagodas, fashions and silks, manners and porcelains, and what seemed to them an exotic "decadence of China" that was subtly erotic.

"Chinese pagodas, latticed 'tea-houses,' kiosks, and 'Confucian temples' " began to spring up in royal palaces and the gardens of castles "in every corner of Europe," wrote Hugh Honour in a superlative account of that era, *Chinoiserie: The Vision of Cathay*. In these Europeanized imitations of Chinese buildings, the kings and emperors amassed vast collections of Sung bowls, Ming vases, and royal concubines.

In France, Emperor Charles V had acquired a set of "China plates" as early as the fourteenth century. Philip II of Spain accumulated more than three thousand pieces of porcelain. Even in "remote and uncultivated" England, Henry VII boasted of owning a single "Cup of Purselaine." By the end of the sixteenth century, factories in China were manufacturing porcelain especially "for the European market."

Mercantile Europe turned its obsession into profit. In 1575, the Grand Duke Francesco of Medici built a factory to produce imitation Chinese porcelain in Italy. Not long after, Marie de Médicis hired a French cabinet maker to set up a workshop for lacquered furniture *à la chinois*. By 1619, the English craftsman William Smith wrote from Rome that he was employed by "the Cardinalles and other Princes" making "workes after the Chinese fashion." And in 1614, when the illustrious Earl of Northampton died, his estate revealed a castle full of fake *à la chinois* furniture, one of the most spectacular pieces being his "bedstead of China worke with the Armes of the Earl of Northampton [engraved] upon the headpiece."

So expensive were these Chinese luxuries that a "cabinet of China worke" given in 1613 as a wedding present to the Princess Elizabeth of England, the daughter of James I (she became known as the Queen of Hearts), was valued at ten thousand pounds sterling, a small fortune at the time.

Not just furniture, but whole rooms and entire castles were created *à la chinois*. One "Chinese room" was built for the Austrian Hapsburgs in the Palace of Schönbrunn, and Catherine I of Russia built another at Peterhof, *à la russe*, while August the Strong built his own "Chinese room" in Germanic style in his castle in Bavaria. Everywhere the fashion became manic. In Germany, Emmanuel of Bavaria had a "pagoda mountain" constructed in the park of Nymphenburg. His son, Prince Clemens August, the bishop of Cologne, outdid his father by building *chinesische Haus*, the "Chinese House" at the castle of Bruhl, while the bishop's brother, Elector Karl Albrecht of Bavaria, outdid them both with his "Chinese pavilion" for his hunting hounds.

On the grounds of his royal castle in Potsdam, Frederick the Great, influenced no doubt by the philosophic visions of his friend Voltaire, built a Chinese tea-house, its roof supported by artificial palm trees and its stillness guarded by German "statues of Chinamen." In the *Musikzimmer* of his castle, where the emperor sequestered himself to play his flute sonatas, his solitude was protected by a guard of "carved mandarins."

Swedish King Adolf Friedrich, in his enthusiasms, went further; he decreed that his architects create an entire Chinese palace for his queen. But in Russia Catherine II surpassed the fantasies of them all by building not only the huge Chinese Palace at Oranienbaum, designed by an Italian architect, A. Rinaldi, but a complete Chinese village at Tsarskoye Selo, designed by a Scottish architect, Charles Cameron.

For centuries the eyes of philosophers and kings of Europe had danced to the dazzling vision of a mythical land that lay beyond the end of the sea. It was the fabled land of all their feudal dreams, of the might of the great khan, Kublai. It was the utopian land of all their philosophical dreams, in a nonexistent Cathay. It was the perfect land of eternal life, in Shangri la. And it was the land of all their fantasies, the land of China.

The Europeans had been fascinated by these images of China that they had created, and they sought to conquer not China, but these images. In some ways the images that Europeans created about China were similar to the images they imposed upon America; for they were wish-fulfilling images of Europeans' own needs and desires.

And, in the end, that was all that Europeans discovered—themselves.

Fable and fantasy, philosophy and science, were forgotten. The *objects d'art* of China crowded Europe like an antique shoppe. It was as if the worshipers, unable to meditate in the Temple of Confucius, decided to buy the temple instead.

In the formal garden of the Palace of Versailles that he had built to enhance his claim to the title of Grand Monarch of Europe, Louix XIV had decreed the construction, *a la chinois*, of a petite white-porcelain "Little Palace of Pleasure," in imitation of a baroque Chinese temple of the Ming dynasty, for his favorite concubine of the winter of 1671—the alabaster-skinned Mme de Montespan, his "Princess of China." A Chinese shrine designed to enshrine French lovemaking!

The eroticism of the *Trianon de porcelaine* was most luxurious, as one might expect, in the bedchamber of the king's mistress. But the *chambre des amours* was not merely the heart of the little palace's existence, it dominated the ostentatiously ascetic lovenest.

In a court romance written a few years later, the story is told of an Emperor who fell in love with the perfect woman, Belle Gloire. The paramour of the Emperor was the Princess of China, "who was unquestionably the most beautiful, and at the same time the most haughty, princess on earth." She disdained the advances of the Emperor, even while she submitted to his gifts. In her country she was so rich that her father, the emperor of China, told her that simplicity was the greatest wealth. Purity was the greatest aphrodisiac, she said. And she mocked her royal lover.

But the Emperor was neither to be insulted nor denied. He desired nothing but to please his lover. And so in the royal gardens—somewhat like Versailles—where the romantic lovers talked, he struck the earth three times with his cane. There in the midst of fragrant jasmines and sparkling little fountains there arose a virginal, petite, simple white-porcelain castle, into which the lovers retreated for their pure lovemaking.

So it was that Louis the XIV built a virginal, petite, simple white-porcelain *chambre des amours* for his "Princess of China." There was in the mind of Europe a vision of the mystique of *l'Orient*, the allure of celestial and heavenly wisdom, and the sensuality of vice and evil that seemed enticingly erotic to the imagination of the Bourbon courtiers.

Said the Emperor of the Romance: "The entirety produced the greatest effect [upon loving] one possibly could imagine." The royal bed was of virginal white; it was hidden by drapes of whitest taffeta hung layer upon layer from its high posts and trimmed in gold and blue, a motif of the Chinese porcelains and embroideries that cast a chilly exoticism upon the bedroom of the royal lovers—so much so, the bed suggested, more than anything, a holy altar of a monastery.

One imagines that Louis XIV, *le roi soleil*—the Sun King—

and his "Princess of China" may have felt exotic as they lay upon their icy bed of love. The fantasy may have been intensified by their pretense that they were Chinese lovers, but Chinese created in a French imagination.

Of the Chinese shrine to royal romance, the poet Denis wrote:

> Let us consider this palace of pleasure,
> See how it is all covered with china;
> The urn of porcelain and many vases
> Causing it to shine with eyes of the universe.

In truth, the *Trianon de porcelaine* was covered with tiles from Delft and Rouen. The walls of the *chambre des amours* were simply of whitish plaster. And though the French furniture was painted white, it was not made of ivory nor lacquered in China, being merely "created in the *fashion* of art works from China," as a court observer noted mischievously.

The enchanting Palace of Pleasure was dismantled after contributing to seventeen years of royal illusions. Mme de Maintenon had replaced Mme de Montespan in the bed of Louis XIV, and she desired a *chambre des amours* of her own design. The fake facades of the imitation Chinese temple of love were torn down and vanished into history, where they have lingered, as illusions do, forever.

V

THE WHITE PERIL

AND THE YELLOW PERIL

The Way of Heaven is fairness to all; it does not suffer us to harm others to benefit ourselves. Men are alike in this in all the world: for they cherish life and hate what endangers life.
—Letter of LIN TSE HSU about
the opium trade to Queen Victoria, 1839

A Chinaman is cold, cunning and distrustful; always ready to take advantage of those he has to deal with; extremely covetous and deceitful; quarrelsome, vindictive, but timid and dastardly.
—ENCYCLOPEDIA BRITANNICA, 1842
7th edition, London

ON THE DESOLATE MOORS of Devon in an isolated farmhouse during the summer of 1798, the English poet Samuel Taylor Coleridge wrote an ode on "Kubla Khan." As he said, he wrote it "without any sensation or consciousness of effort," for he was most likely quietly delirious with opium, to which he was addicted. The ode was more truly, as he subtitled it, "A Vision in a Dream," in celebration of his indulgence in English fantasy, not in Chinese reality.

The Chinese dream world of his opium dream was both familiar and fanciful; for it was Marco Polo's vision of Cathay, revived after five hundred years—fantasy land of European wish-fulfillment, where:

In Xanadu did Kubla Khan
A stately pleasure-dome decree . . .

And yet, in the last lines of "Kubla Khan" the agony of the addict who was addicted not merely to his opiate but to the fantasies it created, painfully emerged. It was an ecstatic, nightmarish, and prophetic message:

> And all should cry, Beware! Beware!
> His flashing eyes, his floating hair! . . .
> For he on honey-dew hath fed,
> And drunk the milk of Paradise.

Cathay of the vision had changed. It was no longer simply a utopia for the salvation of Europeans' ills; it had become "A savage place!" And it was more "holy and enchanted" due to that. Evil was as seductive a prospect as was heaven to the Englishmen of the nineteenth century—if not even more so—and the "milk of Paradise" was to become the juice of the opium poppies that nourished the entire British Empire in the halcyon days of its great Victorian era.

Even so, the realities of China lay beyond the "deep romantic chasm" that separated the East and West, said the poet. If the traveler crossed the chasm he was greeted, in his fantasies perhaps, by "an Abyssinian maid" who, on the "dulcimer she played," cried out to him "Beware! Beware!"; for his opium was as deceptive as a "demon-lover" and it would drive him mad.

In England, at the time, Chinese opium was as fashionable among many intellectuals as Chinese ideas were among many intellectuals in France. The opium possessed all the fantasies and mysteries of the vision of Cathay the English imagined China to be.

And yet the irony of this was that Chinese opium was really English opium. The poppies were grown in India under the supervision of the British government, the opium was manufactured by the East India Company under a royal charter of the British government, and the opium was shipped to China—in violation of Chinese law—under the protection of the British fleet. Some of this opium made its way to England and America, where its use was the original cause of the widespread traffic in and addiction to opiates that was to follow. And that was, perhaps, the even greater irony.

For many centuries the effect of opium, in China, had been like that of wine; it was less a sedative than a meditative drug. And, like wine, it was taken to transcend, not obliterate, the self. In the tense days before the beginning of the Opium Wars, one of the themes of the imperial examinations in Peking was a line from Li Po's poem "On Drinking Alone on a Spring Day." It was a time, said the poet, when "Nature and I are one." In the Way of the Tao, thought transcended thought, as the self transcended the self.

So opium was a means to an end, not an end in itself. Then, with the coming of English opium, there came a new kind of addiction. In old China, the opium had been mild, but this new opium of India was so strong that it was popularly believed that the "foreign devil" English had combined the opium with the sacrificial "flesh of little girls" and the dry corpses of crows.

Poppies that bore the fruit of the opium were not native to China. They seem to have developed along the Mediterranean Sea and Euphrates River in mythological times, when opium was sometimes known as "lion's milk" and "lion's fat." Not until the seventh century were opium poppies known in China, and not until the seventeenth century did opium smoking become "the vice of the Far East"; the deadly addiction was a gift of the ancient civilizations of Greece and Mesopotamia, but the bearers of the gift in its greatest abundance were the emissaries of the English Empire.

England's embrace of the opium trade was wholly practical.

It was, as John Quincy Adams later said, merely an offer of "the liberating arm" of commerce to "anticommercial" China.

To those gentlemen of the Foreign Office and the East India Company who had originally created the commerce with the "milk of Paradise," it was not a matter of morality, nor was it a Machiavellian plot to insidiously dilapidate China. It was not a clandestine traffic run by criminals. It was an economic necessity of the royal exchequer, aimed at halting the trade deficit and loss of millions of pounds sterling, in silver bullion, due to the costs of endless wars and Chinese teas. And the distinguished, though devious, diplomats who thought of using the opium trade to balance the trade deficit and pay for Chinese teas were duly honored for their service to the empire. One of the richest opium traders, Sir James Matheson, was knighted by Queen Victoria. One of the largest, William Jardine, was elected to Parliament.

In the earliest days of England's exploration of the seas, its captains of piracy had known of the riches and temptations of the China trade, long before it was possible for them to succumb to either. By 1592, the sea historian Richard Hakluyt was enviously cataloguing the cargo of a Spanish carrack, *Madre de Dios*, which had been captured on its return from Asia by pirates of Elizabeth I's fleet—whom Hakluyt preferred to call "adventurers." This vessel was a treasure house of "spices, drugges, silks, calicos, quilts, carpets and colours &c" worth "no less than 150,000 li in sterling," wrote Hakluyt, "which being divided among the adventurers (whereof her Majesty was the chiefe) was sufficient to yield contentment to all parties."

So great a treasure on so small a ship had inspired a group of London merchants, in 1599, to form an association to trade with the East Indies. One year later Queen Elizabeth granted a royal charter to the East India Company giving it a monopoly on all Asian trade to reach England.

But the English were too late. Dutch and Portuguese traders

had sailed into these seas and had taken command of the China trade by seizing control respectively, of Macao, at the entrance to Canton, and the Spice Islands of the Indies. The English had been understandably preoccupied with the conquest of Africa and India, not to mention America.

And so the English had to seek a way by diplomatic wiles and commercial stealth and the skilled seamanship of old-fashioned piracy for their ships to enter the China Seas. They did, with triumphant and disastrous result.

Not the sweet aroma of opium but the sweet taste of tea enticed the English into the China Seas. In the unpredictable perversity of life that so often gives birth to history, it was the English addiction to tea that led to the Chinese addiction to opium and to the trade that was to harbinger the collapse of both of their empires.

The beginnings of the tea mania may be traced to a picaresque inn, "Sultaness Head Coffee-House, in Sweetings Rent, by the Royal Exchange, London," where, Thomas Rugge in his *Mercurius Politicus* noted, the "excellent and by all Physicians, approved, China drink, called by the Chineans Tcha, by other nations Tay alias Tee, is sold." The year was 1658. So popular was the "China drink" to become that the East India Company, which had imported a mere twenty three pounds in 1666, by the end of the seventeenth century was importing twenty thousand pounds annually.

Year by year the English addiction to tea increased. Though a few obstinate souls opposed the "China drink"—Dr. Samuel Johnson fumed it was "stuff fit only for a wench"—the ordinary Englishman—and woman—ascribed to the brew all the magical and mysterious healing qualities that the Chinese were believed to possess.

England's insatiable thirst for tea became a severe drain on the royal exchequer. Those millions of pounds of tea had to be paid for in millions of pounds of silver sterling. Emperors of China would accept nothing less, for the simple reason, as the Ch'ien lung emperor had explained to King George III: "Our Celestial Kingdom possesses all things in prolific abundance and lacks no product within our borders," and so there was "no need to import the manufacturers of outside barbarians." If the Celestial Kingdom benevolently permitted the English to import teas, it was due to the emperor's "principle to 'treat strangers from afar with indulgence' and to exercise a pacifying control over barbarian tribes [such as the English] the world over."

All this was due to the request of Lord Macartney, the British ambassador, that the two nations consider establishing free trade and diplomatic equality. The emperor replied that it would create "inevitable friction between the Chinese and your barbarians," and "your barbarian merchants would have made the long journey for nothing."

"We possess all things," said the emperor to George III. "Tremblingly obey and show no negligence." Though the Ch'ien lung emperor's message has seemed "arrogant" and "self-righteous," even "naive and amusing," to Western historians, it was not unrealistic. Joseph Needham, the historian of *Science and Civilization in China*, has said of the underlying realism of this Chinese conceit:

"One of the reasons for the abominable opium policy of the so-called Honourable East India Company, at the end of the eighteenth century and the beginning of the nineteenth, was the fact that the Westerners could not produce all the things they wanted, e.g., silk, lacquer, tea and porcelain, while the Chinese were content with what they produced, and did not want any of the manufactures of Europe. It was therefore in searching for something which would operate to stop the drain of gold and silver to the East that the Honourable Company hit upon the opium trade."

There may have been a more immediate reason for the opium trade. And that was the American Revolution.

In 1773 the East India Company was granted the monopoly of the opium trade, and in 1779 it was granted the monopoly of its manufacture. It was during those years that smuggling opium into China dramatically increased and became a decisive element of English diplomacy in China as well as on the entire Asian continent. The threats of war with the rebellious colonists and the strain its costs were to place on the already drained royal exchequer well may have weighed on the English govern- ment in approving the opium trade. And there was the added irony: it was the colonists' rejection of Chinese tea that increased England's need for opium revenues.

Before the American Revolution trade of opium to China was less than 200 chests a year. By 1800 it was more than 2,000 chests, by 1816 it was 3,211 chests, by 1831 it was 16,000 chests, by 1838 it was 40,000 chests, and after the Opium Wars it rose to 70,000 chests.

The poppies were flowering into a phenomenal source of profit. In 1813, one chest of good quality opium could be bought for 237 rupees and it could be sold at the export auctions for 2,428 rupees, an effortless profit of 1000 percent. When the opium was smuggled into China, the opium traders' profits were much higher, "as high as $1,000 a chest," said the trader William Jardine—an enormous sum at that time, totaling many millions of silver pounds annually. The English colonial government in India, with its usual ingenuity, placed a legal tax upon the illegal shipments of opium, which surpassed one million pounds sterling by 1830; the government's revenue from opium amounted to one-tenth of its annual revenues.

"Opium is a good cash crop, especially for undeveloped regions," the Encyclopedia Britannica noted laconically a century later in an article on "Opium" by N. B. Eddy, of the National Institutes of Health, at Bethesda, Maryland. The opium trade, said Eddy, "led" to the Opium War.

The milk of Paradise flowed from India to China in an ever widening torrent. It addicted millions of people. So catastrophic was the effect that Chu tsun, a high official of the emperor's court, called it a "flowing poison" and demanded that it be banned once and for all.

Emperors of the past had issued edicts banning opium endlessly—in 1729, in 1796, in 1800, in 1813, in 1815, in 1821. The opposition to opium by the emperors was political as well as moral; the English were not only ruining "the mind and morals" of the people, but violating the sovereignty and laws of China. But the edicts of the emperors were never enforced or obeyed by the court officials or by the merchants who profited from the bribes and corruption that accompanied the smuggling of opium. Then, in 1829, the opium trade became more than a matter of morals or sovereignty. The balance of trade *had* changed from China's to England's favor. So much opium had been smuggled into China that, for the first time in the long history of the country, the Chinese began to export silver to pay for the opium of the "barbarians" of the West.

Morally and financially the strength of China was being weakened by opium. In Peking, the Tao kuang emperor summoned his court officials to present him with a plan to halt the English opium traders and to enforce the ban on opium. But the court officials were hopelessly divided. Most of them supported the opium trade.

The minister of the Court of Sacrificial Worship, Hsu nai-chu, believed that banning the opium trade would enrage the barbarians; besides, he said, it was not all evil since it shortened the lives of the peasants and decreased the overpopulation of the country. The minister of the Court of State Ceremonial, Huang Chueh-tzu, charged that the emperor's opium ban was being sabotaged by greedy court officials for their own profit and could be halted if these officials, the foreign opium traders, and the Chinese opium smokers were all severely punished; he urged the ban be enforced.

In an effort to resolve the debate, the emperor called for a vote of his provincial governors and viceroys. Eight of these high officials voted to support the emperor's opium ban, while twenty voted that the opium trade ought to be permitted to go on.

Infuriated, the emperor summoned Lin Tse hsu, royal viceroy of Hunan and Hupeh provinces, who was the strongest advocate of forcibly ending the opium trade. He appointed Lin an imperial commissioner in command of the naval forces of Kwangtung province, where the opium port of Canton was situated, and in the spring of 1839 ordered him, at "the risk of body and limb," to suppress the English opium traders by force. Lin issued an edict banning foreign opium and demanding it be surrendered. Within two months the English and American opium traders turned in two million pounds of opium (20,283 chests)—perhaps the largest drug seizure in history.

On the beach of Humen the opium was burned in a huge bonfire. The fire stank "atrociously," said Lin.

In his "Sacrifice of Apology" to atone for what he had to do, Lin had written an "Address to the Spirit of the Sea," begging forgiveness for his polluting of the sea with ashes of opium. "O Spirit whose virtue makes you the chief of Divinities, whose deeds equal the opening and closing of nature," Lin wrote, "wash away all stains and impurities." Praying to the goddess of the sea "that creatures of the water move away for a time to avoid being contaminated," Lin made offerings of wine.

The goddess of the sea was Lin's deity. Often he began his day as commissioner by burning incense in the Temple of T'ien hou; for he, like the goddess, came from Fukien province, and they had the same clan name of Lin.

A man of scholarly dignity, more a poet than an official, Lin seemed a ghost of the Ming dynasty. The Mandarin, the English called him. In the midst of the Opium Wars that followed, he mused upon a line from Mencius, the theme of the provincial examination in Foochow, his home town: "The great man is one who in manhood still keeps the heart of a child." And as the English threatened war, he relaxed by writing a poem in praise of some green lychee nuts, which reminded him, he said, of "Eighteen young girls, each with the same smile."

Most of all, Lin Tse hsu was to be remembered for his eloquent letter to Queen Victoria that began "The Way of Heaven is fairness to all; it does not suffer us to harm others to benefit ourselves. Men are alike in this all the world over: that they cherish life and hate what endangers life . . ." And then Lin went on to plead with the queen: "O Majesty, control your wicked," for "there is a class of foreigner that makes opium and brings it for sale, tempting fools to destroy themselves. . . . O, Majesty, you can order the opium not to be grown, the fields hoed over, and sown instead with the Five Grains, and thus show the sincerity of your politeness, and humility, so our countries may have peace, together."

Some say Lin's letter was never received by the queen. It would not have mattered. These civilizations spoke in moralities that were as incomprehensible to one another as were their languages. One may wonder at the effect of this letter from the Confucian gentleman in China upon the young Queen Victoria, had she seen it. There is no evidence it was ever shown her. In any event, it was too late to deny that which was now inevitable.

England responded by its invasions of China, not once but twice. In the desultory warfare of 1839–44 and 1856–60, neither government was to distinguish itself with particular military honor. Though the opium traders won a decisive victory in "opening the doors" to the ports of China to the misnamed "free trade" in opium, the real battle was fought not on the battlefields nor in the peace conferences, but in the global balance of these two civilizations and their concept of each other.

After the wars neither the English nor the Chinese saw one another in the same ways they had before. The conflict had ended the romantic myths each had believed about the other, and reshaped and distorted these myths into grotesques of "the enemy" that were, if anything, even more stereotyped and less human.

Now the Chinese and the English began to look on one another with fear and xenophobia. It was as though their perceptions had been tainted by the opium and its nightmares. All that once had seemed exotic and mysterious, fascinating and wondrous, had suddenly become sinister and evil.

In the eyes of the Chinese, the foreigners were no longer merely barbarians. They were "foreign devils" who were said to "kill little girls for purposes of black magic," and they "were in the habit of buying Chinese children" to satiate their "perverted European sexual appetites." An officer of the emperor, Pei Ch'ing ch'iao, said of some of the heathen practices of the English: "They carry off young men and shave their heads, paint their bodies with black lacquer, give them some drug that makes them dumb, and so turn them into black Devils, using them to carry heavy loads."

So evil were these foreign devils that in the Temple of Ningpo they had stolen the sacred gowns of the God of Black Death. They were seen not only to don his gowns, but to sit upon death's throne.

On the walls of Canton a popular placard warned: "The English barbarians are born and grow up in wicked and noxious villages, beyond the pale of civilization, have the hearts of wolves and the thoughts of foxes." And, it was said, "by nature" these foreigners would do "anything for money"; they were "unnatural animals."

There is no wrath like that of a people whose image of itself has been defamed by history. Nor is there a contempt like the contempt of a defeated people toward those who have humiliated their sense of dignity, unless it is the contempt that the conqueror feels for the conquered.

In the eyes of the English, the Chinese, too, seemed less than human and surely less than English. They were said "to drown their infants in the village wells." They drank "the blood of little girls when they were starving." They were pagans, after all, who "worshiped their dead ancestors." And so they were fit to be no more than "coolies," the word of degradation used in India by British colonial officials that literally meant a "beast of burden."

So "passive" were the defeated people, they seemed as if dead, "entombed with the city walls," English correspondent George Cooke reported. Even more disheartening, the Celestial Kingdom, once thought to be so majestic and heavenly in its might, was "in awe of the people," said a disgusted Foreign Office dispatch.

The nearly "complete extinction of the cult of China" was

due to the defeat of the Chinese Empire, and the rise, "the prodigious progress of European civilization," which "gave to Europeans a sense of superior power," wrote G. F. Hudson in *Europe & China*. In the years after the Opium Wars, "the European now felt himself to be preeminent. Especially the Englishman," the English historian happily declared. And he felt a "moral elevation" in his attainment. "With so much moral progress it is no wonder that England and Europe as a whole ceased to entertain the admiration for the Chinese rationality and virtue which had been prevalent in the eighteenth century." And there was this: In Europe "the new *bourgeois* ascendancy" was "republican and democratic," wrote Hudson; it celebrated "the eclipse of Chinese cultural prestige."

Once the English were victorious they had defeated more than China. They had destroyed the European image of the Celestial Kingdom as a font of all wisdom. They had demolished their vision of Cathay as a magical and mystical land to be viewed with awe and trepidation. They had degraded China, and they felt contempt for its degradation, as though somehow China had betrayed them by not living up to their own myths about her.

". . . The curtain which had been drawn around the celestial country for centuries had been rent asunder," said Robert Fortune, in his *Wanderings in China*, of 1847. Fortune was disillusioned because the "enchanted fairyland" he sought did not exist. The self-righteous "Englishman might now be shocked by the venality of the mandarins," not his own, and might "shake his head over the evils of oriental licentiousness," not his own, as Hudson wrote wryly of the remarkable English ability to remain virtuous, no matter what.

And yet, if the Celestial Kingdom had underestimated the powers of the modern world, the West had underestimated the powers of the old world. Of all the ancient empires, China alone had kept the Europeans from its gates for hundreds of years. Even in defeat, most of China was never to be conquered, or even occupied, by the West.

Seldom in its history had China defeated invaders. It absorbed them. It made Chinese of them. And when that seemed unlikely, as the Ch'ien lung emperor had written England's George III, "Even if you were able to acquire the rudiment of our civilization, you could not possibly transplant our manner and way of life to your alien soil." Even then, the Chinese were content and confident in waiting for the yin and yang of life to reassert itself, as it always did.

In all of this there was a perverse sort of balance, if not justice. Foreigners had taken from the Chinese many of those qualities that had sustained the land and people for millennia (and the foreigners had given the Chinese, in return, many of those qualities they had brought with them). So, in the end, the foreigners in many ways became what they imagined the Chinese to have been.

When China lost the aura of its greatness and acquired the mantle of its weakness, those foreigners who had defeated it strangely seemed to begin to fear it. The European yin and yang of contempt and fear, superiority and guilt, conquest and Christianity, re-formed the image of China held in the West to one of a people both passive and sinister, pathetic and frightening, "timid and dastardly," as the Encyclopedia Britannica had intoned.

And so the Yellow Peril was created by the White Peril—of opium.

VI

CROSSING THE PACIFIC

IN A ROWBOAT

Floating, floating, what am I? Between earth and sky, a gull alone.
Night thoughts on a boat.   —TU FU, 712–70

Being from a race of dwellers upon the sea coast, the emigrants
have desired to go thither and have regarded California as a land
of abundance. They have also rejoiced in the freedom of the
United States. Hence they have not gone there as a result of
deceit, or by being kidnapped, nor under contract as Coolies,
but have flown thither as the wild geese fly.
       —LI HUNG TSAO and PAO CHUN, treaty commissioners
of the emperor, 1880

THERE WAS A MAN who crossed the Pacific Ocean in a rowboat.

He had become impatient waiting for passage on the foreign
ships. And, it was likely, he did not trust the captains of these
foreign ships, who treated the Chinese worse then they treated
their cheapest cargo. The man was not a bag of rice or a bale
of jute, and he refused to be treated like cargo.

So he decided to cross the Pacific Ocean by himself.

One day he rowed his boat down the Estuary of Humen,
from the harbor of Canton into the mouth of the Pearl River,
and out to sea. The boat he had was a small sampan, a low,
flat-bottomed wooden riverboat meant for trading in the harbor
and not meant for sailing in the open sea. In the lightest waves
the water would fill it, and it would easily capsize. For it was
not designed to battle waves and wind, but to loll in the gently
idling water of a harbor, like a water lily.

In the sea, his boat was like the paper boat of a child in the torrent of a spring shower. As soon as the boat had left the harbor, the waves began tossing it about helplessly. From the beginning it seemed certain that the man would surely drown. The boat would not survive more than a few days at sea.

Whether the man was a fisherman from Whampoa Island or one of the river people, the Tan Chia, who lived upon the Pearl River at Canton, was not certain. He would not likely have decided to cross the ocean if he was not experienced in handling a boat in the ocean. But he might have.

The small boat had sailed past the Dragon's Eye, a gaunt rock that guarded the estuary, through the Mouth of the Tiger and the Sea of Lions. It sailed farther, passed the haunts of the pirates on the islands of Lingting Bay, passed the fleets of war junks of the Imperial Navy hidden in the coves of the outer islands, and passed the old Portuguese trading port of Macao. And it came at last to the open sea.

Before it lay the vast oblivion of the Pacific. The man set his course toward America.

Either the man was a fool or a hero; perhaps a bit of both. His boat had a makeshift sail and no rudder to speak of, so its ability to sail across the ocean was less than dubious; it was clearly an impossibility. The passage from China to America lay across seven thousand miles of the world's greatest sea, and even the largest and fastest of sailing ships often did not make it. Perhaps, at most, the foolishness of the man might be thought of as a courageous act of suicide.

The strange thing was that the man was not alone in his foolishness. Eight small boats sailed forth on that day in 1852, and each boat was steered by its own Chinese Don Quixote of the sea.

Of these eight boats, six never were heard of again.

On the coast of Kwangtung province near Canton, the daring and skill of the boatmen were legendary. There was a tradition of mastery of the sea that dated from antiquity. It was in the port of Canton that the ancient mariners had largely built and equipped the great fleets of the Tang and Ming dynasties. And the seamanship of the local shipbuilders and sailors was a matter of inherited pride. These were an obstinate and independent people. The freedom of spirit that has distinguished them throughout Chinese history may well have arisen from their kinship with the sea.

Of the Chinese who crossed the seas to America, almost all came from Kwangtung province, and almost all of those came from a handful of counties around Canton. It has been said that half to three-quarters of the Chinese in the United States are the descendants of emigrants from just two counties, Chungshan and Toishan, sea-swept peninsulas south of the mouth of the Pearl River that are all but surrounded by the South China Sea. Often these villagers were old hands at seamanship and sea voyages.

Emigrants sailing to the "Gold Mountain" of California may have been embarked on a new journey, but not at all on a new pursuit. "These adventurous emigrants have for centuries penetrated through the Indian archipelago, have pushed through the Indian Ocean to Ceylon and Arabia, have reclaimed Formosa and Hainan, have established remarkable trade with Cochin China, Cambodia, and Siam, and have introduced useful arts into Java, the Philippines, and the Malay Peninsula," wrote Pyau Ling in the *Annals of the American Academy of Political and Social Sciences* in 1912: "Today they venture southward to Australia and far westward to Peru, Mexico, Canada, Cuba and America."

So their spirit of adventure, the exploration of unknown seas, and the skilled seamanship of the Cantonese and Kwangtung people were nothing new. They were merely new to America.

And these fishermen and peasants had even older spirits of independence. In the hills and on the coast near Canton, the people were descendants of the Yueh tribes, known as the Chuang, who in the third century B.C. established their own independent State of Nan Yueh. Ever since then, tribes of the "Hundred Yueh," sometimes named the "Hundred Clans," had fought the domination of the dynasties of the north, from the Han to the Manchu. These "aboriginal Yueh tribal peoples," as they were called by Jen Yu wen, the founder of the Kwangtung Institute of Historical Culture in Canton, resisted assimilation by the northern conquerors, holding onto the "indigenous language and customs" that were to become the unique and dramatic characteristic of the Cantonese.

"Forced by geography and climate" to be self-sufficient, thought Jen, the "people of Kwangtung acquired the qualities of pioneers, growing more adventurous, energetic, independent and nationalistic." To this Pyau Ling added that their history developed in them a stubborn "unbending spirit."

It was on these southern shores that the Mongols, who defeated the Sung dynasty, and the Manchus, who conquered the Ming dynasty, met the "fiercest and most heroic resistance," Jen wrote. So intense were their battles against the Manchu that the "Tartar Emperor" ordered that the coastal villages be removed fifteen miles inland and that the fishermen and seamen be forced to become peasants. In Canton, the citizens' resistance was so great that more than 700,000 people were slaughtered by the Manchu, wrote Jen Yu wen.

The "spirit of independence" of the people of Kwangtung became so "unruly," said Pyau Ling, that "their northern neighbors designate [it] 'savageness,' and they call the Cantonese tauntingly 'the southern savages.' " And he added: "Whether savage or not, Kwangtung preferred independence to servile submission to despotic rule" by invaders. Not surprisingly, Kwangtung became known as "the cradle of revolutions," and the lands by the southern seas seemed to become a birthplace of nationalistic movements.

"A seafaring people," C. P. Fitzgerald had written in *The Southern Expansion of the Chinese People*, "the Yueh regions fought against incorporation in new empires." To this day, "in Kwangtung, the homeland of the 'Cantonese' retains . . . their distinctive character and restless attitude toward northern rule," he wrote; for "the main constituent of the population of Kwangtung and also in Fukien is a stock originally non-Chinese and largely Yueh."

Who were these people? "The Yueh people, from whom the old kingdom had taken its name, were in ancient times widespread along the coast of eastern Asia. . . . Vietnam is the modern center of the Yueh, and the word *Viet* is simply the local pronounciation of the Chinese form *Yueh*," Fitzgerald said. "The more northerly Yueh were annexed by the Han empire and lost their national identity, although it is probable that a very large proportion of the present inhabitants of Fukien and Kwangtung are descendants of this people."

These seafaring people were among the masters of the seas. From the beginning of known history, faced with rugged and poor lands, the "coastal people turned to the sea, as long tradition suggested," wrote Fitzgerald. "They had, probably before the Christian age, moved south across the sea." And "the pattern of Chinese emigration therefore settled, at a time which has not been fully recorded, into a shape which it has retained until modern times."

It may have been these traditions that made them so self-reliant and independent. They fought foreign invasions with the same resilience with which they fought the storms at sea.

When the English launched their Opium Wars by invading Kwangtung, they were—not unexpectedly—met by a popular uprising. The high officials of the emperor may have connived and cajoled, and the emperor's army may have retreated more often than it fought, but the Cantonese and Yueh people resisted with their customary fury. In the coastal villages the gentry and peasants, fishermen and seamen, formed the Ping Ying Tuan (the Quell the Foreigners Corps) to drive the invaders out. They nearly did.

Several thousand villagers gathered at the town of Sanyuanli. They attacked the English army with bamboo rods and rattan shields, pikes and scythes. And the commander in chief of the English land forces, Sir Hugh Gough, ordered a retreat. In disarray, the invaders withdrew. One-tenth of the expeditionary force had been killed and the army routed. An English historian later called it the Lexington and Concord of China.

In the West the popular resistance to the Western invasions is not well known. But it appeared wherever the foreign armies appeared. On the Chungshan peninsula the fishermen organized the Water Braves and harassed the English fleet; in Ningpo seamen organized the Black Water Party for the same purpose; in Kwangtung the Sheng Ping Sheh Hsueh (the Peace Societies for Education) gathered a hundred thousand adherents and fought both the English and the Manchu for years after the Opium Wars had ended, as did the Red Turbans.

Some of these groups grew into the "secret societies" of later years. Of these, the Tien Ti Hui (the Heaven Earth Society) and the San Ho Hui (the Triads) became most famous and

feared, though, in truth, they were secret only to outsiders—
and were no more secret than the Green Mountain Liberty
Boys in America.

In the aftermath of the war the countryside was devastated
even more than by the war itself. As always, the burdens of
inflation and taxes to pay for the costly war fell upon the people
with the brutal force of the emperor's tax collectors. "It is difficult
for good people to live peacefully," a high official, Tseng Kuo
fan, wrote to the emperor in 1852: "The unjustified imprison-
ments are too many" because of the high taxes, he warned,
and discontent was growing. The burdens were heaviest on the
people of Kwangtung, where the war had begun and where so
much foreign opium had been destroyed.

"Songs of Oh, dear, Oh, dear!" was how the times were described by Pei Ch'ing ch'iao in his book of laments. The name
was an allusion to the despair of the fourth-century general,
Yin Hao, who on being stripped of his rank sat around all day
tracing the words, "Oh, dear, oh, dear, what a strange life," in
the air with his fingertip.

Once again it was the people of Kwangtung and neighboring
Kwangsi, those "impulsive, straight-forward, volatile" people, in
the words of Jen Yu wen, who arose in rebellion against the
Manchu emperor. The revolution of the Society of God Worshipers, known as the Taiping Revolutionary Movement, swept out
of the southern hills northward to the very gates of Peking.
Born in Kwangtung, its visionary prophet, Hung Hsiu ch'uan,
came from a Hakka clan in a poor peasant village, and his Heavenly Kingdom of Taiping promised a peasant utopia that combined the Christian spirit and the communal kinship of village
life. It was a revolution of rural reforms and Chinese nationalism.

"Land shall now be farmed by all, rice eaten by all, clothes
worn by all, money spent by all. There shall not be inequality

and no person shall be without food or fuel. For under Heaven all belongs to the great family of the Heavenly Father," declared the Taiping prophet.

The vision of the Heavenly Kingdom of Hung Hsiu ch'uan had an exhilarating impact upon the self-image and self-confidence of the peasantry. In a few years their armies had not merely reconquered much of China from the Manchu, but had almost toppled the emperor himself. China was to be reborn. It was a time of exaltation. Proclaimed the Patriotic Manifestos of the Taipings: "We consider the world is China's, not the Tartar's. China is the head and Tartary the foot. China is the Holy Continent and Tartary that of evil spirits. We raise this army of righteousness in order to invoke the Vengeances of God and to liberate the masses for the sake of China. This is hereby proclaimed to all under Heaven, so that everyone may hear it and know it."

And so, the emigration to America began amid the despair and defeat of the Opium Wars, and amid the triumphant, rising hopes of nationalism of the Taiping Revolution. It was an escape from, and an affirmation of, the Chinese spirit.

On coming to America, the independent village peoples of Kwangtung and the urbane city dwellers of cosmopolitan Canton were not those passive and defenseless coolies that they have been portrayed as being. They were not simplemindedly tricked by suave labor contractors and "shanghaied" onto the ships wholly against their will. They were not all refugees and sojourners. They were more often adventurers. And they came to the Gold Mountain of California not in fear and servility, but with the courage and boldness that inspired the emigrants from Europe; perhaps more, for they came from twice as far away.

The man who crossed the Pacific in the rowboat was one of

these adventurers. Who was this man? Where did he come from?

No one knew how long he sailed upon the sea. If there was any log of the voyage of his nameless sampan, it has never been found. Nor is it likely to be. There are no records of the storms he may have encountered. There is no word of what may have happened to his "lost" companions at sea. His voyage will be forever shrouded in mystery.

Somehow it is more fitting that way. The image of a man in a small boat appearing in the morning fog one day off the coast of California coming out of nowhere like a ghost, seems appropriate to a legend of the sea.

Even the course he sailed from Kwangtung to California is unknown. It is thought he may have crossed on the winds and tides of the Kuro Shiwo, the Black Stream, as did the ancient mariners. The crossing, if he came that way, would have taken him about six months—a long, but not impossible, journey. Many had done it before. And he would not be the last.

There was once a photograph of the man in the boat in a dusty museum in San Francisco's Chinatown. In this photograph the man was seen sitting on a small wooden boat on a beach in California. He was smiling.

He was a good-looking man—not gaunt, but thin, and self-possessed. The look in his eyes was one of amusement and of determination, as I remember it. Mostly he seemed pleased with himself, and a little smug.

The man's name, it was said, was George Hew. Beneath the old photograph there was a typewritten caption that read: GEORGE HEW SAILED FROM CHINA, IN 1852, IN THIS BOAT THAT HE IS SITTING ON. HE LANDED IN CALIFORNIA. That was all it said.

The old photograph is now missing from the museum. So,

in a sense, not only the man's face has disappeared; his name is gone, his boat has vanished.

And yet the old people who remember that story of the man in a small boat who sailed across the Pacific Ocean say it does not matter if all the records of his remarkable feat were to disappear. The legend of his voyage is its own truth. For the written memory of man is not the only memory written in the sea.

He was, after all, one of those men of Kwangtung. And a man of Kwangtung could do anything.

BOOK TWO

The Chinese

Who Built

America

VII

CONQUISTADORES FROM CHINA

Barbarians of Spain are tall and have high noses, pupils like cats'
eyes, and a mouth like a hawk.
—HUANG CH'ING CHIH KUNG T'U, eighteenth century

The Paradise of the West
and its infinite power
are but transformations
of its lotus blossom.
Pilgrimage to the West, Wu Cheng-en, 1510–80

TO THOSE GREEN HILLS where the "hundred thousand antelope
were seen" under the purest blue and unpolluted sky of the
"Island of California," as the Spanish called it, there came a
band of settlers. In the name of Charles III, king of Spain,
they founded the village of El Pueblo de Nuestra Señora la
Reina de los Angeles de Porciuncula, in 1781. The adventurer
known as Antonio Rodriguez was one of the daring pioneers
in this venture.

He was Chinese.

The man from China who was one of the "Spanish" founding
fathers of Los Angeles may not have been entirely alone in his
disguises. He might have known, as no one else could, how
many other Chinese there were with Spanish names among these
settlers. But if he did, he surely would not have revealed their
names. In Manila, where the Spanish galleons of the Pacific
set sail for America, there were many Chinese tradesmen and

craftsmen who let themselves be baptized as Catholics so that they might continue their trades. On coming to America, these men, known as the Spanish Chinos, the Chinese Spaniards, wore their christened names like masks. And for many reasons there were many other "Spanish" founding fathers who did the same.

Of the twenty-three "Patrons de los Angeles" who came on that *entrata* of original settlers, nine were Mexican Indians, eight were mulattoes, two were black Africans, one a mestizo, and there were two who were said to be *Españoles*, besides the Chino Antonio Rodriguez. These latter-day conquistadores of Spain were a cosmopolitan mixture of cultures and bloods. Yet they were all "Spanish"—even those who were Chinese.

All of these men and women came from Mexico, where there were many descendants of the Chinese merchants and seamen who had come to the New World on the Spanish galleons from Manila, beginning in the sixteenth century. These Chinese conquistadores were among the unheralded pioneers of America, and they were among the earliest, coming to the shores of the Pacific coast long before the Pilgrims crossed the Atlantic.

Merchants of Portugal had reached the coast of China in 1514. By bribing the local Ming officials, they established a colony at Macao, near Canton. Five years later, in 1519, the Portuguese navigator Fernando Magellan, sailing under the flag of Spain, landed in the Philippines. From that date the modern beginnings of oceanic commerce from China to America and back to China may be said to have begun.

On the famous "Manila galleons" of Spain this China trade was launched in 1565, when the first of these great ships sailed from Manila. The passengers and seamen, from the beginning, were Chinese in significant numbers, not surprising considering that the ships and the cargoes were almost wholly the products of Chinese manufacture and skill.

So many Chinese had crossed the ocean by 1635 that the Spanish barbers in Mexico City had petitioned the Municipal Council to protest the competition of Chinese barbers in the capital. They were duly banished from the city. But it was not merely the Chinese barbers who troubled the Spanish shopkeepers—there were physicians, tailors, weavers, silversmiths and ironsmiths, shipbuilders, carpenters, merchants, and mandarins who came from China. Many of these skilled professionals had been baptized with Spanish names in Manila. Many took Mexican wives in America. And yet, no matter in what guise the Chinese came, they remained Chinos.

The seaport of Acapulco, where the Manila galleons landed, became known as the *ciudad de los Chinos*, the city of the Chinese. Its citizens "consisted of Indians and Orientals, and of mestizos and mulattoes of every possible degree of mixture," wrote the historian of *The Manila Galleons*, William L. Schurz. And Simon de Andes, who described the port as an "inferno" of venomous serpents and tropical heat, noted with surprise the numbers of Chinese and Filipinos who were settled there. In Mexico City, all these emigrants were simply called Chinos, the Chinese. So, too, the road on which the goods brought by the galleons traveled from Acapulco to the capital was known as the China Road—El Camino de la China—the road of the Spanish Chinos who had become Mexican Chinos.

Even the Manila, or Spanish, galleons became known in the Americas as the China ships, the *naos de China*, for the fabled galleons were actually Chinese. Though these ships were likely so named because they carried Chinese goods, the truth was that the Spanish Manila galleons in the Pacific were almost all built by the Chinese.

Ships from Europe were pitifully small on the vast expanses of the Pacific. They had neither the cargo space nor the weight for a journey across an ocean that was twice the width of the Atlantic, a voyage that could last as long as six months. Nor were they designed to survive the peculiar furies of monsoons and typhoons upon those treacherous and unfamiliar seas.

And so the Spaniards had decided to have native artisans build ships native to these seas. The shipbuilders came from China, mostly from Canton. In using their centuries-old experience in ship construction and their deep-sea knowledge, the Chinese redesigned the Spanish galleons and adapted them to the styles of the majestic seagoing junks of the Ming dynasty.

In the large shipyards of Cavite on Manila Bay in the Philippines, these great galleons were entirely built by Chinese and Malayan shipbuilders who "carried on the work of construction and repair," Schurz wrote. Some of the galleons weighed in excess of two thousand tons, an unheard of tonnage at that time, ten times the weight of Columbus' flagship. The designing of the ships was done almost wholly by Chinese ships' engineers and architects. The hulls were built by Chinese carpenters. And the metalwork and casting of cannon were done by Chinese smiths. Even the elaborate designs on Spanish baroque themes were done by Chinese artists.

No wonder the graceful crescent-shaped hulls and the huge cargo holds of the Manila galleons resembled the seagoing junks of the Ming dynasty as much as they did the many-oared galleasses of the Mediterranean for which they were named. They were more Chinese than European.

Shipbuilding in China had been "a very ancient art, known long before the days of Tarshish" when the biblical vessels of the Old Testament brought ivories to the court of King Solomon, as the historian Charles Walcott Brooks noted years ago. In some ways, the Manila galleons were among the masterpieces of the Chinese art of shipbuilding.

On these galleons the riches of China reached the east—not

Europe, but America. In the colonies of Spain in the New World, colonial aristocrats lived as luxuriously as the courtiers of the royal court in Madrid—perhaps more so. Their taste for the silks and jewels, perfumes and spices, porcelains and jades of China was phenomenal. One galleon came laden with a cargo of 50,000 pairs of silk stockings. One brought chests with 80,000 jeweled combs of ivory. One was deeply weighted with 22,300 pieces of Ming dynasty porcelains and precious temple carvings, manufactured especially for export. But the Spanish colonialists were not too discriminating in accumulating wealth—so long as they could accumulate it.

"All these people live most luxuriously. All wear silk," the viceroy of New Spain wrote the king in 1602: "Gala dresses and clothes of the women are so many and so excessive that in no kingdom of the world are such found." An Irish priest who lived in Mexico City during the 1600s noted with a mixture of awe and disapproval that "Gallants, Ladies, and Citizens" promenading in the afternoon "spare no Silver, nor precious stones, nor Cloth of Gold, nor the best silks from China, to enrich them." And by 1720 a royal memorial stated matter-of-factly that "Chinese goods form the ordinary dress of the natives of New Spain."

The extravagances of the Spanish colonialists were paid for by the silver and gold of Mexico and Peru. In the early 1800s the Spanish archives record that in a single year more than two and a half million silver pesos were shipped to Manila to pay for the treasures of the Orient, and that of this fortune one and a half million were given to the merchants of China. From 1565, when the first galleons sailed across the Pacific, until 1815, when the last galleons docked, the Chinese trade was estimated to have cost the Spanish Empire, in contemporary values, from ten to twenty billion dollars.

And this China trade became "the most fortunate and lucrative of all in Europe and America," Tomas Ortiz de Landazil, royal treasurer of the Council of the Indies, had proclaimed when it hardly had begun. In a few decades the port of Manila, as home port of the galleons, became "the Magazine of the richest commodities in the world," the English geographer Morden wrote in 1673. "Manila is the equal of any other emporium of our monarchy, for it is the center to which flow the riches of the Orient and the Occident," the Jesuit father Colin had said. It was the "new Venice," the "warehouse of the faith"— *almacén de la fe.*

Manila had become much more than a port of trade. It was the "gateway to the East" for thousands of seamen and merchants from China who were to cross the Eastern Sea—the Pacific— to America. Not only did the city's trade come mostly from China, but so did most of its traders. Chinese merchants had established commerce with the Philippines hundreds of years before the Spaniards arrived. They soon dominated not merely the buying and selling of goods for the Manila galleons, but retail trade on the island as well.

Don Antonio Morga, soldier and historian, praised the Chinese merchants as "very skillful and intelligent traders." But, he complained, they outwitted his fellow Spaniards by "innumerable frauds and deceits in their merchandise." The Spanish soldiers were as uneasy with the deft and subtle methods of the Chinese traders as the Roman soldiers had been at the time of the Caesars. "Although they do not rob here or plunder the foreigners, yet they do it by other and worse methods," said one report to Madrid. So astute were these Chinese and so practiced in the guiles of commerce, that "each Chinese man appears to be the devil incarnate," wrote the xenophobic Ríos Coronel.

A tale that the Spaniards often told voiced the popular feelings about the commercial and professional expertise of the Chinese.

It was recorded by Father Casimiro Diaz, in 1669: "A Spaniard who had lost his nose, by a certain illness, sent for a 'Chinaman' to make him a new one. The workman made him so good a nose that the Spaniard, in great delight, paid him handsomely, giving him twenty *escudos*. The 'Chinaman,' attracted by the ease with which he earned so much, loaded a fine boatload of wooden noses in the following year and returned to Manila. There he discovered he would have to cut off all the noses of all the Spaniards to sell his merchandise." It might have been one of the fantastic tales of Don Quixote. But to the Spaniards in Manila, it was neither a fantasy nor a fiction.

Not all the royal officials were quite so xenophobic. One of the earlier governors, Lavezaris, had advised the king that the Chinese merchants were essential to the colony. "Each year their commerce increases," he said, "and they supply us with sugar, wheat and barley flour, nuts, raisins and pears, silks, choice porcelain and iron." It was the Chinese who clothed and fed the conquistadores and who made possible the Manila galleons' trade with America.

The Chinese came to Manila, in the beginning, as merchants, as they had to Europe and later would to America. They were everywhere pioneers in the establishment of commerce. In 1586 there were said to be ten thousand Chinese in Manila, a majority of the city's population. When the Spaniards "deported" twelve thousand, ten years later, it was reported that as many remained. By 1636 the Chinese population had risen to almost thirty thousand, and by 1749 it was forty thousand.

In all those years there were not more than a few hundred Spaniards in the entire city. So the Chinese were relied upon not merely as traders and builders and seamen who maintained the fleet of galleons, but as artisans and professionals of the city.

"From China come those who supply every sort of service, from physicians to barbers, to burden bearers and laborers. They are the tailors and the shoemakers, metal workers, silversmiths, sculptors, locksmiths, painters, masons, weavers, and finally every kind of servitors," wrote Father Chirino. Even Ríos Coronel had to admit reluctantly that the "community cannot be maintained without them." It was true. They came in great numbers to Manila bringing the skills and experiences of their civilization, which they offered at a good price to those less fortunate non-Chinese.

Since the third century B.C., this was the way that Chinese had most often gone overseas. They went as merchants. They went as adventurers. In many ways these emigrants who came to the Philippines and later to America were not unlike the earlier pioneers and explorers who settled throughout Southeast Asia, from Cambodia to Java. Neither as conquerors nor as sojourners, but as Chinese who happened to be living overseas they came and went, lived and died, much as they would have at home.

The merchant comes with his way of life in his head and in his pocket, as the craftsman comes with his skills in his hands. Neither needs to conquer and possess the land to exist and prosper. If either acquires power, it comes less from conquest than from the skills that each offers to the people and to the state, which are in themselves necessary and beneficial.

So the merchant and the artisan may precede the soldiers—and outlast them. They come independently of those clashes of national sovereignty that often follow them. For they are freer men.

And so it was with the merchants and artisans of China who came to America on the Manila galleons. The emperors of the Ming dynasty sent no soldiers after them. In the millennia since the founding of the dynasties, the emperors had learned that the perversity of military conquest of foreign—non-Chinese—lands often led to the dissipation of a nation's resources and strengths as it emptied the national treasury; while the conquest of an enemy by merchants, on the other hand, enriched a nation and increased its treasury. So the emperors rarely sent armies to foreign—"barbarian"—lands. Instead they preferred conquest by commerce, and their merchants became the conquistadores of China.

These then were the Chinese who were to come to America, beginning with the sixteenth century. In Mexico City, in Acapulco, in Mazatlán, and wherever they settled, the emigrants established themselves with the skills they brought with them, and they profited from their labors. And they endured here, as they had elsewhere, quietly.

Not that they were uniquely quiet people. They were not. It was more that merchants did not need or wish to upset the economy or cause disturbances. Rather, they sought to adapt their trades, if not themselves, to the existing ways and to develop what existed. It earned them the false but useful reputation of being passive and silent.

In truth, the merchants from China were simply realistic. The emigrants were almost all men. So, as was natural, they mated and married native women, and their children were not only Chinos, but mestizos. They were in double jeopardy from the racial legal codes of the Spanish Empire. At the time, the colonial rulers of New Spain had devised rigid and racist laws that divided the people into eighteen categories of purity, or "whiteness." Salvador de Madariaga, in his *The Rise of the Spanish American Empire*, caustically observed: ". . . as time went by mestizo blood became tainted with illegitimacy. This was the chief cause of the anxiety which the 'Whites,' Creoles and

Spaniards showed in later years to claim absolute white blood."
In these degrees of purity there was no category for the Chinos.
So many decided that it was wisest to be as silent and as invisible
as possible.

They succeeded. Not merely did they hide behind Spanish
names, as did Antonio Rodriguez, the founder of Los Angeles,
but they disappeared into the graying shadows of history.

Some three hundred years after the Manila galleons set sail
for America, during the Ming dynasty, there were descendants
of those Chinese who landed on the Pacific shores of Mexico
who reemerged from centuries of silence as Mexican Chinos.
They exuberantly joined the Gold Rush to California. It was
recorded in the shipping charts of San Francisco that in the
first six months of 1852 twenty-nine boats arrived with emigrant
Chinese gold miners. Of these, twenty-eight came from China.
But the twenty-ninth boat inexplicably came not from China,
but from the port of Mazatláan on the western coast of Mexico.
For all those three hundred years it was as if the Chinese emigrants who had traveled on the Spanish galleons to Mexico had
been waiting for that day.

The mysterious arrival of Chinese miners from Mazatlán must
have been confusing to the California officials. Even the coming
of these Mexican Chinos did not explain where they had come
from or why.

From the beginning of the Manila galleons voyages there had
been an obvious connection between the Spanish colonists' desire
for the riches of China's dynasties and their search for the riches
of America to pay for these extravagant luxuries. One desire
led to another. And the unearthing of the vast silver mines of
Alamos, in the State of Sonora in northern Mexico, and the
illusions of even richer mines in the Seven Cities of Cibola
whetted their appetite for further conquest. The Manila galleons

and the Spanish *entratas* into the American Southwest were related.

One of the founders of Santa Fe, New Mexico, in 1610, the oldest Spanish capital in the country, was, for example, Don Pedro (Gomez) Duran y Chavez. Earlier in that very year, he had been the royal tax collector on the Manila galleons in the port of Acapulco. Don Pedro was the patriarch of one of the powerful and distinguished governing families of the Spanish Southwest. His family's fortunes originated in large part from the profits of the ships of China, the *naos de China*. And he was not alone. Even Admiral Zevallos of the Manila galleons journeyed north to New Mexico, in 1614, to become the provincial governor. He, too, brought the skills and profits of the China trade with him on his *entrata* to a personal El Dorado.

These *entratas* of the Spaniards to America were more than quests for pesos of silver. On the religious and military expeditions there were cosmopolitan mixtures of cultures and peoples that characterized the Manila galleons. And they laid the foundations for La Raza, that complex and many-nationed people of the Southwest. Eugene Bolton, an old historian of the Spanish borderlands, had written: "In every frontier Spanish colony the soldiery was to a large extent made up of castes—mestizos, coyotes, and mulattos." To this, Carey McWilliams commented in *North from Mexico:* "It is quite obvious therefore, that the present Spanish-speaking population is of a very mixed racial origin, with the Spanish strain being the least important element in the mixture." And George Sanchez, the venerable native historian of New Mexico, said, "Biologically they range over all the possible combinations," but they were "untouched" by "Western civilization."

Were the conquistadores from China amongst these mixtures? It is difficult to say. The feats of the "Antonio Rodriquezes" of Chinese ancestry remain largely unknown and unrecognized in the history of the American West.

In the provinces of northern Mexico and what is now the southwestern United States there is a hidden history of the Mexican Chinos. There are tales told by the Mayo and Yaqui, by the Hopis and Apaches, of these "strangers." There are documents that tell of their comings and goings preserved in the high monasteries of Tibet, which once were described to me by a Shinto priest from Japan who said he had seen them, reciting names of emigrant families to verify his claims. For all that, there still is no written history of these pioneers.

Many who came returned to China. Many stayed. It never will be possible to know their numbers for, strangely, the Spaniards, who kept exact records of almost everything, seemed to be uninterested in the numbers of Chinese who crossed the oceans on the Manila galleons. The Chinos were spoken of often enough in official documents and personal memoirs so that their presence was remembered—but it is a half-forgotten memory, elusive and vague.

The comings and goings of these conquistadores of China have nonetheless left indelible traces of their exploits on both sides of the ocean. For it was a bold feat that they accomplished, though it has been so little recognized. As the merchants of China brought their skill and daring to America, so did they bring the knowledge and achievements of native American Indians to China. Early in the sixteenth century they had introduced crops such as Indian corn and peanuts to the Ming dynasty. By the end of the 1500s they had brought sweet potatoes and native tobacco to the court of the emperor. The Chinos were extraordinary bearers of both cultures.

In the old days of the Spanish missions, the word Chino was spoken in pride. The cultural heritage of these Chinese "Spaniards" was one that symbolized the spirit of independence and toughness of a frontier people.

There was even a horse known in old California as a Chinese horse, the *caballo chino*. It was a breed that was famous for two characteristics. One was its sturdy build and endurance. ". . . the old timers say the *chinos* were *muy guapos* (very tough)," wrote Arnold Rojas, in his *California Vaquero;* and the other was its curly hair. Rojas, using the old ranchero patois translated the *caballo chino* as "the curly-haired horse." It was said that these horses of the vaqueros, the first cowboys, descended from the fierce Mongolian horses with which the great khans conquered, and they were in turn the ancestors of the mustangs of the West.

On the Pacific coasts of Mexico and in the southwestern United States, Chino is still a common name among Mexicans and Indians. Few who have it know the history that it holds. It is, after all, "Spanish."

Though it too has been disguised by history, and is often mistaken for its masks, the inheritance of these pioneers remains. One may see evidence, for example, of the Chinese influences in Mexican embroidery and pottery. Native floral designs and brilliant colors suggest a similarity to the Ming dynasty damasks and silks, jades and porcelains brought by the Manila galleons— not too surprising, since the clothing industry of Mexico had its modern beginnings in the use of raw Chinese silks. In the early 1600s the viceroy of New Spain wrote that so much raw silk had been imported from China that fourteen thousand Indians were employed in Mexican factories converting the materials into robes and mantillas, dresses and altar cloths.

Since then the designs have been re-created with a Mexican flair. The style of dress has been altered, much as the colonial Americans changed the fashions of the English to suit their nature and environment; but the heritage of the Mexican Chinos remains.

One of the most fascinating Americanizations of Chinese customs was the use of Buddhist temple lanterns to celebrate Christian religious holidays. In the Southwest these paper lanterns were once known as *faroles de China*, the lamps of China. They too were brought to America on the Manila galleons. Here they were converted by the Catholic priests of Mexico into *farolitos de Navidad*, the little lamps of Christmas, to celebrate the birth of Jesus.

These *faroles de China* nowadays are made of brown paper bags bought in the supermarket. The imitation lanterns are weighted with a handful of sand, in which holy candles are set and lit. And the soft glow of the flickering flames seen through the brown paper bags makes the night seem like an altar surrounded by votive lights.

On Christmas Eve, throughout New Mexico, these Buddhist temple lanterns burn for Jesus.

VIII

THE FOUNDING FATHERS

> Long are the roads that divide us
> > and black the dust of the enemy riders.
> I watch the wild geese flying eastward.
> Would that I could fly with them
> > and be with you . . .
> Should I die here
> > how will you find my bones?
> > > —*Seven Songs of a Refugee* by TU FU, 759 A.D.

> From one generation to another, everybody tries to send a man overseas.
> > —*Longtime Californ'*

ONE OF THE FIRST English forts on the northwest Pacific coast of America was built in 1788 by armorers and carpenters from China. At Nootka Sound on Vancouver Island, these Chinese pioneers constructed the earliest frontier village in the Northwest. There they built a small but sturdy two-story fort that served as a fur trading post for the East India Company, four years before the English established an English settlement.

In 1788, an English sea captain, John Meares, had sailed from Kwangtung province in China for America with an adventurous crew of from fifty to seventy Chinese pioneers, a band consisting of carpenters, coopers, armorers, seamen, helmsmen, ships' pilots, architects, engineers, and craftsmen from Canton and Macao. They had signed on for the voyage across the Pacific in "much greater number than could be received," Meares noted in his ship's log; and though the captain was impressed, he was not surprised. After all, he wrote, the Chinese had a long history of seamanship, and they were "generally esteemed an hardy and industrious, as well as ingenious race" who had "navigate[d] every part of the China Sea."

Still, he was bemused. It was not every day that the Chinese built forts for the British Empire. And there had never before been a frontier settlement of Chinese pioneers so far north along the Pacific coast—not that the English captain knew. And little was then or is now known of these Chinese frontiersmen.

In the woods of Vancouver Island the settlers built a village. Using handhewn wooden boards and handmade nails, they constructed not only houses but a wharf and small ship's drydock, as well as their Chinese version of an English fort.

They did more than that. On the shores of Nootka Sound these pioneers built a forty-ton schooner, the *Northwest America*. It was probably the first seagoing vessel to be launched on the northwest coast of America by other than native shipbuilders. Surely it was the first "British" vessel to be built in the north Pacific. And on its maiden voyage to the Queen Charlotte Islands, it was commanded by a crew of English and Chinese seamen— a curious setting for the unfurling of the flags of the British Empire.

Although the English abandoned the fort the year after, many of these settlers from China remained in America. They traveled up and down the seacoast and explored the rivers and woods from Alaska to Puget Sound, in Washington State. They were among the first explorers in many of these regions of the Northwest.

Some fifty years after the English had left Fort Nootka, there were several reports of Chinese men living among the native tribes. These pioneers had become settlers, while the English were mere sojourners.

These settlers of Nootka Sound, by their endeavor, had paradoxically established the English claim to the land of the Canadian Pacific. Although Captain James Cook had explored the
region ten years before, in 1778, he had never built a settlement.
And so, when in 1790 the Spanish relinquished their claim to
the northwest coast, the treaty of these European nations by
which they divided the Pacific shore of North America between
themselves was symbolically titled the Nootka Convention in
recognition of the settlers from China, who were not of course
asked to sign it.

Sadly enough for the English, the Nootka settlement had been
captured by the Spanish soon after the Chinese settled. And
yet, before the village was abandoned, two more ships owned
by Captain Meares had brought another twenty-nine Chinese
pioneers to America, and a ship of the American Captain Metcalf
brought forty-five more in 1789.

More than one hundred pioneers from China were settled
on the northwest Pacific coast in the late eighteenth century.
These Chinese emigrants preceded, by almost two decades, the
famed expedition of Lewis and Clark, which set forth to "discover" the Pacific in 1804, and they had explored the coastline
for several years before Alexander Mackenzie crossed Canada
to the Pacific in 1793.

For all that, these Chinese pioneers and explorers have received
little recognition in the histories of the West. Their explorations
and achievements remain largely unrecorded by American and
English historians. It seems especially strange since their settlement was so crucial in determining the course of empire in
the West. The founding fathers of the British Empire in the
Northwest were nonetheless mostly Chinese.

The souls of these pioneer men had been set afire by an "in-
born, independent idea, the seafaring spirit, the early contact
with western nations, the stress of war, the 'Golden Romance,' "

the historian Pyau Ling has written. And these characteristics of the people of Kwangtung and Fukien made them into "a migratory people."

In these ways, the spirit of the frontiersmen from China was perhaps not so greatly different from that of many other pioneers. It demanded a sense of adventure and arrogance to cross an unknown ocean to an unknown land. Even more, the men who risked their lives to pursue a vision had to possess a daring and a boldness sufficiently foolhardy to be heroic. In all of these ways, the Chinese pioneers were similar in spirit to the seamen on the Manila galleons and the pilgrims on the *Mayflower*. They, too, were ironic heroes.

To the pioneers and explorers, the seamen and settlers from China, the land of America had long been a fabled place. It was the miraculous land in "the Eastern Sea" where the sun rises. It was the enchanted land of wealth. It was in many ways the Cathay of China.

Ever since the fifth century, when the legends of the "Land of Fusang" had spread through the court of the Sung emperors, America was dreamt of as the paradise of innocence and abundance—where there were neither wars nor taxes. The wealth that came to China from the Americas, beginning in the sixteenth century, on the Manila galleons of Spain did little to dissuade that fantasy. Travelers returning from Mexico and Peru told of treasures so vast that their tales had impressed even the blasé Ming emperors. Surely America was the "Golden Mountain" long before gold was discovered in California.

In America there were conquistadores from China with Spanish names, like the Chino Antonio Rodriguez who became one of the founders of Los Angeles. There were the Chinese merchants and traders whose goods made possible the profits of the trading routes of the Spanish and English empires in the

Pacific. There were the Chinese shipbuilders who built so many of the Manila galleons of Spain. There were the Chinese seamen who sailed the ships across the Pacific to America. And there were the Chinese explorers and pioneers who settled in the Americas from Peru to Canada.

No one knows, or will ever know, how many settlements and villages these Chinese established in America. The Europeans, for many reasons, were not eager to recognize the Chinese colonists within their colonies. And the Chinese could not do so: The penalty for leaving China, by the decree of the Manchu emperors, was death by decapitation—not a reward conducive to the faithful recording of history.

So there were understandably few records of the Chinese pioneers. In the scant and scattered notes on life in sixteenth- and seventeenth-century colonial Mexico there was casual mention of settlements of Chinese pioneers in Acapulco, Mazatlán, and Mexico City, and of Chinese frontiersmen in California and New Mexico. But the historical tribute to these Chinese founding fathers (they were almost all men) was written with a deliberately vague and shadowy hand.

Nonetheless, these pioneers from China, and the merchants in China, had a profound effect on the future of American history. They influenced the founding and shaping of the nation. And they belied their silent and unobtrusive presence by the perverse force they exerted on the way the European empires governed the economy of their colonies in America and on the way the American colonists revolted against them.

The influence of the Chinese upon the American Revolution was subtle and indirect. It was like the colonies of pioneers and frontiersmen from China—unseen and unremembered. But it was as crucial as if the Manchu emperors had dispatched their navy, the largest in the Pacific, to sever the economic lifeline of the British Empire by bombarding Boston harbor. Instead, they sent their tea. The effect was as explosive.

England (as I've noted) had become addicted to the teas of China. In the late eighteenth century the prices of these "celestial herbs" were seriously depleting the royal exchequer; for the Chinese emperors insisted that English merchants pay for their tea addiction in silver, much as they forced the Spanish to pay in silver coins for the luxuries they bought from China. And in so doing, they created a disastrous trade deficit for both European empires and nearly bankrupted both.

In time, the English would solve this crisis of commerce by the ingenious opium trade and Opium Wars. But in the 1770s the prime minister agreed to a less imaginative and much more practical policy: He ordered that the colonies be taxed increasingly to pay for the English taste for Chinese teas. The American reaction to these taxes is history.

The symbolic beginning of the American Revolution—more significantly than anybody knew at the time—was the dumping not of English teas, but of Chinese teas into the waters of Boston Harbor. On that night, those colonists, dressed as Mohawks, who hooted and hollered as they tossed the chests of green Hyson and baskets of black Bohea teas overboard sang with misplaced fervor:

> And tell King George
> We'll pay no more taxes
> On his foreign tea.

The American revolutionaries were as ignorant of the reason for England's need to increase its taxes as the Chinese merchants were ignorant of the effect that their haughty trade policy was to have in hastening the American Revolution. And yet the growth of the American nation was intertwined with these faraway cycles of the China trade. As the cost of England's defeat in the American Revolution made the opium trade to China seem all the more economically attractive, England's victory in the Opium Wars was to open the ports of China to the Yankee ships of the American revolutionaries.

On the China Seas, the passages and trade routes had been the "preserve" of England's imperial companies, as Sir John Pratt had said. The ships of the colonies were prohibited. It was as if the seas were fenced and the oceans closed. But as soon as the Europeans had forced the Chinese to open their ports to the opium trade, schooners and clippers of the Americans slipped through. The Yankee sea captains approached China with naiveté and admiration. In the beginnings of New England's trade with China, these whaling and sealing captains seemed innocent of the Europeans' jaundiced view of the Chinese. The sea logs of the Yankee captains, studied by the historian Stuart Creighton Miller in his *The Unwelcome Immigrant,* showed little prejudice toward China; if there was any, it was more fantastic than racist. Enthusiasm for China was reflected by the Yankee sealing captain Amasa Delano, one of the earliest of New Englanders to arrive in Canton; he forsook his usual tight-lipped commentary to exult: "China is the first for greatness, riches and grandeur of any country known."

On George Washington's birthday in 1784, when the *Empress of China* became the first yankee ship to clear New York Harbor for the Orient, the occasion was one of patriotic speeches. The captain, John Green, was himself a hero of the Continental navy, and the "supercargo," Samuel Shaw, who was to become the first American consul in China, had been an officer in the Revolution. A "Great Number of Inhabetants," wrote Captain Green in his sea log, "Salluted us by giveing Three Cheers"; for emotionally, if not economically, the "New People," as the

Chinese named the Americans, felt they were challenging the British Empire on the high seas. The psychological effect upon the young nation was exhilarating.

In this, the China trade was more than a matter of profit to the Yankee captains—though it was that. While the English were already shipping opium to China, the *Empress of China* sailed with a cargo consisting four-fifths of ginseng root, a medicinal herb as popular in China as it was among the Iroquois tribes who grew it. The Yankee ship was indeed carrying coals to Newcastle. In his innocence, the purser wrote home: "We brought too much ginseng."

Most of the American colonists had not the slightest notion of where China was or what it was like. Their horizons did not grow noticeably longer after they achieved their own place in the sun. And so it was not at all surprising that when the country's leaders thought of China—when they thought of it at all—it was as if it were an imaginary land. George Washington was not alone in his belief that the Chinese people were "white." He seemed somewhat puzzled to learn that they were not. But he had never met anyone from China in his entire life.

In colonial and revolutionary America not everyone was that happily ignorant, it was true. In his notes on the Continental Congress, the worldly John Adams had knowingly written that "China is not larger than one of [our] colonies"; he had been so informed by one of the country's most sophisticated intellectuals, Dr. Benjamin Rush. There were many equally knowledgeable. In the scholarly library that Thomas Jefferson sold to the Congress after the British had burned the national library during the War of 1812, there was evidence of *his* knowledge of China. Of six thousand volumes, there were three concerning China, all in French. But that was a considerable improvement upon the library of Richard Henry Lee, the "best scholar in Virginia," whose library had not a single book on China.

There was thought to be but one volume of the works of Confucius in all the colonies. And that was in the library of the bibliophile James Logan, who, it was said, collected "anything."

Even old Benjamin Franklin, who wrote that "if he were younger" he'd be delighted to visit China, for he was "fond of reading" about its philosophers, gave no evidence of ever having done so. The sage of Philadelphia seemed no more knowledgeable than Washington, who in his self-effacing way had said that all he knew about China was that its people were "droll in shape and in appearance."

Of the fascination with China that came later, much developed from this ignornace. The historian Ping Chia kuo once wrote of the first Yankee traders who visited Canton: "Their interest in China was, in the main, hardly more than an interest in the exotic, a fantastic striving to escape [from] drabness." And of such ignorance was born the image of China as a land of "darkness," as a missionary paper wrote. The Chinese became "an enigma wrapped in mystery"; they were "inscrutable."

If the Founding Fathers of America knew little about China, it was likely the Sons of Han were much more knowing about America. The earliest known maps of the New World had appeared in Peking in 1584, when Jesuit missionaries had presented a global map to the Ming emperors. But Chinese merchants and traders "may have already possessed knowledge of the New World" before that, said researchers of the Chinese Historical Society of America; for there was abundant evidence of sea explorations and trading missions from China to America that dated back to antiquity.

The scholars of China may have known of few of the events of the American Revolution, but their knowledge of the long history of relations between colonies and empires gave them an insight into its global effects. Some of the more perceptive scholars sensed its impact on the future of England and on China. "When England lost [the American colonies], it almost lost its color," commented Tse Chi-yu in his *Manual of Geography* in 1848; for without its colonies, England would be no more than "a handful of stones in the western sea."

From this, these geopoliticians of China had foreseen the rising of a great nation in America, a new "Fusang." The Chinese pioneers who had been coming to the New World since the beginnings of the Spanish Empire had long ago written of this.

There were, at the time, not more than a dozen American pioneers in China, wrote James Kirker in his history *Adventures in China: Americans in the Southern Oceans, 1792–1812;* but there were hundreds of Chinese pioneers in America. For two centuries before the founding of the nation, these pioneering men of China had been influencing the form of the colonies on the Pacific coasts of America.

On the east coast the Founding Fathers hardly were aware that the west coast existed. Nor had they ever heard of the Chinese pioneers. Even if they had, they probably would not have recognized them as pioneers. They did not behave as pioneers should, for they made no attempt to possess the land they explored, and the emperors of China did not send their navy, the largest in the Pacific, to invade America,

Pioneers on the frontier came to conquer. The ethic and the ideal of the pioneering Europeans was to remake America in their own image, as was fervently expressed in those lines of Walt Whitman's "Pioneers! O pioneers!"

All the past we leave behind,
We debouch upon a newer mightier world . . .
Fresh and strong the world we seize . . .
Conquering, holding, daring, venturing as we go . . .

The pioneers from China had come with a different mind.
For to possess and to conquer the land was a foreign idea to
them. Here and elsewhere they came to savor the adventure,
to explore with curiosity, and to become wealthy. It was not
their need to remake America into an image of China; the
thought was absurd.

So, to the Americans, the Chinese hardly seemed pioneers.
They dismissed them as "sojourners" who had no desire to be
Americans. The Americans did not understand that exploration,
in China, was as ancient a form of conquest as emigration, but
that it was guided by its own beliefs and goals learned from
millennia of history. The art of pioneering without ever leaving
home was a peculiarly Chinese art; it consisted, in part, of enticing those to be conquered in coming to the conqueror.

One of the few American historians who recognized the unique
nature of the Chinese influence on the creation of this nation
was that venerable curmudgeon Charles A. Beard. In *The Rise
of American Civilization*, his text had ranged from the shores
of California, where "the Chinese was first to bear the impact
of the collision with the Nordic," to the shores of China, where
this country "for the first time" formulated and applied a foreign
policy of "imperial design."

Beard, in his sweeping prose, embraced a century within a
sentence. He wrote with a clear and dramatic style that deserves
to be quoted in full.

"The very year after Cornwallis surrendered to Washington

at Yorktown, the *Empress of China*, fitted out partly at the expense of Robert Morris, merchant prince and 'financier of the American Revolution,' sailed from New York to Canton, carrying the American flag into the midst of the Dutch and British pennants that fluttered in the breezes of Chinese waters. . . . Before the Fathers completed the framing of the Constitution, at least nine voyages had been made to the Far East by enterprising Yankees.

"In the year of Washington's inauguration, ten ships from Salem plowed the waters of the Indian Ocean. Before he delivered his 'Farewell Address' warning his country against foreign entanglements, American captains were at home in the ports of China. In 1797, the date of his retirement to Mt. Vernon, a crew of thirty boys, the oldest not over twenty-eight, took the *Betsy*, a boat of less than a hundred tons, on a voyage around the world by way of the Horn, Canton and Good Hope, netting on an outlay of about eight thousand dollars the neat profit of a hundred and twenty thousand.

"Meanwhile Congress under a Constitution formed, as Webster remarked, mainly for the advancement of commerce, granted to merchants trading with the Far East protective rates and special privileges of royal generosity, advantages that assured magnificent returns except in the most adverse of circumstances. As Senator from Pennsylvania and a promoter of business with China, Robert Morris could speak with authority among his brethren. . . .

"In the decade ending in 1840, American business with China alone amounted to nearly seventy-five millions, a sum greater than the total debt of the American revolution which timid souls in Hamilton's day thought the country could never pay. By that time American manufacturers, especially cotton spinners, had come to view China's teeming millions as the marginal customers who were to keep their wheels whirling and coffers full. In 1875 over a hundred and fifty American ships cleared from Indian ports carrying goods worth upwards of ten millions.

"When the guns of [Fort] Sumter echoed over the plains and through the valleys of the United States, shrewd American business men had already gathered into their ships more than half the trade to and from the port of Shanghai and had made themselves masters of the lion's share of the commerce up and down the turgid current of the Yangzye. The challenge of the planters to the captains of industry slowed down this enterprise in the Far East—but only for a day. . . . In this titanic process disputes over slavery and even the Civil War itself were incidents. . . ."

Never has a historian so forcefully described the decisive influence of China on the formation of the American nation, and on America as a world power. And yet, this is the history of the influence of China on America—not of the Chinese in America.

The pioneers of China, the colonies they once established in the West, and the ships and the settlements they built that were to become the mythic legends of the China trade, have seemingly vanished into history. Of the few documents that have remained to tell their stories, many are deep in the dim archives of Spain and the remote archives of Peking. For, like ghosts, their memories have faded into the elusive shadows of the American past and are denied to their progeny.

Nonetheless, pioneers of every new nation always become the new Eve and Adam, the First People. And, in time, the Chinese explorers and seamen, settlers and merchants of the West, will again become legendary heroes, more likely remembered in fantasy than in history. An aura of myth has already begun to surround them in this generation. One aged man in San Francisco's

Chinatown remembered the pioneering life of his own father in this way:

"When my father was young, that was the time for heroes for the Chinese in America. It was the hardest times, because of what they've been through, but they were the greatest ones."

Of the "brave pioneering Chinese who preceded us," California Superior Court Judge Harry K. Low told a Bicentennial Conference on "The Life, Influence and Role of the Chinese in the United States" from 1776 to modern times, that the "pioneers blazed a trail," not merely for their compatriots from China, but for all Americans.

"History, like beauty, is in the eye of the beholder," Judge Low said. "As a Chinese American it is hard [for me] to speak of our 'influence.' Like every participant, or artist, we dip our brush in our own soul. And paint our thoughts in how we view history."

But these Chinese pioneers were not a romantic myth. They still exist in the history of America. On the shores of the Pacific in a hidden cove, among the scattered logs of a forgotten fort, amid the ruins of a frontier village, or deep in the woods surrounding a secluded settlement of an Indian nation, as in the graying waters of Boston Harbor, there exist the spirits of the Chinese pioneers of America. The silence that clothes them is merely ignorance. Somewhere there are the Chinese Paul Bunyan, the Chinese Davey Crockett, the Chinese Wovoka, the Chinese Geronimo, the Chinese Murieta, patiently waiting for history to recognize their existence. For there were Chinese founding fathers of America whose names no one knows.

IX

MASTERS OF THE GOLDEN

MOUNTAIN

The call of the Gold Mountain, the name given by the Chinese
laborers to California, was ringing in the air. . . . Those who
had made their fortune returned and spread the news of the
"Golden Romance." —PYAU LING, 1912

I beseech the Golden Heaven Spirit for an answer to my question
by his roadside shrine, but the Golden Heaven Spirit does not
answer me; he is more melancholy than a mortal being . . . when
I heard his speech my sadness grew sadder; Heaven sends down
disasters we cannot control, and if a Spirit cannot escape calami-
ties, why should we curse and praise the Lords in the East?
—WEI CHUANG, 836–910

SOME WERE SCHOLARS, but mostly they were merchants who
had come to California to engage in commerce with the gold
miners, and little more. They had no desire to dirty their hands
by digging gold. They were men of culture. Resplendent in their
silk robes and gold brocaded jackets and carved ivory fans that
concealed their eyes from the dust of the muddy streets, the
elders of the Chinese community were an incongruous sight as
they led their solemn procession through the filthy alleys of the
Barbary Coast.

On the streets lay the refuse of the night before, animal and
human. The city had no sewage or sanitation system. So the
streets of San Francisco were an obstacle to a horse and wagon,
much less to the silk-gowned merchants with their silk slippers.

These gentlemen must have walked with some distaste upon

the debris. But they were on their way to being honored by the city and they continued on their way with as much dignity as they could maintain, hiding their displeasures and amusements behind the fluttering of their ivory fans.

Miners from the gold fields, who had never seen so many Chinese, marveled at their "dignified manners and general appearance." And spectators, who seemed astounded by the elegance of these merchants, applauded as they marched past. There were cheers.

On that summer day—it was August 25, 1850—the clergymen and dignitaries of the city had gathered to pay their respects to the Chinese merchants by "converting" them to Christianity. Some biblical tracts had been printed in Chinese, in Canton, for the occasion. The mayor, John Geary, was on hand to distribute them. So was the Reverend Albert Williams, the founder of the First Presbyterian Church of San Francisco, who described the tribute to the "celestial men of commerce" as an expression of the "pleasure shared in common by the citizens of San Francisco at their presence."

In "the hope that more of their people would follow their example [by] crossing the ocean to our shores," the city's fathers all but promised any new emigrants who came from China the keys to the city; for America "needed" them. Go tell your "friends in China that in coming to this country they will find welcome and protection," they proclaimed. That, said the Reverend Williams, was an "encouraging omen" for the future. Sadly, he was quite wrong.

The speeches on that day outdid each other in praising the "China Boys," as these subtle merchants were called. Speaker after speaker extolled the virtues of the Chinese character. "We have never seen a finer-looking body of men collected together in San Francisco, in fact, this portion of our population is a

pattern for sobriety, order and obedience to laws, not only to
other foreign residents, but to Americans themselves," editorial-
ized the *California Courier*. To this the *Alta California* added:
"These celestials make excellent citizens and we are pleased to
notice their daily arrival in large numbers."

So much warmth and friendliness in welcoming the Chinese
to California may seem suspect in light of the later vehemence
with which the newcomers from the east demanded that these
newcomers from the west be deported. But the reasons were
practical enough.

In the early days the port town of San Francisco was nothing
more than a cabal of shacks huddled on the hills. The settlers
had few of the simplest necessities. Even food was scarce. Goods
and supplies had to be brought from the east, around Cape
Horn, a long voyage of many months, so treacherous that many
of the ships were lost and many of their cargoes swept overboard.
And the journey by wagon train across the continent was even
more hazardous.

The passage from China was more direct, and in many ways
easier. Merchants of Canton had been regularly crossing the
Pacific on trading missions in the Manila galleons of Spain for
two centuries. So these Chinese merchants became the suppliers
of grain and rice, sugar and tea, dried fruits and spice, to the
gold miners of California. "Soon as the news of the discovery
of gold reached [China's] ports, ships were loaded and dispatched
to the California market," noted the Reverend Williams. Not
merely foodstuffs but a vast array of manufactured products—
tools and utensils, textiles and clothes—were exported from the
Old World to the New.

"Were it not for the Chinese we might have starved the
first year," one Yankee miner wrote in his diaries.

Enthusiastic, too, was the response of the mercantile houses, such as Finley Johnson & Company and C. B. Post & Company. In fact, it was John Osborn of Osborn and Brannan who proposed the establishment of the first steamship mail line from San Francisco to Canton.

The Chinese goods and foods were a welcome sight on the docks, but even more welcome were the skilled craftsmen and technicians who accompanied these shipments. Few professionals were practicing in California. As soon as they arrived they headed into the hills for the gold camps, where there was a shortage of artisans of all types. In recognition of this, the unofficial "American ambassador to California," Thomas Larkin, had written in 1848: "One of my favorite subjects or projects is to introduce Chinese emigrants into this country. . . . Any number of mechanics, agriculturists and servants can be obtained."

And so they came, the physicians and engineers, merchants and fishermen, farmers and ironsmiths. It was the carpenters among them who built the famous prefabricated "Chinese houses" that became so popular in San Francisco. The movable houses were often transported by wagon to the new mining towns, where they became the unknowing precursors of a later life-style in California.

These Chinese houses were "the prettiest, the best-made and the cheapest," wrote a French journalist, Etienne Derbec, while the correspondent for an eastern magazine wrote: "From early morn until late in the evening these industrious [Chinese] men are engaged in their occupation of home builders." In amazement he noted that "a great number" of the houses had been brought all the way from China, and they were merely assembled in America. It puzzled him.

Some of the prefabricated houses were indeed shipped from China, because it was widely believed that the "white barbarians" in America would not be able to construct them. And the Chinese workers did not think that they could teach them how to do so.

The emigrants from China were utterly convinced of their superiority, and the rough and crude vulgarity of the mining camps and frontier towns did little to lessen this conceit. So sublime was their belief in the superiority of their ancient culture and practical knowledge that these Chinese forty-niners tended to be overly polite and patronizing to the Yankee settlers, whom they treated like amusing and uncultured children. And yet, they were stern. The elegance of their silk gowns amidst the filth and excrement on San Francisco's streets was a wordless way of expressing their contempt for these surroundings, as though they were above such aesthetic backwardness.

So the procession of the merchants on that summer day in San Francisco in 1850 may have had two purposes. One was the city fathers' desire to ingratiate themselves with these men who had brought enormous profit to the mercantile houses; and then there was the desire of the Chinese merchants to impress the Yankee barbarians with the benevolence of their wisdom and worldly wealth.

On Portsmouth Square, in front of the old Mexican Customs House, a ceremonial platform had been built. There the Reverend T. D. Hunt not only welcomed the "celestial China Boys" to the city, but offered them an invitation to the Christians' heaven. Although he knew, he said, that they came from a "celestial country" there was "another celestial country above, much better, much larger, than their own," where their dead ancestors were waiting for them.

When his remarks were translated, the Chinese merchants "broke into roars of laughter." The benevolent ministers were understandably shocked.

In the early days these men who crossed the ocean to this

strange land were bold and outspoken. They may have been wary, but they were not intimidated. So boisterous was their behavior, in the spirit of the frontier atmosphere of San Francisco, that the pioneer Yankee settlers spoke of them as too conceited and "haughty." The Reverend Williams sought to explain that, "like other immigrants, they came as adventurers," but that did not soothe the feelings of uncertainty and confusion among the Yankees.

Still, it was not their boldness but their haughty manners that made the Yankees uneasy. The word "haughty" was most often used by the white settlers to describe the men of China.

"Emigrants [from China] to this day constitute the most respectable type of emigrating class, and are, perhaps, as little open to the charge of being the scum of the population as any emigrants in the world," Sir Walter Medhurst was to write in his *The Chinese as Colonists.* The "predominating element" among them formed "the backbone of trade and have as much interest in leading a quiet, well ordered life, as a colonist who leaves the shores of Great Britain for the purpose of bettering his prospect," said Medhurst.

And so they were "welcomed, praised and considered almost indispensable," Mary Roberts Coolidge said in her classic on *Chinese Immigration.* They were not only "respected," but "desired."

In that year of 1850, there were only a few hundred Chinese in California; the figures vary. Almost all figures agree, however, that by 1852 there were twenty thousand or more young men from China who had sailed to the Golden Mountain to seek their fortune. And one decade later, by 1860, there were between thirty and fifty thousand people, mostly from Kwangtung, in California.

Few of these young men, and most were in their twenties,

were thought to be merchants or professionals. They were the sons of "fishermen and small farmers" from the seacoast villages of south China. And yet less is known of their origins and occupations than of their characters, which were, if anything, even bolder and more adventurous than those of the lordly merchants. Pyau Ling has described the impetuous daring of these young men: ". . . 'To be starved and buried at sea are the same,' said some young adventurers. 'Why not plunge right into death, rather than wait for death!' " Pyau went on: "With this spirit they even embarked in their crude old junks and combatted with the dangerous elements of the sea without fear or the idea of receding.

"Liberty, above all, is the star that guides these people to America," said Pyau.

Some historians believe, as many did at the time, that the young Chinese came as coolies and contract laborers. But there is little evidence that they were either. The governor of Hong Kong, Sir John Rowring, said in 1852 that the great majority of emigrants who passed through his port "paid their own way." Rowring spoke of "the marvelous exodus of the Chinese" as "one of the most remarkable ethnological circumstances in modern history," and prophesied that it would have an "extraordinary and lasting result" wherever they went.

An English agent sent to recruit coolies for the plantations of the West Indies lamented that the "best workers" were "those who pay their own expenses to California." They were too independent and shrewd, he complained, to listen to his promises.

One of the rather typical broadsides issued in Hong Kong in 1862, to recruit miners for Oregon, gives some idea of the enticements that were offered to the young men who accepted the challenge of coming to America: "To the countrymen of Ah Chan!" began this appeal. "There are laborers wanted in the land of Oregon, in the United States of America. They will supply good houses and plenty of food. They will pay $24 a month and treat you considerately when you arrive. There is no fear of slavery. All is nice. The money required [for the voyage] is $58. Persons having property can have it sold, or borrow money of me upon security. . . . Signed, Ah Chan."

This contract for coolies was in fact a financial loan secured by property. It was a straightforward business deal between a shipping agent and would-be passengers who demanded a great many guarantees. And these emigrants never resembled the "yellow hordes" of "coolies" who so terrified the Yankee miners, for that specter never existed. It was simply a myth. Somewhat backhanded and patronizing praises of the Chinese emigrants by the contemporary historian H. H. Bancroft refuted the coolie myth: "It was not the lowest grade of laborers who came hither; the infamous coolie system never obtained to the United States. John [Chinaman] is no time server, this little fellow from the celestial hills, nor [is he a] pauper."

Men who paid their own fares "to the last cent," as Sir John Rowring said, were treated differently from contract laborers and steerage passengers. There were some captains of clipper ships who overcrowded their holds inhumanly, with resultant tragedies of death and disease. But these death ships were an exception.

On these voyages to America there often was a mutual respect. It was evident in the elaborate banners that the emigrants presented to their captains, as did the passengers of the *Ellen Foster*, the *Persia*, the *Archilles*, and the *Australia*. When the *Balmoral*, commanded by Captain J. B. Robertson, completed its Pacific run, the Chinese emigrants honored the ship's master with the gift of a gold ring, made "of California gold," apparently brought from China. On the tallest mast they raised a "magnificent silk flag" embroidered with Chinese characters that proclaimed to all San Francisco harbor: "Presented to J. B. Robertson by 464 of his Chinese passengers who have experienced much kindness and attention from him during the voyage from Kwangtung to the Golden Mountain." There was a sense of grandeur and majesty among these peasants.

Once they landed on the shore of California their dreams faded. The life that beckoned them was one of hardships they had not expected and of insults they could not understand.

Going to the mines, most of these young men had to walk, for horses were for vaqueros and Anglos. The journals of forty-niners often commented on the "long lines of Chinese on foot" to be seen along the roads. And they made their way through mountain passes beneath loads so huge that the Yankee miners would marvel as the Chinese miners sweated.

The strength of these young men—or their spirit—seemed extraordinary. It caused the editor of the California *Madisonian* this outburst of uneasy enthusiasm:

"Chinamen are heavy in the pack. While the heathen is apparently physically deficient, he can carry a load that would disgust— not dismay, or astound, but disgust—the boss mule of a pack train. . . . It was a mystery how [these Chinamen] managed to tote [this] weary load along so gracefully, and not grunt or groan."

In the mountains, from the beginning, the adventurous young men of China had been among the first prospectors. They came as soon as gold was discovered. One month after James Marshall found a small gold nugget in the tracings of Sutter's Mill, in January of 1848, three Chinese miners were reported to have arrived in the gold country by Charles Peters in *The Mother Lode Country*. That was even four months before Mexico had ceded California to the United States.

These miners took to placer mining "like a duck to water," and working sluice boxes "appeared to be especially adapted to their use," wrote the amazed Peters. Even more astounding to the Yankee miners was the highly developed technology of mining that the Chinese introduced. By the use of "the Chinese water wheel" and a mechanized system of bailing buckets on rope pulleys, the Chinese drained the rivers to retrieve the gold from the river bottoms, while the Yankee miners merely panned the gold dust from the fast-flowing rivers. They discovered gold "the more impatient Caucasians would not tarry with," said Peters; and in this way, "they reworked successfully claims given up as worthless by others, and this led to jealousy and hatred and numerous outrages."

One Yankee miner put it bluntly: These "little yellow men were hated by most of the white miners for their ability to grub out fortunes which they themselves had left—for greener pastures." Not the superiority, but the inferiority of the Yankee miners caused their hatred of the Chinese.

When the Chinese bought an abandoned claim, if they mined it profitably they were usually run off at once. That happened, in a typical incident, to four Chinese miners in the Long Hollow camp, near Round Trent, California, who had purchased one "worthless" claim for a few hundred dollars. In just two days they mined $4,000 worth of gold. So swiftly did a "rush of white men" overrun their claim, said an observer, that "the Celestials considered themselves fortunate to get away safely with their tails hanging behind them." They may have felt less fortunate than furious.

The Chinese way of mining became known as "scratching" for gold, and the mining technology they used was disparaged as that of "Chinese diggings." Nonetheless, there was a certain aura, an awe, that surrounded these ingenious miners; for as

Ping Chiu wrote in *Chinese Labor in California*, quoting a white contemporary: "They appear to have reduced this kind of mining to a science."

Soon the gold was all but gone from the rivers. The time of hardrock or deep mining had begun, and the search for "the yellow stones" went underground in hastily dug haphazard tunnels deep beneath the mountains. It was evident at once that the Chinese miners had an uncanny skill in hardrock mining. One mine owner discovered, to his surprise, that they "surpass the white man in the same mines," and another mine owner was to predict that "ultimately the rough work in our mines will be done by the Chinese."

The "Chinese rank with the most successful foreigners in the mines," declared E. C. Capron in his *History of California*, published in 1854. While that was disturbing enough to the Yankee miners, even more disturbing was the "demonstrated ability" of the Chinese young men "to learn the skills of the [deep mining] trade," as a historian of hardrock mining, Richard Lingenfelter, put it. And so skilled were many of these Chinese miners that, for this and equally uneconomic reasons, they were banned from most of the deep mines. If they were permitted to work they often became exemplary miners, as did S. Yanda, who was given the honor of guiding the party of General Ulysses S. Grant when the former president toured the Comstock lode of Virginia City in 1879.

Some of these young Chinese miners were in fact old gold miners. They came from a fifty-year-old tradition of overseas gold mining.

On the islands of Borneo, since the early 1800s, there had been as many as thirty thousand Chinese miners who both operated and worked the gold mines. And it was said that three thousand emigrants came to and from these mines each year.

No one could know for certain how many of these experienced Chinese gold miners may have come to California, for no occupational records were kept; but, no matter what their number, the traditions and knowledge of gold-mining technology were not unknown in Kwangtung. The San Francisco newspaper, *Alta California* believed that the migrations of Chinese miners to California were modeled on their earlier experiences in the gold fields of Borneo, a training that gave them an unfair advantage over the inexperienced Yankees from the east.

Even before Chinese miners had begun to dominate the gold mines of Borneo, the mining of tin in Malaya had become "a Chinese monopoly." These tin miners settled in Malaya in the late 1700s, and by the end of the eighteenth century they controlled the mining industry. The advanced technology they brought from China, such as methods of dredge-mining ore from the rivers, was later used to mine gold in the Sierra Nevadas of California.

Not merely were the miners in California from many of the same districts as the miners of gold in China—they were often the same men. Among these men who crossed the Pacific in the Gold Rush were many experienced Chinese gold miners. They were men who had been toughened by the jungles of Malaya and the incessant wars of the sultanates against them. And they were "well armed and led by men of courage, enterprise and ability," English historian C. P. Fitzgerald said of them.

The young men of Kwangtung were not, then, the naive novices in mining they pretended to be. Nor were they, as the Yankees believed them to be, gentle and self-effacing men content to work "leftover" claims abandoned by others because they were afraid to stake their own claims.

Not only did the Yankees and the Chinese mine gold differently; they looked at it differently and attributed different values to what the Medoc people of the mountain tribes prosaically called "the yellow stones."

In the mountain streams the Yankees were forever seeking the one nugget that would make them rich: The Bonanza! The Glory Hole! The Lucky Strike! Once they had filled their dreams with gold they could change the whole world; for gold was a panacea, the miraculous substance, the heavenly metal that turned lice-ridden, filthy miners into millionaires and transformed a dirty, miserable mining camp into utopia. The young republic had never known a "golden era," as had the older empires, and the California Gold Rush represented the beginning of a new empire.

To the men of Kwangtung the Yankees' dreams must have seemed naive. In China the mysteries of gold were known from ancient history; and that history taught that these "Magesteries of Gold" brought men both immortality and death, poverty and wealth. In such times, wrote Shih mo in 511 B.C., "The high banks become valleys and the deep valleys become heights." That being so, the paradoxes of life were nothing new. And the young men of the peasant farms of Kwangtung had a sophisticated philosophy of wealth that was as old as their sophisticated mining technology.

On the edges of the crevices of the mountains and by the crying rivers, the peasants from China and the peasants from Europe confronted one another, not for the conquest of a continent, or even for a job—though that was soon to come—but as the bearers of two cultures that were incomprehensible to each other. The Chinese, at least, had faced foreigners before and had learned to keep their peace.

And "to the somewhat unlearned and inexperienced mid-continent Americans," wrote Bancroft, the Chinese seemed at times to be "more Christian than many Christians," and at times "heathen." But what confused the Yankee miners most of all was how these "little men," as a forty-niner wrote, "hardly 4' 10" and weighing no more than 120 pounds," could work as hard as and more successfully than Yankee miners almost twice their size.

Once the veins of gold had given out and there was little left but dust, the Yankee miners turned on the Chinese. They praised them with envy:

> We're working like a swarm of bees
> scarcely making enough to live
> And two hundred thousand Chinese
> are taking home the gold that
> we ought to have . . .

"So many [of these Yankee miners] went home disgusted," declared Dr. Jacob Stillman in his *Gold Rush Letters, 1849 to 1850*, because they discovered "gold washing is very hard work" and this is something "a large part of mankind do not relish." The good doctor ruefully wrote: "Many who went to the mines returned unsuccessful, and report that the exertion in getting gold is too great. Some are leaving the country—for the Sandwich Islands, in disgust."

In the saloons of their mining camps they lamented the loss of their dreams and claims to the Chinese:

> We used to think 'twould always
> last with a perfect ease,
> If Uncle Sam had only stopped
> the coming of the Chinese.

But it was too late to undo what had been done. The frontier spirit of the mining camps that had been so Chinese in many ways had become a ghost of its past. Still, the memory embittered the Yankee miners:

John Chinaman, John Chinaman,
  But five short years ago,
I welcomed you from Canton, John,
  But wish I hadn't though.

Oh, John, I've been deceived in you,
  And all your thieving clan,
For gold is all you're after, John,
  To get it as you can.

Of all the songs they sang, "The Lousy Miners Song" was the best—and worst—expression of their despair:

I was covered with lice, coming on the boat,
I threw away my fancy swallow-tailed coat,
And now the lice crawl up and down my back;
I'm a lousy miner and a pile is all I lack.

"Seeing the elephant" is what it was called. The phrase was defined in 1844 by Kendall on his Santa Fe expedition: "When a man is disappointed in everything he undertakes, when he has seen enough, when he gets sick and tired of any job he may have set himself about, he has Seen The Elephant." This was the theme of one of the most popular saloon songs in the mining camps, a lament of every lonely miner, whether Chinese or Yankee:

Because I could not pay my bill
They kicked me out of Maryville
I stole a mule and lost the trail
And fetched up in the Hangtown jail . . .

And yet, in his despair, the Yankee miner often did, as the Chinese miner did not, victimize his opposite to expunge his frustrations and his humiliations:

And I filled the town with lice,
Robbed the Chinese of their rice,

People said, "You've got the itch!
Leave! You lousy Son of a Bitch!"

The men of China who were so much farther from home than the Yankee miners seemed much more capable of enduring and surviving their hardships. And they seemed more tolerant of their sorrows. It may have been the wisdom learned from an older tradition of exile and exploration; but it may have been simple necessity.

In this, too, these Chinese miners seemed to have an advantage over Yankee miners. Emigrants from Kwangtung were almost all men, but they were a community of men, coming from the same villages and clans. Men who knew one another, and one another's families, were able to work together in ways the more individualistic Yankees did not. And coming in groups, as they did, the men in these Chinese camps had both a greater cohesion and diversity. For the peasants were often accompanied by men of many skills and professions. It was not uncommon for the village's doctor, the money lender, the local scholar, the carpenter, and the blacksmith to come to the Golden Mountain with the men of a village.

In the most remote and isolated mining camps, the Chinese community often seemed remarkably stable because of this. On the distant frontier, in the Black Hills of the Dakota territories near Deadwood for example, the scattering of Chinese pioneers reported by the census takers included, besides the expected forty miners and ten prostitutes, four merchants, a barber, two "real estate speculators," ten young firemen who formed the "World Champion Fire Hose Team," and a doctor.

Many of the professionals and intellectuals in the mining camps were unknown to outsiders unless they ventured beyond the Chinese community. They were nonetheless the men who made life on the frontier bearable for the miners who had exiled themselves in the crevices of the Golden Mountains.

One of the Chinese intellectuals who became known to the Yankees was the man they named Ah Sang—the "Doc." His medical treatment of his fellow miners in the Yankee Hill camp was so successful that the white miners begged him to open a doctor's office. He did, and so proficient was his practice of medicine that the hotel he rented for his clinic soon proved too small for all the patients who came to him, and he had to rent four other buildings as well. In time, Dr. Ah Sang was directing a hospital with fifty beds, the largest in the mining camps and at the time one of the leading hospitals in California.

The dedication of this doctor in the pioneering of modern medicine in the remote and wild mining camps—treating men who were to him little more than "barbarians" with few medicines and fewer facilities—was one of those courageous acts in medical history that, had the situation been reversed, and had he been a white doctor in China, would have been honored as the work of a missionary of science. But Dr. Ah Sang was Chinese, a sad-eyed man of impressive stature, seen in an old photograph dressed in an elegant silk robe with a faraway look in his understandably wistful eyes.

Men such as Dr. Ah Sang civilized the mining camps as best they could. They were the culture bearers of morality and civility among the "strangers in a strange land." Gold and silver were the lure and cause of much of the exploration and settlement of the West. But neither was noted as the creator of high levels of civilization. The mining camps were the original sin that enticed the white pioneers across the prairies and brought about the founding of our western cities and wealth; "the lodestone," as Ray Allen Billington has said, of the "march of [white] civilization across the American continent"; the guiding light of gold.

More than that, the wealth of the mines was the foundation upon which the future of the West was built. The money, the capital investment, that made possible the financing of agriculture and industry came, in a significant part, from the riches of the earth itself and the labor of the men from China.

Such is the irony of history that almost one-third of these miners of the West were "yellow men." The Chinese miners who were counted by the census of 1870 numbered 27 percent of the total; but the census takers, for reasons ranging from the exclusiveness of the Chinese to the statistical racism of government officials, never counted nonwhites quite completely. There were most likely more miners from China in the heavens and hells of the frontier than the government ever knew.

In California, the census of 1870 counted 34,933 Chinese miners. That was 25 percent of all miners in the entire state.

In Washington State the Chinese had been among the first settlers of the territory and were 25.4 percent of the region's miners.

In Montana, of 6,270 miners, 1,415 were Chinese. That came to 22.6 percent of the miners, or one of every ten people of the total population of the territory.

In Idaho, of a population that numbered 14,999, 4,274 were Chinese; and of 6,579 miners, 3,853 were Chinese, or 58.6 precent.

In Oregon the percentage of miners from China was even greater. Of the 3,965 miners recorded by the census of 1870, there were 2,428 Chinese miners, or 61.2 percent.

The newspaper *Alta California* had prophesied in the early days of the Gold Rush that the "prosperity of our State, and the happiness of society generally, are in a great measure affected by those who've come from foreign climes to seek their fortune in this country." Since, as late as the 1870s the great majority of the miners and settlers in the West were foreigners, either from Asia or Europe, this was something of an understatement. Almost everywhere in the West the foreign-born outnumbered the native-born; and the Chinese were the most numerous of all.

So obvious and crucial was the influence of these Chinese miners upon the State of California that Daniel Webster, in 1850, described the land as "Asiatic in formation and scenery." The same may have been said of much of the West.

And yet the memory of these miners from China has been reduced to a footnote to history. It is thought enlightened to sympathize with them as a persecuted minority, an exotic curiosity. Much has been written of the segregation and discrimination that defaced their presence, and little of their daring accomplishments in the shaping and developing of the cities and industries of the West. These dramatic portraits of the Chinese miners and pioneers who settled the American West have been all but washed from our history, diluted by ignorance and insult, until merely the faded outlines of their achievements remain. Still, these men were not merely the victims of America's past. They were the builders of the future of the American West.

An old-timer in the mining camps of Hornitos, Frank Salazar, once recalled what happened to one Chinese miner who refused to be insulted and banished from history by being reduced to a stereotype. Remembering him by the dubious name of Ah Sin, the old man retold his story with a rare sympathy.

In those days Hornitos was known as a singularly rough town; it was the hideout of the band of Joaquin Murieta, the scourge of the mine fields. "Certainly, seldom before in the history of the mining camps had there been so much murder, fornication, adultery and incest packed into such a small group of people," Salazar said. Life in Hornitos was fit solely for "the quick and the bold." Ah Sin was both.

Several hundred Chinese men, many of them merchants whose stores and saloons covered an entire street, lived in the midst of this "roaring camp." These men were as tough as the rest; they had to be to survive in so lawless a place. The camp was notorious for its hangings and shootings, and even lawmen rarely ventured there. For their own safety the Chinese citizens dug tunnels underneath the town's streets, connecting their establishments and homes, so that in case of attack they could escape. Later, Murieta and his band used these tunnels in their attempt to drive the Yankees from California.

In spite of their rough and ready reputation, the Chinese miners of Hornitos were "constantly bedeviled by small boys shouting 'Yellow Chink' and 'Pigtail' at them," Salazar recalled; for the Chinese were not thought of as real westerners. But Ah Sin was not the sort of man who accepted insults. He was a hardened, well-armed miner, and known to be perhaps a bit too quick on the trigger.

One day, in anger, Ah Sin took his pistol from its holster and fired a shot into the air to frighten away his tormentors. The bullet ricocheted off a stone wall nearby and struck one of the small boys in the leg.

The crowd that gathered seized Ah Sin and dragged him to the town jail. In the night he was awakened by the friendly voice of a man at his barred window who offered him a pipe and opium to soothe his insulted pride. Not knowing that his benefactor held a short-looped *reata*, a lariat, in his fist, Ah Sin thanked him for the gift. Then as he reached for the window, a "loop dropped over his head and was pulled taut."

Salazar, who later turned the jail into a museum of mining

camp history, then told what happened next, in his pithy, matter-of-fact voice:

Ah Sin's "head was smashed again and again against the stone wall, until his brains were knocked out. In later years the walls were roughly calcimined to hide the stains of blood and brains," said the old man, "but some of the hair remains to this day."

On the wall of the jail the mark of history is still there indelibly, as if the Chinese miner had signed it with his blood.

X

THE CHINESE RAILROAD MEN

Men of China (the Chinese railroad foreman said) were skilled at work like the big job. . . . Their ancestors had built fortresses in the Yangtze gorges, carved and laid the stones for the Great Wall [of China].
                                        —*The Great Iron Trail*

There was no train to Jerusalem, and the Lord of Life rode into the city in the humblest guise, upon a donkey.
                                        —*The World on Wheels*, Chicago, 1874

AND THEN the day came when the final spike, the "Golden Spike," was to be hammered down to hold the last length of track. The iron rails had spanned a continent. In celebration of the occasion, the dignitaries came—bankers and railroad tycoons, politicians and railroad men—to be photographed at the uniting of the nation. Of the hundreds of people in that memorable photograph taken at Promontory Point in Utah, on May 10, 1869, there was one large group who were wholly invisible.

The Chinese . . .

Nowhere to be seen were the thirteen thousand railroad men from China who had dug the tunnels, built the roadbeds, and laid the track for half of the transcontinental line—that of the Central Pacific Railroad—crossing the most precipitous mountains and torturous deserts of the West. These Chinese workingmen had become faceless. They had disappeared.

One oil painting of the event later symbolically depicted three railroad men crouching beside the tracks as they drove in the

Golden Spike. Two of the three were Chinese.

That famous painting was reprinted in hundreds of thousands of copies; it proudly hung in saloons and brothels throughout the West for years. And yet, in the reproduction of the painting a curious thing had happened. Beneath the painting there was a drawing in which the people who had gathered for the joining of the tracks were outlined, each face numbered, so the viewers might identify who was who. But there was no drawing of the three railroad men.

Once again, the Chinese railroad men had been rendered faceless. They had vanished from history.

Men of China not only built the western half of the first transcontinental railroad, they built the whole or part of nearly every railroad line in the West. In spite of that, or perhaps because of it, their labors were belittled and their heroism disparaged for a century afterward; the white workers on the western railroads were resentful of the skill and strength of the "little yellow men" whom they contemptuously compared to midgets and monkeys.

From the beginning, the white railroad men had ridiculed the young men of China as too "effeminate" to do a "real man's work," such as laying iron rails. They were too "delicate." They had "too small hands." They were much too small. A railroad historian reflected the popular prejudice of the time when he described how "the Chinese marched through the white camps like a weird procession of midgets."

So convinced were the white railroad men that these "celestial monkeys" could not do the work of white men that when James Strobridge, the tough-minded Irish work boss of the Central Pacific, was ordered to hire Chinese men he exploded with rage: "I will not boss Chinese. I will not be responsible for work done on the road by Chinese labor. From what I've seen of them, they're not fit laborers anyway. I don't think they can build a railroad."

His contempt was a commonplace. When Leland Stanford, one of the owners of the Central Pacific, was elected governor of California, he condemned the Chinese emigrants as a "degraded" people who were the "dregs of Asia." They were unfit for honest labor.

The "lack of manhood" of the men from Kwangtung was evident not only in their diminutive size, but in the ways they dressed and bathed. In the rugged frontier camps, after work they religiously washed in hot bathtubs made from empty whiskey kegs. Every man soaped and rinsed himself "like a woman," in "flower water," and emerged "smelling of perfume." Surely to the Yankees from the puritan East who were roughing it in the wilderness, and to the peasants from Europe to whom bathing was an aristocratic vice, these habits were suspiciously feminine.

Stranger still, and more suspect, were the odd ways they ate. It was said "the Celestials devoured mice and rats." In their work camps their cuisine was even more exotic. They refused to eat the manly diet of beans and beef that the white men consumed. Instead they imported their food from China: dried oysters, dried fish, dried abalone, dried fruits, dried mushrooms, dried seaweed, dried crackers and candies, and an endless variety of roasted, sweet and sour, and dried meats, poultry, and pork, rices and teas. Each group of twelve to twenty Chinese workmen had its own cook, who prepared dishes to fit the local palate. And each cook had the duty not only of preparing these feasts of "Un-Christian foods," but of brewing the barrels of tea that had to be served all day long in tiny cups such as "ladies see fit to use."

In these customs of the Chinese the Yankees imagined dark, mysterious rituals. These men from China were not merely "heathens," they turned ordinary things into "heathen" and somehow "feminine" practices that were deeply disturbing to the men of the frontier.

And yet the dreams of conquest of the railroad owners were more powerful than their workmen's prejudices. Though the Central Pacific had been founded in 1861 to construct the western section of the dreamed-of transcontinental railroad by 1865, it had succeeded in laying only thirty-one miles of track. Not only were the owners humiliated by the lack of progress, but the work was frustrated by the lack of responsible workmen. Strobridge needed five thousand men, he said, but his work crews rarely numbered eight hundred. Even these were untrustworthy and worse: The Sacramento Union sarcastically referred to these white workers as the "enterprising cutthroats" who either ran off to the gold camps or preferred to work at "robbing Sacramentans at the alley corners." Those who did stay on the job were more trouble than those who did not, for they tended to be "drunken and wayward."

"Hire Chinese!" was the order of the railroad's General Superintendent Charles Crocker.

Strobridge, a stubborn Vermont man, unwillingly hired fifty Chinese workmen; he assigned them to menial jobs such as filling dump carts. They were too "frail" to swing a jack hammer, he insisted.

On the day these men were at last permitted to work at grading the roadbed for the tracks, it was reported that "the coolies' right of way was longer and was smoother than any white crew's." It was embarrassing, for the Chinese were so inexperienced that many had never been on a railroad or even seen one.

Enraged, the white crews vowed to avenge their shame. In the days that followed, they not only worked at top speed, but voluntarily halved their lunch break. Still, at the end of a week the roadbeds of the Chinese workmen were the longest of "any gang on the line." The white railroad men "who wouldn't work within a hundred rods of them" threatened to strike or quit, and many did.

An observer wrote that this was surely "the cruelest blow of all to the ego of the whites."

The muscular young men from China were given the jobs that the whites had abandoned. "Wherever we put them, we found them good," said the delighted Crocker. "And they worked themselves into our favor to such an extent, we found if we were in a hurry for a job of work, it was better to put Chinese on it at once." Even the stubborn Strobridge barked, "Send up more coolies."

And they came as the gold miners had come before them, from the same regions of Kwangtung province on the Canton delta, mostly from the sea-swept maritime districts of Sunwui and Toishan, in the area known as Sze Yup. They came by the thousands and tens of thousands. So many young men wished to come that the ships of the Pacific Mail Line, which brought most of them, were often overloaded by their captains with a third too many passengers. At the inevitable congressional investigation of this lawlessness, the captains were redundantly accused of greed, though no one asked the young men of Kwangtung to testify as to why *they* were so eager to come to America that they crowded onto the obviously overloaded ships.

Of these men it is said that most were the sons of farmers, but on the land of their fathers, near the coast, the traditions of the seas were as alive as the sea's winds. These were the lands where the seamen and adventurers of China had come from for centuries, and these young men were aggressive and pugnacious. Even more than the gold miners, they seemed to enjoy, to relish, to seek after the challenge of unknown and exotic foreign lands and the adventures they offered. And working on the railroad they found them.

On the undulating hills of those ridges of rock that form the spine of the Sierra Nevada foothills, the serpentine iron rails climbed in winding arcs. The ravines and valleys in between had to be filled by untold tons of dirt or be bridged by great trestles. Some of these trestles, such as the one at Deep Gulch, rose one hundred feet high and were five hundred feet long. They were built of logs, felled and tied by hand, for there were no steam or power tools; even the tons of dirt had to be moved entirely by hand. In awe of the strength and skill of the men from China who did this work, Albert Richardson of the New York *Tribune*, who had been Horace Greeley's most distinguished correspondent during the Civil War, attempted to describe the epic scene:

"They [the Chinese] were a great army laying siege to Nature in her strongest citadel. The rugged mountains looked like stupendous ant-hills. They swarmed with Celestials, shoveling, wheeling, carting, drilling and blasting rocks and earth . . ."

Soon the "great army" was to face ever greater mountains. On a high, sheer cliff towering above the gorge of the American River, the roadbed of the railroad was to climb fourteen hundred feet up the sides of the precipitous rock face. There were no ledges. There was not even a goat trail. The blasting crews chipped away at the seventy-five-degree incline for days. Inch by inch, they advanced less than a foot on some days.

The tale is told of how one day a Chinese work foreman came to see Strobridge. He politely waited, hat in hand, until he could speak. "Maybe, we can be of some help," he supposedly said, "My people, you know, built the Great Wall of China! Of stones."

The carving of roads that clung to cliffsides, like bird nests on inaccessible ledges, was a very ancient art to Chinese engineers. One spectacular reminder of their skill was depicted in the famous painting of Emperor Hsuan tsung's retreat from his Tang dynasty capital, in 775 A.D. Upon a mountain in the painting there is a winding road that is supported by logs and dug into the side of a sheer rock face; it is perched on the mountain as though suspended in air.

Feats of road construction such as this had been commonplace in China for thousands of years. If the ability of the men from Kwangtung to hang from cliffs at dizzying heights and to blast a road out of midair seemed amazing to their Yankee bosses, who "sneered in disbelief" at the thought, it was not new to Chinese technology.

Skeptical as ever, Strobridge gave his begrudging approval. He had nothing to lose.

The men wove great baskets, large enough to hold several workmen, of tall reeds and vines. On the waist-high baskets they knotted four eyelets, in the directions of the Four Winds, and inscribed them with the proper prayers. Ropes were tied to the eyelets and the baskets, each holding two or three men, were slowly lowered from the edge of the cliff down to the site of the marked roadbed hundreds of feet below. In the swaying wind, the Chinese workmen set dynamite blasts in the rock face and swung away for their lives with all their might. Many fell below. Many died. But in a few weeks the roadbed had been blasted from the rock. They were "becoming expert in drilling, blasting and other rock work," said the railroad's engineer, Sam Montague.

The summit lay ahead.

In the icy winds that whistled through the infamous Donner Pass, which rose to 7,042 feet in the High Sierras, the crews were snowed under during the winter of 1865. The engineers had planned a tunnel that was to be dug beneath the summit, exactly 1,659 feet long and wide enough for two tracks. But the rock was so hard the "blasting powder merely shot back out of the holes." And the Chinese tunnelers were forced to camp, in thin canvas tents, under ten- to twenty-foot snow drifts. For month after month, they lived like seals, huddled together in padded cotton clothes. Several of their camps were swept away by avalanches in the arctic oblivion of those mountains, and the dead were not recovered until the snow thawed.

Spring brought a renewal of work on the tunnels. There was not one but fifteen tunnels to be dug and hundreds of ravines to be crossed before the railroad could go through. And by the winter of 1866 the tracks still had not reached the summit. Not willing to wait for another spring, the railroad owners ordered that three locomotives be pulled over the mountains by hand. It seemed an impossible task.

In the snow that was higher than a man, hundreds of young men from Kwangtung hitched themselves to mule teams that were to attempt this feat. The men cleared a path two hundred feet wide through the forests on the mountainsides. "Not Yankee trees" is the way an official described the giant trees. And yet "the tiny lumbermen" cut a roadway in the snow that was miles long. On log sleighs that they greased with pork lard, they pulled the locomotives and an entire wagon train of highly volatile nitroglycerin and supplies up the mountainside.

Said a historian of the railroad: "The yellow man had proven his superiority by hard labor."

In their desperation to span the mountains before their rival railroad builders did, the owners of the Central Pacific forced the Chinese crews to work from dawn to dark, seven days a week. Still, the Irish crews of the Union Pacific had the advantage of easier terrain and wealthier owners. That meant better wages and entertainments.

On the dry flats of the deserts of Utah, the Chinese crews of the Central Pacific, coming from the West, and the Irish crews of the Union Pacific, coming from the East, met head on. They literally blew each other up. In the race of the railroads to lay the most track (the government subsidized each mile at $16,000 to $42,000, plus hundreds of millions of acres of right-of-way), the rivals ordered their crews to lay parallel roadbeds for hundreds of miles. In grading their roadbed, the "Irishmen were in the habit of firing their blasts without giving warning to the Chinamen," reported a surveyor for the Union Pacific, Grenville Dodge, and "from this cause several Chinamen were severely hurt." The Chinese crews, "appreciating the situation," responded in kind. One day they set off a dynamite charge right above the Irish crews, and several Irishmen were buried alive.

"From that time the Irish laborers showed more respect for the Chinamen, and there was no further trouble," said Dodge.

In the race of the railroads to outdo one another, these Chinese crews were to distinguish themselves in more productive ways. Crocker, in bravado and some say on a bet, announced that on a single day, April 28, the Chinese crews would lay ten miles of track; the "Ten Mile Day," he named it. Together with eight Irish rail handlers, they did just that, laying ten miles and fifty-six feet of new track, spiking 3,520 rail lengths to 25,800 wooden ties.

The feat was a fitting finale to the completion of the great transcontinental track less than two weeks later. On Promontory Point, where the nation was joined together by the "iron nerves" of the iron rails and orators proclaimed "This way to India!" the historic event that created a truly United States was symbolized to a contemporary writer by the image of "the Anglo Saxon and the Celt met in friendly greeting [with] the tawny Asiatic"— a fantasy that was more real than the fact.

Years later, in his testimony before the Joint Special Subcommittee of the Congress in 1876–77, which was deciding whether the Chinese had the "right" to remain in the West they had pioneered and built, one of the railroad builders, West Evans, declared forthrightly: "I do not see how we could do the work we have done here without them; at least I have done the work [on the railroads] that would not have been done if it had not been for the Chinamen . . . work that I could not have done without them."

On the prairies and in the mountains of the West there were few railroads that these young men of Kwangtung did not build, in whole or in part. They helped build the Southern Pacific in the deserts of the southwest and the Northern Pacific in the forests of the northwest. They worked by the thousands upon the Canadian Pacific as well. They built the roadbeds and laid the track of almost every railroad from Texas to Alaska: the Atlantic and Pacific; the California Central and California Southern; Nevada's Virginia and Truckee; Eureka & Palisades; Carson and Colorado; and Nevada; California and Oregon; the Oregon Central; the Seattle and Walla Walla; Texas Pacific, and the Houston and Texas Central; the Alabama and Chattanooga; and numerous smaller lines.

And thousands of these young men gave their lives in the building of the railroads. The dead were never counted, nor have they been memorialized. Some twenty thousand pounds of bones were gathered from shallow graves along the roadbeds and rights-of-way, according to a newspaper of 1870 quoted in *The History of the Chinese in America*, by Philip Choy and H. Mark Lai. These bones of about twelve hundred Chinese who died in the building of the transcontinental line were eventually shipped home. But many others lie to this day in unmarked graves in every western state.

The ghosts of these Chinese railroad men hovered over the mountains and lingered beside the roadbeds and haunted the whistle-stop depots long after they had gone. On the prairies, where there was "not a tree nor living thing in sight," one early traveler on the transcontinental trains recalled coming upon a bowl decorated with "some quaint pattern for Chinese ware," like a specter of the past; and at Omaha, one day, he was surprised by the sight of a "steam caravan come in from what used to be 'forty years in the wilderness' region, direct from the Golden Gate." That, he said, was "a tea train from the Celestial Kingdom." Surely "the Iron Horse" was the "Angel of Abundance" and the "arm of Christendom," for "its mountain-eagle elocution" would carry civilization into the wilderness and "whistle [the] barbarism of the Orient down the wind." By 1874, the year this was written, the travelers on the transcontinental railroads had already forgotten that those Chinese men who were buried beside the roadbeds had laid many of the tracks they traveled on.

And it remained for a stranger from Europe to perceive the blindness of those white men who could not see the Chinese as humans. On his tour of America in 1879, the Scottish novelist Robert Louis Stevenson traveled to California in a third-class "immigrant car" on the Union Pacific Railroad. He grew troubled by the segregation of the Chinese railroad men in a separate car; but even more disturbing to him was the attitude of the white passengers toward those who had helped build the railroad they were traveling upon—"the stupid ill-feeling," he called it.

Of these white Americans' conceptions of the Chinese railroad men, Stevenson wrote: "They seemed never to have looked at them, listened to them, or thought of them, but hated them *a priori.*" They did not see them at all.

Still, there were quiet nights along the rails when the ghosts emerged. On those nights, in the darkness, the history of the railroad men from China reappeared as an apparition, a folktale, a fantastic legend.

One of these folktales was reported in the *Daily New Mexican* of Santa Fe, New Mexico, on the twenty-seventh of March, in the year 1880.

At Galisteo Junction, the terminus of the Atchison, Topeka and Santa Fe Railroad, south of the territorial capital of New Mexico, the specter appeared. Soon after the arrival of the evening train from Santa Fe, the station operator and a few friends had taken a stroll along the tracks. Coming "from above them" in the sky they heard loud voices and, looking up, they were startled to see a "large balloon coming from the West"! Whoever was in the gondola of the balloon was talking in a strange language, "entirely unintelligible" to the people on earth.

The marvelous balloon was "monsterous in size," the newspaper said. More wondrous than its hugeness, though, was its design, for "it was in the shape of a fish." Painted on its sides were "very elegant" and "fanciful characters" of an unknown but obviously Asian language, which added to its mystery.

As the fish-balloon sailed overhead, its mysterious occupants dropped two objects onto the desert below. One was a "magnificent flower" made from a "fine, silk-like paper," and the other was an earthen cup, perhaps a teacup, with a blue design.

Sounds of music and of laughter drifted down from the fish-balloon. In the cool of the evening air it fluttered there, like a cloud, for a moment. Then, as silently as it had appeared over the Sierra Colorado mountains, it disappeared. It simply sailed away.

On the evening of the following day a "collector of curiosities" on horseback happened to ride by the isolated depot in the desert. He bought the silklike flower and the cup for a large sum of money. Being a connoisseur of curiosities, he was asked where, in his learned opinion, he thought the fish-balloon might have come from, and he answered at once, without hesitation, that the "balloon must have come from Asia."

XI

FISHERMEN AND FARMERS

Those peach and plum trees
Planted by my hands
Are not without a master.
                                    —TU FU, 712–770

Sure, all Chinese! Everything was Chinese in those days. They started everything, you know. Oh, a lot of things in agriculture, in farming. When they started fishing shrimp, they got all their nets from China. The Americans said, "Those Chinese are really able to do a lot of things we never thought of!" Oh, there's many things the Chinese started.
                                    —LELAND CHIN in *Longtime Californ'*

IN THE SMALL GARDEN of the wooden house near De Land, Florida, there was a citrus tree on whose branches oranges and grapefruits grew side by side. There was a cherry tree full of currants that looked and tasted like wine grapes. There were rosebushes with many different colored roses on each stem. There were tomato plants on which all the tomatoes were exactly the same size and weight. There were orange trees where clusters of ripening fruit hung, firm and sweet, sometimes for two years or more.

The magical garden was the laboratory of Lue Gim Gong, a botanist who became known as the "Chinese Burbank." And it was in this garden that he mated, with loving hands, the seeds of reluctant and unlikely plants to create their delectable offspring.

One of his creations, the famous Lue Gim Gong orange, became the father and/or the mother of the Florida and California citrus industry. For that fruit the United States Department of Agriculture, in 1911, awarded him its highest honor, the Wilder Medal, a remarkable achievement for a man who had come to America in 1872, alone, at the age of twelve, with neither schooling nor money.

As a boy he had sailed from Hong Kong on a small schooner with a crew of adventurers. The journey lasted for two months. On reaching San Francisco he was shocked by the prejudice against the Chinese in that city and quickly volunteered to be a contract laborer in a shoe factory in North Adams, Massachusetts, unaware that the plant was on strike. He was no more welcome there. (One hundred years later Lue Gim Gong's arrival in North Adams was proudly memorialized in the United States Senate by Edward Kennedy.)

In that dank New England mill he acquired a knowledge of English and developed tuberculosis, as well as a passion for the sunlight, the gardens of his homeland, and fresh clear air. When he was befriended by Miss Fanny Amelia Burlingame, a spinster cousin of the United States Ambassador to China and a patroness of bright young Chinese boys, he immediately became her gardener.

She taught him many things. And it was in Miss Fanny's garden that Lue began his botanical experiments. He became fascinated by a then exotic fruit called the "love apple"—the lowly tomato. But his health deteriorated. The doctors told him he had one year to live, and he returned to his home in China, believing he would die at the age of fourteen.

He did not die. Instead, he found "he had become so Americanized" that life on his family's farm bored him. And when Miss Fanny cabled him offering a home and land in sunny Florida to protect his weak lungs, Lue sailed again for America.

In Florida, Lue began his romance with the orange. At that time the citrus orchards were plagued by heavy rains and seasonal rot that were destroying the harvests year after year. The delicate oranges that had been brought to America from China had as much trouble becoming acclimatized to their new surroundings as did the sons of Chinese farmers, such as Lue; the fruits, too, were suffering from a culture shock.

The sweet oranges from Kwangtung had been imported into the New World hundreds of years before by the Portuguese. In the early 1500s these traders gathered orange seeds from the groves surrounding their colony at Macao and sought, not too successfully, to grow them in Portugal. Later, when they had gained a foothold in South America, they tried again in Brazil, but there too the fruit had trouble assimilating. And when, in the eighteenth century, the oranges were brought to Florida by the Spaniards, the trees were beset by diseases and the oranges were mottled and decayed on the branches. Neither the Portuguese nor the Spaniards knew how to grow these Chinese fruits. But then, it is understandable that Europeans would have difficulty growing Asian fruits in America.

In his garden Lue mated the Chinese American oranges with a hardy European variety from the Mediterranean. Long before, in China, Lue's mother had taught him how to pollinate flowers, according to a writer, Chih Meng, director of the China Institute of America. She would take the pollen from one plant and place it upon the pistil of another with her fingers. Then she would cover it with a paper bag to keep the winds and the insects from carrying the pollen away. A few days later, when the flowers had been fertilized, his mother would uncover the plant and pluck off the half-dead blossoms so that the newborn fruits might ripen and grow beautiful. In this way Lue grew his new fruits from the old fruits. Though he mated the pollen and pistil of flowers that were strangers to one another, the offspring of his botanical matchmaking had the strongest qualities of both lovers.

And so, in this way the ancient methods of pollination became the new methods of hybridization. The Americanization of Lue's oranges was successful. On his farm in Florida he merely "practiced what his mother had taught him" on their farm in China, said Chih Meng. And the exotic orange, which had been considered an aphrodisiac, was soon to be squeezed into puritanical orange juice.

Often the seeds of many fruits and vegetables—from cherries and teas to celery and asparagus—made the botanical journey from China to America easily. But growing them here was another matter. Entire villages of farmers were sometimes brought to the Americas specifically for the purpose of planting and growing tea (the drink of the King, the Portuguese called it) and only the Chinese grew it. In Brazil, the first colonies of Chinese were settled in 1812 in this way.

In many countries the farmers from Kwangtung became not only the masters of vegetable gardening but the connoisseurs of food, the merchants, and the restauranteurs. Especially was this so in the western United States.

On the frontier of California almost all the farm and ranch workers were Chinese. The Reverend A. W. Loomis, writing in the *Overland Monthly* in 1869, observed: "On many ranches *all* the laborers are people whose muscles were hardened on the little farms of China . . . Go through the fields . . . the vineyards and orchards, and you will learn that most of [the] fruits are gathered or boxed for market by this same people." In the wheat fields and on the vegetable farms the story was the same; it was the Chinese who planted, cultivated, and harvested the crops of the West.

And as late as 1886 the California Bureau of Labor estimated that 87.5 percent of "all labor on the farms" in the state were Chinese. While the *Los Angeles Times* in 1902 declared flatly: "The Chinese are the only people who will do ranch work faithfully." The native born were unreliable, said the newspaper, for they tended to be "tramps."

Be that as it may, the historic truth was that in the beginning American agriculture in the West was largely Chinese agriculture. These farmers from Kwangtung contributed not only the seeds and the sweat that transformed the deserts of California into a pastoral cornucopia but they contributed their knowledge of agricultural science and technology as well. One of many examples of this were the vineyards of California where the Chinese vintners built "the roads, stone bridges, rock walls, wine cellars and irrigation ditches," as well as picked the grapes, according to the Chinese Historical Society's, *A History of the Chinese in California*.

In the vineyards they were the judges of the wines even after the anti-Chinese riots had driven them from the fields. They served as wine tasters and masters of the brew. They had been expert vintners for hundreds of years and their knowledge and skill helped create the wines. And the wine industry.

Not just the fruit of the land but the land itself was shaped by these Chinese farmers. They reclaimed and re-created with the might of their own bodies some of the richest farmland in all of California.

Some of these lands were underwater. There were endless acres of marshland and tule swamps that covered much of the northern San Joaquin and Sacramento valleys. And along these riverbanks the flooded bottomlands stretched for five to ten miles in either direction. It was the Chinese who reclaimed them.

Though the Congress in Washington had ceded such swamplands to state governments in 1850 (some 2,192,505 acres were ceded to California) nothing was done to drain and reclaim them until the Chinese miners came down from the mountains in the 1860s. It was their experience and skill in engineering and hydrology that made possible the building of the levees and irrigation systems and waterways.

Since the draining of the swamps was largely done by hand, shovel by shovel, wheelbarrow by wheelbarrow, it has often been thought that the Chinese contributed nothing but their sweat and perserverance. That they were only "coolie" laborers. They were not. On the frontier there was a shortage of artisans and technicians, and the Chinese were among the few who had any experience with levee building. Considering the millennia of engineering genius that had gone into such feats of construction as the Grand Canal it should not have surprised anyone that the Chinese manned and directed the reclamation crews.

"Chinese labor is used almost entirely in making the levees," noted Charles Nordhoff in his book on northern California in 1877. That theirs was more than "coolie" labor was evident in Nordhoff's eyewitness comment that the "engineer or master in charge of the work deals only with Chinese foremen," who were responsible for "the perfect organization of [the] Chinese labor."

In ten years more than a quarter of a million acres of land was reclaimed by the Chinese. Now it has indeed become the richest farmland on earth. But even then the labor of the Chinese increased the value of the land from six to seven dollars an acre to up to one hundred dollars an acre—after reclamation (it originally had sold for one dollar an acre). By the mid 1870s, the former Surveyor General of California estimated that the labor of the Chinese on the reclamation projects and the railroads was worth at very least $289,700,000 to the economy of the state of California.

For working on these reclamation projects the men were paid from nine to twenty-five cents for each cubic yard of dirt they moved. If they were extraordinarily tireless they could earn as much as one dollar a day for changing the direction of the rivers and remaking the face of the land.

These men from the river banks of China and the seacoasts of Kwangtung knew not only the flow and flood of the rivers, they breathed the ebb and tide of the sea. The provinces they came from were bounded by and were given their character by the moods and angers of the waters.

Such men, in generation after generation, developed an inner sense of mastery of their environments. Even as farmers they learned the ways of the waters as intimately as they knew the ways of the lands. And so, in the fields and cities on the coasts of California they became pioneering fishermen as naturally as they had become farmers.

They founded the fishing industry of the West.

On the shores of the Pacific the native people had for millennia fished both in the rivers and the sea. They were skilled fishermen who built entire civilizations on the mysteries and wonders of the seas. But the white frontiersmen who settled in the West had little interest in fish or fishing. And they did little fishing; they were largely "bean and beef eaters," to whom fish, like greens, were a lesser food.

And so it remained for the coming of the Chinese for the abundance of food in the sea to be recognized. In the beginning these new fishermen may have learned by watching the old fishermen, the Indians, who knew the best waters for fish and shellfish up and down the coast. The fishermen of Kwangtung were not content, however, in imitating the Indians and they quickly introduced their own methods and tools for fishing.

In the fishing camps they established they built sampans and junks, as they had in China. Many of their fine mesh nets were brought from Kwangtung. And so were their fishing gear and sails, though these were later fashioned in America when the building of junks became more and more an Americanized trade.

One visitor to the Chinese fishing camp on the Sacramento River, in 1873, described these American junks as "strongly built, but narrow and pointed at both ends, and constructed in the Chinese fashion . . . with Chinese sails. The whole air and look of these crafts was decidedly foreign, and I might say oriental."

The fishermen with their finely made nets and boats became so successful that within not many years they dominated the fishing waters from Southern California to the state of Washington. In San Diego nearly all fishing boats were owned by the Chinese, and in San Francisco every one of the shrimp camps were run by the Chinese, and on the Columbia River eighty percent of the salmon cannery workers were Chinese. Everywhere the fishermen from Kwangtung surpassed all others.

Flounder, halibut, mackerel, shark, bluefish, salmon, cod, sardines—there was no fish they did not catch in abundance. But most notably they introduced the eating of shellfish—crabs, lobster, shrimp, and mollusks into the West. Most of all the abalone, a popular delicacy in China but unknown in America until its shell became fashionable as jewelry.

So successful were these fishermen that as early as 1860 a special and discriminatory tax of four dollars a month was levied by the state of California on only Chinese fishermen. And by the mid-1870s laws were passed regulating and prohibiting the use of fine mesh nets, such as the Chinese used, especially in shrimp fishing. In the 1880s still another tax was levied in the form of fishing licenses. But by then many if not most of the Chinese fishermen were being forced from the sea. Often by strong-arm methods and gang attacks their boats were sunk, their nets were destroyed, and their crews were murdered.

In 1897 San Francisco Bay had twenty-six shrimp camps; by 1969 there was merely the decaying remnant of one camp left. There are now none. Some say not only the Chinese fishermen but even the shrimp were driven from the Bay by the building of the great bridges that destroyed their breeding beds and by the industrial pollution. Now the commercial fishermen have to go far to sea for fish that were once near the shores. And now few of the fishing crews are Chinese.

"All of them are gone," said Jennie Linn, of the old Hunters' Point Shrimp Company, in a recent interview: "The guys I had all are dead."

These farmers and fishermen, who came from China, cannot be forgotten, however. Some may be remembered by the names which still identify the fruits they created—like the Bing cherry. Some will always be remembered for the food they contributed to the growth and survival of the American West, though no one knows their names.

Nonetheless, few are now honored by statues and plaques that pay homage to their remarkable and patriotic efforts. The country takes most of their offerings for granted.

Even the fruits of Lue Gim Gong no longer have his name. He lived in obscurity and poverty. He became a recluse. He died alone. Neighbors later remembered that he went to town—just two and a half miles from his home—not more than four times in the last eighteen years of his life. If he was mourned at all, most likely it was by his faithful, thirty-year-old horse, "Miss Fanny," and his pet rooster, both of whom he taught to bow their heads in grace.

His grave is untended.

XII

THE CHINESE COWBOYS
AND INDIANS

My people think of people as people. It doesn't matter if they
are black or Italian or Chinese. They are all part of our family.
— MEDICINE MAN FROM CHINLE

"Don't you know there's no such thing as a real Chinaman
in all of America? That all we are are American Indians cashing
in on a fad?"

"Fad? Don' call me fad. You fad youselv."

"No, you're not Chinese, don't you understand? You see it
all started when a bunch of Indians wanted to quit being Indians
and fighting the cavalry and all, so they left the reservation, see?"

"In'ian?"

"And they saw that there was this big kick about Chinamen,
so they braided their hair into queues and opened up laundries
and restaurants and started reading Margaret Mead . . ."

— *Food for All His Dead*, by FRANK CHIN

ON A WOODED ISLAND in the River of No Return in Idaho,
known now as the Salmon River, before the end of the nineteenth
century there lived an old rancher by the name of Luke Billy.
He tamed wild horses and raised cattle. Even on his island people
came to steal his horses and cattle, and he guarded his small
herd with his rifles. Billy was a tough old Indian; he was a loner,
and he had only one friendly neighbor, a mountain man and
prospector from China.

The old man's daughter recalled their neighbor fondly. She
said of him, "He talked Chinamen to me."

As a girl on the island, she had had the job of rounding up

the cattle for the winter. She was good with horses, too, and broke the wild horses for her father. In those days a young Indian girl learned at an early age to do all the things boys had to do. She shared the work of her family and of their Chinese neighbor. That was the only way to survive in the wilderness.

She was eighty-three years old when she reminisced about those days. Her name was Josephine High Eagle, and she had been born into the family of Weaskus of the Nez Percé people, led by Chief Joseph; her mother's family had lived in the Snake River Valley, to the north, and the city of Lewiston had been built on the ground where she was born, in 1893. "I was born where they hold the Lewiston Roundup," she said with a laugh. The thought of being born in the rodeo arena pleased her.

When her mother became the wife of Luke Billy, she went to live on his island. One day her mother fell from a horse and died. After that the little girl lived alone on the island with her father and their mountain-man neighbor, the Chinese back-woodsman.

Sometimes she teased their quiet neighbor about his "China-men talk." But he simply smiled at her. "When I said, 'Take me to China!'" she recalled, he answered that he "didn't want to go across the ocean." He liked Idaho.

North of the Salmon River, gold had been discovered not very long before her father built his ranch on the island. In a few years their mountains swarmed with miners, mostly white men; they came searching for riches, but they soon gave up the search. The mountains would not give up their secrets. And when the white men gave up, the men from China came to try.

These were rough woodsmen, with dogged stubbornness and old-timers' determination, and they soon were quite successful— so successful that the white miners began to resent and hate them. A fury of racial feeling swept through the mining camps and railroad towns of Idaho; there were lynchings of Chinese shopkeepers and mass burnings of Chinese homes and lootings of Chinese gold miners' cabins.

Some of the men fled into the mountains for their lives. Some returned to the isolated safety of the Chinatowns of California. Some booked passage back to China. And some of them hid among the Indians.

Were those who escaped into the wilderness, like Josephine's father's neighbor, welcomed by the tribes? If so, did they settle down and marry Indian women and become Chinese Indians? The "squaw men" have been depicted as French fur trappers who became "Indian"; but what about those Chinese frontiersmen of the West for whom living with the native people was a matter of life and death?

The old woman was amused by the thought, for her full, moonlike cheeks rounded into a broad smile and her eyes squinted mischievously. But she would say little. All that she would say was that her father's neighbor, "He talked Chinamen to me . . ."

In the fading years of the nineteenth century, an era was dying. One by one the mining camps were abandoned to become ghost towns as the gold was taken from the rivers, and when the work on the railroads was done there were few jobs for the white men from the eastern cities. These men were not settlers, nor were they ranchers or cowhands. It was a lean time for many of them. They were hungry, restless, embittered men. And the riots that erupted in town after town against the Chinese were begun by these fearful men, who in their desperation had become brutal and even murderous.

And so hundreds and hundreds of men from China, isolated and scattered throughout the mountains and deserts, became as invisible as they could. In the Sonoran deserts of Arizona many became traders and merchants living among the Colorado River tribes. One bolder soul opened a saloon in Yuma; but most retreated to the remoter Indian villages. From the mountains of the Apaches Chinese farmers would emerge from time to time, bringing vegetables into the white mining camps. Then they would disappear once more. Several men were reported to be living with the Paiutes in the deserts of Nevada.

In the land of the Navajo people the same thing had happened. One man in New Mexico recalled: "The Old People say after the railroads were built, many Chinese ran away from the white man and lived with us." He remembered how his grandparents had talked of this. Many people from the tribes that lived along the railroad tracks remembered stories like this. The history of these people had not disappeared, it was merely hidden with the Old People.

On the northern Columbia River, in British Canada, a Chinese lumberman was seen living among the Cree tribes. In the deep woods he had established a small logging camp that supplied wood for the river steamers. And in Texas there were reports of several Chinese who, disguised by Spanish names and Mexican clothes, were working as vaqueros on cattle ranches.

In the late 1870s when the work on the railroads ended and the mining camps were stilled, there were tens of thousands of Chinese men living throughout the West. Many had been in America for twenty years by then. They had become old-timers in a young country who had learned to respect and to fear its majesty—youthful veterans of the frontiers where all foreigners, white or yellow, were newcomers.

They were as experienced in the wiles of the wilderness, by that time, as were the white frontiersmen—more than most, for their work as gold miners and railroadmen had been wholly with the earth itself, and they knew its mountains and valleys, rivers and deserts, in a most personal way. They had developed an intimacy and affinity with the land. And, because of this, the Chinese workmen and native people may have found a common bond that surprised both.

When the British abandoned Fort Nootka in 1789, many of the Chinese who had built this English outpost on Vancouver Island decided to stay with the native people. They went into the woods and were accepted into the encampments of the local tribes. Five years later, in 1794, the American sailing ship *Jefferson* stopped at Nootka Sound and picked up two of these Chinese exiles who were still living with the peoples of Vancouver. And then nearly fifty years later, in 1834, several Chinese men one day appeared at the gates of Fort Nisquallie of the Hudson's Bay Company, happily informing the startled Englishmen that they were survivors of the Nootka settlement. They were old men by then. Some said they had been held "prisoner" by the Indians. Some said they had simply been living peacefully with the tribes, where they now had families and children.

As the Chinese merchants of the Manila galleons had settled into the villages of the Mexican Indians years before, the Chinese frontiersmen of North America lived among the western tribes. They were accepted, when they were, because they came not for conquest but for solace, and to escape the white men. That, too, was a bond between them.

In the mining camps and towns of the whites, the Chinese had met few Indians. There was, in the beginning, a natural suspicion and caution in their meetings. One old miners' song, "John Chinaman's Appeal," printed in the *Gold Diggers Song Book* of 1856, told of such an encounter as seen by a popular writer of the day:

I met a big stout Indian once,
  He stopped me by the trail, Sir.
He drew an awful scalping knife,
  And I trembled for my tail, Sir.
He caught me by my hair, it's true,
  In a manner quite uncivil,
But when he saw my awful queue,
  He thought I was the devil.

The fears were real. Army cavalrymen were not known to risk their lives for the Chinese miners, and the white railroadmen and ranchers simply abandoned their Chinese employees when the native tribes attacked them.

Many of the bedraggled and rugged gold miners went to work on ranches as cowhands. But the Chinese miners, in spite of their centuries of experience as horsemen, were confined to jobs as servants and cooks. It was widely believed by white men that these men from China did not know how to ride a horse.

One old story tells what happened to a Chinese chuck-wagon cook on the vast ranch of Peter Finch, the Oregon cattle king. His was the famed Diamond Ranch, a great spread of 120,000 acres in central Oregon, which had arbitrarily fenced the richest valley land of the native people.

All winter sorrow had been brooding in the encampments of the local Indian tribes, for without their pastures and rivers they were starving. When the spring came, a band of young men put on warriors' signs and set forth to punish the rancher. It was spring roundup. The angry young men surprised the rancher and his cowboys in the field, and the white and Mexican vaqueros fled, leaving the Chinese cook behind. He mounted the nearest horse and tried to escape, but he was thrown from his mount in the path of the warriors.

Looking back, the rancher became alarmed. He ordered his cowboys to rescue the horse.

Paradoxically, it was the building of the railroads that was to bring about a more human confrontation. The iron rails of the white man showed the yellow man and the red that they had more in common than their hostility to their treatment by the white man or the frustration they felt at being treated like minorities when together they were the majority in the West. It was an irony that appealed to both.

As the railroads cut deeper and deeper into Indian lands, they were increasingly attacked. On the prairie the crews of the Union Pacific were severely slowed by the resistance of the tribes. To soothe the wrath of the people whose most fertile lands were often selected for the right-of-way, the owners of the Central Pacific decided to invite the native people of Nevada to work alongside the Chinese crews. And they did so "with nonchalance and ease." It was reported that the Indian women worked so hard they "outdid the men." Gratified by the response of both the Indians and the Chinese, the railroad owners offered a "special treaty" to the Shoshone and Paiute bands, giving the tribal leaders free seats in their passenger cars; the "common Indians" had to be content with riding in the freight cars.

The camaraderie of these Chinese and Indian crews amazed the white foremen; both delighted in raucous and practical jokes, which they played upon one another with great exuberance. And they worked amicably side by side, without hostility—something the white railroad men could not have done, since they refused to work beside either the Chinese or the Indians.

And yet, though it was the white man who brought the Chinese and the Indian together, there must have been something within themselves and their beliefs, elusive and intriguing, that captured their curiosity about one another. They seemed to share many attitudes and ways of behavior. Even though they came from differing cultures, half a world distant from one another, these clansmen from southern China and western America undoubtedly were equally fascinated and confused by the things they had in common. It may have seemed magical to them.

In the encampments during these long nights when they talked, there must have been an unusual excitement in the mountain air. As they sat around their fires and compared their clothes and beliefs, their ideas and foods, in the way that travelers do, the things they believed in common may have interested them more than their differences. For though their cultures were worlds apart, their world views were not.

Reverence for the wisdom of the old ones was shared by both people. So was their humble and self-effacing respect for the spirits of the past, embodied in a sense of continuity, the circle of life in which the past and present coexisted, as did the good and bad, the yin and yang. In this sense, Chinese and Indian alike were thought by whites to be "serene" and "stoic." They both envisioned the world ruled by a myriad of spirits and forces beyond the meager power and intelligence of human beings. Because of this, they both tended to be not falsely, but scientifically modest and soft-spoken.

There were religious rituals as well that they shared: the corn dances of many American bands and the Oriental corn cults of the Kwangtung farmers; the homage to the Chinese dragon and the plumed serpents of the Aztecs, and the real serpents of the southwestern desert Pueblo people, which were used similarly; the Death Songs of the plains people and the ancestor worship of the Chinese, in which Hartley Burr Alexander thought he had observed "conceptions [that] are somewhat similar."

Of all the similarities between the two peoples, the one that most likely made living together the easiest was the mutual almost religious devotion to the family. The concept of filial loyalty, not merely to father and family but to the clan, first of all, dominated Indian and Chinese life. And both shared the communal ways of living and of thinking that were at the heart of their extended families and clan societies; it was something that the white man could not understand, and the Chinese man didn't have to try to.

Some of the similarities in the ordinary things of life seemed equally startling, if only because they were so commonplace. Some were not, in fact, similar, but were the same. One of these was the red war paint of many of the western tribes.

On the banks of the Missouri and the Colorado there were many pits of red clay. When a hunter or dancer wished to brighten his or her face and body with the color of life, the red clay often seemed weak and lifeless. It did not evoke the red blood of birth and death, life and sacrifice. So many people began to use the red dye, vermilion, that the white man brought in trade.

People of the plains "bought large amounts" of the vermilion dye from the French fur trappers, said the artist George Catlin. It was much sought after and highly prized by the Arikara and Sioux, the Pawnee and Chippewa; for it was a vibrant red, deep and bright as blood.

In the East the vermilion dyes had been worn by the Iroquois and Algonquin people long before the American Revolution. They were a tribal tradition, but they were not Indian. They were not even French. They were Chinese. The dyes came from China, where they were made from an old Buddhist formula, with the leaves of the henna plant, a fragrant herb used for centuries by the Buddhist monks in their temple ceremonies.

Chinese war paint in America! *Aiiee! I am Red as Father Sun! Aiiee! I am a Hearer of Buddha! Aiiee! I am! Aiiee!*

The red banners and placards of the Chinese New Year's celebrations are emblazoned with the brightest vermilion, as are firecrackers and greeting cards. Centuries before red became a flag of Chinese revolution, it was the color of birth and rebirth, creation and re-creation.

In the Hako ceremonial of the Pawnee, on the plains of America, "red paint, symbolizing the coming of the day, the rising sun, the vigor of life," proclaimed the appearance of the Giver of Life, Tirawa. A ritual of the Arikara people began with a stone—the "Grandfather," the "Aged One"—set facing the entrance of the medicine lodge and "painted with red, the sign of life."

"It is entirely true that there are analogies, at first glance astonishing," Alexander wrote in *The World's Rim*, "not only between the material forms of Old and New World cultures, but what is yet more impressive, between the reflective and imaginative expressions of the peoples of the two hemispheres. Consequently, it is facile to find striking samenesses of Chinese or Buddhist thinking with [the] American [Indian] . . ."

Not merely the Chinese, but whites marveled at the "samenesses." The hogans of the Navajos somewhat resembled the yurts of the nomads of Asia. And some saw in the faces of the Apaches and the Sioux the uncanny mirror images of the people from Kwangtung and of the Manchus. One scholar, who was studying the language of the people of Taos Pueblo, became intrigued by the Indians' "Chinese name," and claimed that a great many words spoken along the Rio Grande sounded like Cantonese.

So strong were these resemblances to the eyes of the whites that in the beginning of their western exploration they were given to calling the Sioux and Navajos the Red Tartars. Some, though, preferred the name Red Hebrews, for they believed that these were the Lost Tribes who had wandered from the Holy Land to America across the Pacific.

One hundred years before it would have been difficult to convince non-Indians that the Indians had come from China. The non-Indians knew better: The native Americans either were the descendants of the Lost Tribes of Israel or the descendants of the Egyptians who, it was said, had built the pyramids of the Mayans and Aztecs. Both these beliefs had been scientifically proven in the eighteenth and nineteenth centuries to everyone's satisfaction except the Indians'. Nowadays, there was a newer belief that had also been scientifically proven: The Indians came from the opposite direction. They were Asians—neither Hebrews nor Egyptians, but either Chinese or Siberians.

". . . The American Indian is a Mongoloid; that is to say, a transplanted Asiatic," wrote archaeologist Charles Avery Amsden in *Prehistoric Southwesterners;* it became a dogma of archaeology pronounced unequivocally by George Willey before the American Philosophical Society: "Little doubt now exists that the first man to enter the New World crossed the Bering Strait from Asia to America" and he was of "the Mongoloid racial stock." To these oft-repeated beliefs a religious blessing was given in 1910, when the Franciscan fathers on the Navajo reservation declared that, for anyone "who believes in the Bible," there could "hardly be any doubt that the Navajo are of Asiatic origin."

"Scholars no longer discuss the question of whether the first Americans came from Siberia; today that is regarded as conclusive," said the archaeological writer C. R. Ceram, in *The First Americans.* But then, he cynically added, "the present certainty rests on a rather indirect type of proof; the fact that all other theories have been eliminated either as wrong . . . or nonsensical."

Many "other theories" do however still exist; and there remain as many questions as there are answers. The similarities between the Chinese and Indian ways may not have been due at all to vast theoretical migrations, but to the ordinary commerce and conflicts between the peoples of the two continents; for modern man has but very recently begun to know, and acknowledge, the skilled seamanship and oceanic navigation that his ancient forebears knew and practiced with remarkable success. From their earliest meetings, the peoples of Asia and America may have traded bits and pieces of their cultures, long before the beginning of our version of recorded—that is, of written—history.

When the Chinese merchants came to America in the sixteenth century on the Manila galleons of Spain, the modern era of "culture trading" began. By the end of the sixteenth century China was importing seeds of native American tobacco, corn, and sweet potatoes. And by the time the first Yankee clipper ships reached Canton in the eighteenth century, they brought cargoes of ginseng roots, grown by the farmers of the Six Nations of the Iroquois.

So, too, when the miners and railroadmen from China settled in the West, often living and working side by side with the native peoples, they brought their culture with them and traded their knowledge for that right. And the Indians, for their part, taught the Chinese the skills of survival. The trading of cultures had to work both ways, or it would not work. The curious case of the Chinese war paint on the prairie was not really as curious as it seemed.

Nonetheless, when these people met and traded, they adapted the new culture to their own needs and stayed as they had been, distinct and unique. The man who most comprehensively traced the "samenesses" of the Chinese and Indian ways, beliefs, and rituals, Hartley Burr Alexander, expressed this strongly: "Nothing essential to Indian cultures can be traced to other than native sources." Of the idea that the Americans were "transplanted Asiatics," he wrote: ". . . the evidence against all such theories is overpowering." The "samenesses" were not archaeological or esoteric to Alexander, but arose from common perceptions of life and of human wisdom, and from the necessities of living on the same earth.

On the frontiers the white settlers knew little of the Indians or the Chinese. Nor were they really interested in these panoramas of human culture that surrounded them; they were struggling to survive in what to them was a hostile wilderness, and they fought voraciously against everyone and anyone who they believed might threaten their tenuous hold on the "edge of civilization." In the eyes of the settlers, both Chinese and Indians were equally potential enemies, as an editorial in the Marin County *Journal*, in California, declared: "We have won this glorious land inch by inch from the red man in vain; we have beaten back the legions of George the Third for nothing . . . if we are now to surrender it to a horde of Chinese. The people of California cannot endure it."

In the East, as in the West, these "heathen" were simply regarded as an obstacle to civilization. Governor Horatio Seymour of New York State, while campaigning for the Presidency as the candidate of the Democratic Party in 1868, expressed the popular mood when he thundered: "We did not let the Indian stand in the way of our civilization, so why let the Chinese barbarian?" More and more, in the rhetoric of the time, the Indian and the Chinese were seen as mutually evil, to be expurgated.

On the prairie and in the mountains, the insult to the Chinese and Indians was more personal and human. They were often described by the same words and cursed by the same prejudices. Not merely were they equally "heathen," but their habits and beliefs were equally condemned as "barbarian" and "fiendish," "uncivilized" and "savage." In a dubious and racial sense, their "samenesses" caused them to face similar prejudices. Men from China had inherited the white man's fear and hatred of the native American. "The Chinaman, of whose civilization almost nothing was known in America at this time, was ignorantly compared with the negro and the Indian merely because of the color of his skin," one observer complained, "such parallels arising in part from ignorance, in part from an instinctive color antipathy." And yet, "It was the habit of Congressmen, and Editors, to draw the most alarming deductions from these comparisons."

To the white emigrants to California any people who were not white were surely foreigners, whether they were Chinese or native Americans; the absurdity of the assumption, since the whites were themselves foreigners, escaped them. In the eyes of these whites, the Chinese and native Americans were genetically equally "semi-barbarian," as the Shasta *Courier* warned in 1853: ". . . if the Chinese are to live amongst us as our equals . . . are we willing that they should marry with our sons and daughters and people our country with a motley race of half-breeds, resembling more the native Digger [Indian] than the Anglo-American?"

A few years later the State of California barred the children of "Africans, Chinese and Diggers" [Indians] from the schools. The children of these "inferior races" would cause the "ruin of our schools," said the white educators.

So widely believed by the white man were these cultural hatreds and racial concepts that the Supreme Court of California sanctified them with the power and dignity of the law. The year was 1854. A murder trial had been brought before the court. Two men had fought, for a forgotten reason, and one man had been accused of killing the other in the fight. In the trial, the defendant had been convicted on the testimony of the "Chinese houseboy" who had seen the crime and so was an eye witness. The convicted murderer appealed on the legal ground that there was a "Gold Rush law" in California, by which a member of an "inferior" people, such as an Indian or "African," was not permitted to testify in court against a white man. Surely, the murderer said, the Chinese were as "inferior" as the Indian or "African."

The California Supreme Court agreed and reversed the murder conviction. In their ruling, the justices decreed prophetically: "To let Chinese testify in a court of law would admit them to all the equal rights of citizenship. And we might soon see them at the polls, in the jury box, upon the bench and in our legislative hall." Since the Chinese were a "distinct people . . . a race of people whom nature has marked as inferior, and who are incapable of progress or intellectual development beyond a certain point, as their history has shown," and because of "differing language, opinion, color and physical conformation [they] should be denied the right to testify."

Said the justices of the California Supreme Court: the "Chinese were Indians."

One hundred years later a Chinese lawyer, Harry K. Low, was appointed to the Superior Court of California. In reading the verdict that "Chinese were Indians," Justice Low was moved to comment with some irony: "I first came across this outrageous decision when I was a Deputy in the California Attorney General's office. As a young lawyer, I [believed] I should check on its current validity. For, if 'Chinese were Indians' I wanted to claim my rights as an Indian. While Indians were also subjected to great discrimination, they were also accorded certain rights for land that was taken from them."

Low grinned: "I wanted my share of oil lands, free fishing privileges, and free camping on [the] Indian reservations."

BOOK THREE

The Chinese

Who Became

America

XIII

THE PAPER BROTHERS

AND SISTERS

When I am silent, I feel fulfilled; when I open my mouth to
speak, I am conscious of emptiness.   —LU SHUN

Were his thoughts with his heart, ten thousand miles away, beneath the billowy wastes of the Pacific? among the rice fields
and plumy palms of China? And now and then, rippling among
his visions and his dreams, did he hear familiar laughter and half-
forgotten voices, and did he catch fitful glimpses of the friendly
faces of a bygone time? It is a cruel fate . . .
          —MARK TWAIN, in *John Chinaman in New York*

THE OLD MAN was not dead. But he had been ill for many
weeks. On the dirty windowsill of his small room in that dilapi-
dated hotel for men, there were four empty flower pots; the
flowers had died weeks ago. Once, years before, the old man
had been a gardener, and he always tended his flowers with
loving care. When he thought he was dying, he decided that
his flowers ought to die too, and so he stopped watering them.
They died, but he did not.

Now he mourned for his flowers. "I killed them," he said.

In the morning he had awoken uncertainly and dressed himself
by habit. Still, weak as he was, he walked with his usual dignity
to his usual bench in the little park at Portsmouth Square. There
he watched the children begin the day. He sat there smiling,
not so much that the children amused him, as that he was delighted to be sitting there at all.

Sitting on that bench meant that he was not dead. Not yet. When he awoke, but was not really awake, he often wondered whether he was not half dead. Sometimes he thought he was. On those occasions he did not get out of bed for hours, even for days at a time, getting up only to buy a bottle of cheap wine or the newspaper. If he was already half dead, he was curious to learn what the rest of death was like, and he waited defiantly to see what was going to happen. But nothing did.

The old man's sorrow for his dead flowers was so deep he refused to plant new ones. In this country, the red geraniums and azaleas had been his only living family. He had no wife. Nor did he have any children whom he knew by name. And he had no name that was his own. The name on his immigration papers, which he was known by, was not his name at all; it was his "paper" name that he had bought when he came to America, because he was told that was what the American government wanted Chinese emigrants to do. It was an odd custom.

"So, you know," he said, "no one remembers who I am, sometime. I forget, too, sometime."

In a strange way, he seemed pleased that he had lived so long with false papers and a paper name. The sly smile on his face was one of guile and shrewdness, not of pleasure; for he was proud he had outwitted the authorities at their own games for so many years. He was a tough old man.

One of the old bachelors, he was one of the generations of men from Kwangtung who, year after year, had come alone to the Golden Mountain without wives or families, illegally, and had created a society of bachelors that had survived for one hundred years. Now they were dying like monks in the aging hotels for men and in monastic cubicles of tenements that, like themselves, had begun to fade like the old pages of history.

No one cared if they were alive. No one knew when they

died. Once these old men had been strong young boys who had come to America as had their ancestors, who had helped build the railroads and mines, farms and fishing industry of California; but no one remembers the sons of heroes when they become old and ill—especially if they have false names.

Many of the old men in the International Hotel in San Francisco's Chinatown, where his room was, were, like him, nameless. They too had paper names. They too were of the bachelor society of Chinese and Filipino men who had no home but their hotel room.

The decaying hotel was a dull red, squat three-story building that its owners believed to be a blight on the city. It occupied a block on Kearny Street, not far from the simulated sex act shows and topless bars of the profitable Broadway tourist area. And it was doomed to demolition to make way for a parking lot for the devotees of simulated sex and the admirers of topless women who had silicone breasts.

On the boarded-up storefronts of the old men's refuge there were defiant posters: WE WON'T MOVE! But they had. The shopkeepers were all gone. Even the old Mabihay Restaurant, whose sign still offered FINE PHILIPPINE CUISINE, was abandoned and empty.

Not too long ago the quiet relic of a hotel had been a lively place. Its shops had often been facades for raunchy and high-spirited gambling games which went on night and day in its back rooms. The elderly men, upstairs in their lonely beds, remembered happily the excitement of police raids and the exuberance of youthful fistfights for winning hands and willing women. But these were fading memories. Everything was gone now except the old men.

"One day soon," the old man said, "we will be gone. When we are gone, no one will remember when we were here. You

know, in America no one remembers anyone. Anything. Any-
time."

In the pale sun of the morning, as the fog was rising, the
old men gathered in Portsmouth Square. They clustered together
like flocks of formal birds. Most of these men were dressed in
dark suits and worn coats and ancient fedoras meticulously cared
for from the days of their youth. And they talked together, as
they had for years, rarely admitting any outsider to their intimate
circle; for the stories they told one another were personal histories
of the West they shared only with those with whom they had
shared them in their lives. No one but another paper brother
was to be trusted with the memory of the past. It was not that
they were secretive and sullen. They were jovial and boisterous,
but they had reasons to be cautious.

Even the old man would not let me know his real name.
No one knew his name in America, he said.

The gatherers of memories, the historians, had recently begun
to collect and collate the lives of the old men of Portsmouth
Square. They inscribed their lives in neat and orderly books.
But the old men smiled tolerantly upon these "story gatherers."
No man told the story of his life wholly to a stranger, when
he rarely told it to himself.

Some of the stories they did tell, but others they did not.
They had more than bitter memories. They remembered things
that were so ugly and sadistic that they wished to forget them.
In the minds of these old men not merely the glory of the
history of the West, but its evils, were preserved. And they
hid these memories beneath their tongues and behind their eyes.
They did not like to talk about their youth as old men do.
And when they remembered there was a visible pain in their
eyes.

Long ago, when these old men were young, many had come

to America illegally. They had to acquire papers and paper names, for that was the only way they could enter the country. They had lived in fear of deportation ever since, though some had been in America for seventy-five years and more.

Even when the old men came legally they were not welcome. They were taken to the island of the Angel, as the Spaniards had called it, in San Francisco Bay, to be rudely questioned by officials of the Immigration Service whose goal seemed to be to deport as many as possible. Some of the old men were imprisoned on Angel Island for months; they lived in dormitories, behind barred windows, isolated and alone, for they were unable to speak English or reach their families, just across the bay. And there they waited for their paper identities. These were men who came legally, but were treated illegally.

Some of the immigrants were young boys in their teens and they were terrified by the ordeal. One old man remembered with defiant hindsight. He told Victor and Betty de Bary Nee, authors of *Longtime Californ'*: "When I first came here, to work on the levees, we were stoned when we got off the ship. We weren't allowed to leave Angel's Island because they said our feces had worms in them. They fed us like pigs because they thought we were filthy. Finally a group of all men came and led us to Chinatown. But on the way people shouted, 'Chink! Chink! Chink!' and threw stones at us again." And then he quietly said: "Before we used to lower our eyes before the white man. Now [after seventy years?], we can look straight at them without being afraid."

Once these young emigrants had come ashore they were welcomed by more than stones. Those who understood English could discern the cry: "The Chinese must go!"; while the less humanistic citizens greeted the shocked newcomers by shouting "Kill the Chinks!"

Fear and hatred of the Chinese had been growing in the West for generations. The decline of gold mining and railroad construction toward the end of the nineteenth century had brought about the demand that the men who helped create these industries be forced to return to China. When they were needed they were enticed to come here, but they were no longer needed. And so, the white populace and its government had demanded that residents be deported and new emigrants forcibly excluded.

Mobs had been storming through the country, from town to town, for many years, forcing the expulsion of Chinese residents from cities they had founded, burning their homes, looting their shops and savings, lynching those men who resisted, and raping the women. From the coast of California to the mountains of Montana, this scourge ranged across the land. In California alone there were riots that terrorized Los Angeles, Santa Barbara, Pasadena, Oakland, San Jose, Santa Cruz, Sacramento, Hollister, Merced, Fresno, Redding, Napa, Sonoma, Yuba City, Santa Rosa, Chico, Placerville, Marysville, Dixon, Wheatland, and San Francisco—to name only the larger cities.

Not only were the Chinese forced from the towns and their homes burned, the white farmers and merchants who employed workmen from China were targets of the mobs' anger. Farms that refused to fire Chinese ranch hands were set afire. Barns and fields were burned. In the agricultural valleys of San Joaquin armed vigilantes roamed from town to town. They were equally severe with the Chinese and the whites who tried to defend them. In the mountain country the mobs of unemployed white workers dynamited the tracks of those few railroads that continued to employ Chinese railroadmen. One observer noted that the situation in the West was "approximating civil war."

For nearly half a century, these attacks had gone on in town after town, in state after state. They had become a way of life and a way of thinking, among both the victims and the vigilantes. Neither the local nor the federal authorities did very much to halt the mobs, for their violence was, in effect, a way of enforcing the many laws aimed at excluding the Chinese residents from the daily life of the West and forcing them not only from their homes but from the country. The mobs were, in some ways, even more effective than the laws.

Of the original settlers of the West, more and more had fled in horror, returning to China. In the late 1880s there were said to have been nearly 110,000 Chinese residents on the sparsely populated frontiers of the West. But thirty years later there were barely more than 60,000. Nearly half of the western pioneers had been terrorized into leaving their homes, refugees from their own land.

None of this was unknown to the new emigrants; they had heard tales from those who had been in America and had had to flee the violence that was sweeping the land. Then why did they come? Surely it was an act of courage—some said madness—to emigrate to this country, where they would be attacked. Even so, they were unprepared for the sadistic nature of the violence that was awaiting them.

The savage and bestial manner of the whites' attacks was extreme. Even in the atmosphere of lawlessness that was celebrated by the vigilantes on the western frontier, the violence against these men from China was peculiarly brutal; it expressed a fury and a wrath that seemed irrational.

Not merely were men scalped and their pigtails cut off. Their ears were amputated. In more than one incident men were branded with hot irons. One Chinese miner was caught by a mob who sliced off his genitals and took them in triumph to a nearby saloon where the severed organ was placed on the bar and toasted as a trophy of the hunt. In one Nevada town an old-timer recalled how a defenseless laundryman was tied to a wagonwheel and the buckboard was driven at high speeds through the town until "the man's head fell off and rolled across the streets like a tumbleweed."

On a single night in Los Angeles in 1871, some twenty innocent Chinese men were lynched or burned alive by mobs of white men in what began as a dispute over a "flower-boat girl." Four men were crucified by being "spread eagled against the sides of 'sagebrush schooners' and executed with knife and gun." One white doctor who was walking by was almost torn limb from limb and left to die in the street. The "blood bath," as the newspapers said, caused an "international incident." And the United States had to offer an official apology to the emperor of the imperial court in China for what were described as the "senseless" killings by white Americans.

No less sadistic and inhuman was the violence that seized the cosmopolitan city of San Francisco. One day in the summer of 1868, the *Times* of that city reported that a Chinese crab fisherman had been beaten to death; his body was found on the waterfront beneath a wharf. It seemed, at first, merely another Barbary Coast murder, but it was not at all. The man's flesh had been branded by hot irons. His ears had been sliced in half with a knife. His tongue had been severed and cut off. "There was apparently no other motive for this atrocity than the brutal instincts of the young ruffians who perpetrated it," wrote the editor of the *Times*. "Such boys are constantly . . . eager to glut their cruelty on any Chinaman who must pass." The editor was compassionate, but he was at a loss to understand the source of this sadism except to blame the "mob" instincts of the uneducated "lower classes." Since the mobs of vigilantes were often headed by the leading citizens of the towns, this explained nothing at all.

In the rural towns and the mining camps the Chinese who were murdered often went unnoted. Neither the newspapers nor the local officials cared to record their deaths. There were kidnappings of Chinese miners on the American River who simply disappeared. There were uncounted Chinese ranch hands who were waylaid on lonely country roads and whose bodies and graves have never been found.

The crescendo of this violence was reached in Rock Springs, Wyoming, in 1885, where some twenty-eight Chinese men were murdered by the local townspeople. It began because the Chinese miners had "dissented" in a strike vote. In the orgy of bloodletting that followed, men were not only burned alive, but their dead bodies were mutilated. One man, found in the "ashes of his hut," had only "the right half of his head and the backbone"; while another's remains consisted of "the bones of the lower half of the body"; and still another was left with only "the sole and heel of the left foot."

Some of "the bodies [of the Chinese], mangled and decomposed, were strewn on the ground and were eaten by dogs and hogs. Some were burned beyond recognition. It was a sad and painful sight to see the son crying for the father, the brother for the brother, the uncle for the nephew, the friend for friend," said a memorial written by the 559 Chinese miners who had survived the massacres. When they had ended, the living were haunted by the dead: "Their sleep is disturbed by frightful dreams and they cannot obtain peaceful rest," the memorial said.

Some of their murderers were not men at all. They were women and children. "Even the white woman who formerly taught English to the Chinese . . . took handkerchiefs" from the dead, and there were others "who took no part either in beating or robbing the Chinese," but who had "stood by, shouting loudly and laughing, and clapping their hands."

In sorrow and lamentation, the survivors wrote: "We never

thought that the subjects of a nation . . . so highly civilized as this, so unexpectedly [would] suffer the cruelty and wrong of being injustly put to death."

The massacres of the Chinese were so commonplace that many chroniclers of the West were either undisturbed by them or so disturbed they could not write about them. And those that did write maintained a remarkable nonchalance toward the death of these pioneers. Samuel Bowles, in *Our New West*, published in 1869, wrote matter-of-factly: "To abuse and cheat a China-man; to rob him; to kick him and cuff him; even to kill him have been things done not only with impunity by mean and wicked men" but by respectable citizens as well "with vain glory." As the editor of the *Montanian* wrote, in 1873: "We don't mind hearing of a Chinaman being killed now and then, but it's been coming too thick of late. Don't kill them unless they deserve it, but when they do, why kill 'em lots."

Mobs might attack Chinese men and women with impunity because the victims—if they survived—could not testify in court against their tormentors. In California the laws prohibited non-whites, such as the Chinese, from appearing in court to confront a white citizen. Since it was not thought to be a crime to abuse someone who had no standing under the law, there were few cases where any white man or woman was ever punished on the frontier for the murder of a Chinese man or woman.

One old tale told of a white man who was brought before Judge Roy Bean's court in Texas, accused of killing a Chinese man. The judge, after consulting his lawbook, decreed: "I can't find nothing where it says it's against the law to kill a Chinaman."

Curiously, in an earlier version of the folktale the victim was a Mexican. And the judge's verdict was exactly the same.

Laws of the West merely enforced the demands of the mobs, who in turn enforced the laws. In city after city local ordinances

were passed that prohibited the Chinese people fr[...]
the city limits, buying or owning property, workin[...]
shopkeepers or farmers, voting in elections and, in[...]
walking on the sidewalk. There was another town, in Montana,
where it was a crime for white people to be seen eating in a
Chinese restaurant.

All these laws legalized the results of the mob violence. In
his veto of Congress' first attempt to halt Chinese immigration
President Rutherford B. Hayes, in 1879, perceived the relation-
ship between anti-Chinese laws and mob rule, when he prophesied: "We shall oppress the Chinaman, and their presence will
make hoodlums and vagabonds of their oppressors."

So severe and strident were the local laws that sought to banish
the Chinese people from American life that in some ways they
equaled the slave ordinances of the South. In some ways they
were worse. The constitution of California had been rewritten,
in 1879, forbidding any man or woman of "Chinese or Mongolian" ancestry from earning a living by working for a white man:
"No corporation now existing or hereafter formed under the
laws of this State, shall employ, directly or indirectly, any Chinese
or Mongolian," and "No Chinese shall be employed on any
State, county or municipal or other public work, except in punish-
ment for crime," it declared. And further, "The Legislature shall
delegate all necessary power" to the towns and cities "for the
removal of Chinese." Lest there be any doubt about the purpose
of these laws, the constitution categorically declared the Chinese
people were "dangerous to the well being of the State." In these
acts the government was echoing the demands of the Workingmen's Party of Dennis Kearny, which had warned the constitutional convention that "the Chinese laborer is a curse to our
land, is a menace to our liberties, and should be restricted and
forever abolished, and *'the Chinese must go!'* "

In 1882, the Congress did enact the Exclusion Act, which decreed that a Chinese man who worked with his "hands," who was a "manual" laborer, henceforth would be prohibited from coming to America. The law specifically outlawed all laborers who were "skilled and unskilled, and those engaged in mining." And the people from China who were already residents were forever barred from becoming citizens, no matter what they had contributed in the building of the West. No other people were ever excluded in quite this way. The Chinese were simply outlawed.

Six years later, in 1888, Congress enacted an even more severe restriction on immigration, the Scott Act, which prohibited any Chinese man, temporarily absent from the country, from ever returning. It was said that this law permanently barred as many as twenty thousand men who were visiting their families overseas; six hundred of them were aboard ship in the middle of the Pacific Ocean.

That year the Congress had amended the Exclusion Act with a paradox. It decreed that men from China might enter the country if they had papers that proved they had a wife, a child, or a parent here. Merchants from China, too, were allowed to come ashore with their wives and children. So were preachers, teachers, seamen, newspapermen, and wealthy travelers. They merely had to have proper papers, or enough money to buy false, but legal, papers, which proclaimed acceptable lies. So the paper fathers and mothers, sisters and brothers were created by the act of the same Congress that had banned the people with real names. The time of the old men with "paper" names was about to begin.

The need for these laws was justified by the patriotic argument that the jobs these Chinese men had created were wanted by white men, and the flow of capital accumulated by those Chinese merchants who were adherents of Ben Franklin's frugal *Poor Richard's Almanack* and sent their penny-by-penny savings back to their families in China, had to be halted. Political reasons were just as logical; the Chinese had been the single largest nationality in the West in the frontier days—at least one-quarter of the population of California and an even greater part of many of the remote western territories. Together with the native Indian and Mexican villagers and clans, they were the majority. So they had to be excluded from civic life and were denied the right to vote, as were the others.

Reflecting the popular opinion of the time, President James Garfield had explained the Chinese "have no assimilation whatever to Caucasian civilization." And, they refused to enter the "melting pot." One United States senator described the problem in gastronomical images: "These people are an indigestible element in our midst, a cold pebble in the public stomach which cannot be digested." Therefore they were potentially a threat to the rule of white men, and to the possession of the wealth of the West.

The money ethic and the profits theory of history were highly esteemed in the West. Commented the Sacramento Record-Union, in 1879; "The Chinaman is here because his presence pays, and he will remain and continue to increase so long as there is money in him. When the time comes that he is no longer profitable *that* generation will take care of him." It was all a matter, wrote the editor, of the needs of business.

And yet these economic and political reasons did not explain the ferocity of the attacks against the Chinese, or the severity of the laws that sought to "abolish" their existence. They were logical and rational explanations, but superficial and obvious.

"Race prejudice" was more likely the cause, thought President Grover Cleveland. It "is the chief factor in originating these disturbances and it exists in a large part of our domain, jeopardizing our domestic peace," he said. The classic history of the *Mining Camps*, by Charles H. Shinn, published in 1884, strongly agreed: "Race-hatred [was] the darkest thread in the fabric" of western history, Shinn wrote; there "the immemorial race-impulse of the Aryan had reawakened with all its ancient force."

Even that did not, however, explain the savagery of the attacks on the Chinese. It was not simply prejudice and discrimination that they faced. Said one observer, Chang Kiu Sing, in 1904: "They call it exclusion; but it is not exclusion, it is extermination." The settlers from Europe did not wish to segregate the settlers from Asia; they wished to eliminate them entirely. Sardonically condemning the epochal angers of the white citizens, the noted preacher the Reverend Henry Ward Beecher had admonished the white congregations of California for their genocidal brutality to the Chinese people, which had turned the paradise of the West into a purgatory. "We have clubbed them, stoned them, burned them and even murdered them. Yet, they refuse to be converted" to Christianity, Beecher intoned: "If we are ever to get them to Heaven" it might be necessary "to blow them up with nitroglycerin." It was just a joke.

Paradise was to be "white." It was ordained in the Heavens by a "Divine Plan" entrusted to "Anglo-Saxon supremacy."

California was a new utopia, a cornucopia, a Garden of Eden, but it was a paradise for white men only. "The Anglo-Saxon race has laid the foundation of our Western empire," proclaimed William Thayer in *The Marvels of the New West;* these "Anglo-Saxons control the destiny of the human family." So it was in the year before the State was admitted into the Union, the San Francisco *Californian* announced matter-of-factly: "We desire only a white population in California." So, too, the constitutional convention had been informed by a spokesman for the white farmers of California: "This State should be a State for white men. We want no other race here. The future of this republic demands that it be a white man's government. . . . All other races shall be excluded." And so the constitution of California duly stated that only "white male citizens" would be allowed to vote.

From this fantasy of a white paradise that never existed, the Workingmen's Party of California created its own all-white dream world: "We declare that white men and women, boys and girls, cannot live as people in this great republic . . . with [a] single Chinese coolie." Some years later Samuel Gompers, the leader of the American Federation of Labor, justified the anti-Chinese racism of labor with a tract, *Some Reasons for Chinese Exclusion: Meat vs. Rice, American Manhood Against Asiatic Coolieism—Which Shall Survive?* Gompers was forthright: ". . . the racial differences between American whites and Asiatics would never be overcome. The superior whites had to exclude the inferior Asiatics, by law, or if necessary, by force of arms." Gompers, a socialist on occasion, was, like so many white men of his era, obsessed by racism.

Remembering "The Days of '49," the old-timers from the Gold Rush in California nostalgically sang about their white paradise that never existed. They celebrated their memory of years when "the boys [were] all white":

> Since that day
> > How things have changed,
> > In this land of liberty.
> Darkies didn't vote
> > Nor plead in court,
> > Nor rule the country.

> But the Chinese question
> Worst of all,
> Then did not exist.
> For the country was right
> And the boys all white,
> In the Days of '49.

Five years before Congress passed the Exclusion Act, all but shutting tight the ports of the Pacific coast to Chinese emigrants, it voted to accept a gift of a great statue that was to stand in New York Harbor, welcoming European emigrants. The statue, was named Liberty and beneath her torch, which was never lit, there were the world-renowned words of blessing: "Give me your tired, your poor, Your huddled masses yearning to breathe free, The wretched refuse of your teeming shore. Send these, the homeless, tempest-tost, to me. I lift my lamp beside the golden door."

But the statue stood with her back to half the world. Her torch did not face toward China.

One of the prominent poets of the day, Thomas Bailey Aldrich, writing in the venerable *Atlantic* magazine of the Boston brahmins, sensed the irony. He greeted the "Colossus" of a statue as the "white Goddess" of liberty for some, but not for all. The paradox seemed to titillate his sense of drama, for he wrote:

> O Liberty, white Goddess!
> Is it well to leave the gate unguarded?

On the Golden Mountain of the West the "golden door" remained shut, and "the gate" was guarded all too well. Not until the midst of World War II, in 1943, did the Congress repeal the Exclusion Acts, which for sixty-two years had been the law of the paper brothers and sisters. It was now possible for Chinese residents to become citizens. And some 105 Chinese were actually to be allowed to enter the country legally every year.

Policies of exclusion had been enforced for so many generations because the acts and attitudes of Congress had continually reenforced them. So did the power of the Presidency. It was contemptuously but politely—more politely than usual—expressed in words attributed to President Woodrow Wilson, in 1917. "In the matter of Chinese and Japanese coolie immigration, I stand for a national policy of exclusion," the President was widely quoted as saying. "The whole question is one of assimilation of diverse races. We cannot make a homogeneous population of people who do not blend with the Caucasian race. . . . Oriental coolieism will give us another problem to solve and surely we have had our lesson."

The repeal of the Exclusion Acts did not repeal these attitudes. Such a change would take as many generations as it took to create the prejudices.

None of these changes helped the paper brothers and sisters. As far as they were concerned, the immigration laws were still anti-immigration laws, whose aim was not to govern the coming of Chinese emigrants to America, but to keep them out. They were still vulnerable to deportation at any moment; it did not matter how long they had lived here.

They were invisible men. And since they were "illegals," they had to be as invisible as possible.

In the dim corridors of the dusty old International Hotel, the retired men found safety from the world "outside." Their narrow rooms, maybe as wide as two coffins, were cosy and familiar. Year after year, they sat by the curtainless windows of their rooms peering down upon the passing parade of Chinatown, which filled Kearny Street with a comforting and unchanging array of faces they knew.

Sometimes they sat there playing a Chinese or Filipino guitar. Most of the time they just sat there, seemingly doing nothing at all. They were alone but not lonely, for they were surrounded by their memories, which crowded their rooms and their minds.

These were toughened old men. In their youth they had withstood the power and violence of a society and government that was determined to declare them nonpersons and nonexistent. But they had resisted and survived; their minds were living archives of a time in history that most Americans preferred to pretend had never happened, and of a heroism that most Americans knew nothing at all about.

Now, in the quiet of their dying days, the old men wished for little more than to die in peace. But this was not to be.

Ever since the landlords of the old hotel had decided to tear it down and build a parking lot upon its ruins, the old men had become a cause célèbre. For nine years they had been living under the threat of eviction. The demolition plans were announced in 1969. And since then thousands of people had rallied around the decaying hotel, at first bewildering the old men and making them uneasy, but finally making them feel the hotel was a bastion and their rooms were parapets guarding against the destruction of their past.

The old International Hotel, built in 1850, was the perfect setting for such a battle. It was destroyed and restored many times in its history, the last time when it fell before the great earthquake of 1906 and arose again from the debris, as it always had.

From sidewalk to sidewalk a banner waved like a great white sail across Kearny Street. It billowed in the evening wind from San Francisco Bay. On the banner, in blazing red letters, were messages in Chinese, Tagalog, and English proclaiming the old men's stubborn intransigence: WE WILL NOT MOVE and FIGHT

EVICTIONS and similar slogans. But one old man seemed to express his neighbors' feelings with a defiant humor that sounded more genuine: "As I see it, these eviction notices they give are just a personal sort of Exclusion Act. But it is too late.

"This is our country, now," the old man said.

On the starry night of August 3, 1977, the City of San Francisco decided to marshal its not inconsiderable forces in a full-scale assault on the old men's bastion. Some four hundred policemen were summoned, and a vast array of riot equipment, mounted horse patrols, emergency ladders, fire trucks, and television cameras and crews gathered at the embattled hotel.

Several thousand defenders of the old men gathered as well. They surrounded the entire building, around the block, in lines six deep.

All night long the lines of people and police moved back and forth. The old men sat in their rooms and watched. In the street the ballet of protesters and enforcers continued until dawn, like a panoramic pantomine. Then, at 5:25 A.M., the first of the old men to be evicted emerged from the hotel, stood there, dazed by the sight of thousands of people, all shouting at him. An old man by the name of Mr. Yip came out wearing a large "Yippie Power" button on his coat lapel. Cursing as he was led away, he cried, "I want to go back to my home."

One of the last of the old men to leave was Wahat Tompao. There he stood, before the empty building, with his jaw set, and a bitter and saddened look began to fill his eyes. Someone, maybe one of the police, had taken a razorblade, he said, and cut his pet goldfish right in half. He lamented: "I am suffering all over my body.

"I do not understand why they do this to us," Wahat Tompao said.

XIV

THE CHINATOWN BLUES

Maybe you can tell me in your next letter how to make chop
suey and chow mein? Many American friends ask for these dishes,
but nobody here knows how to prepare them. Yet they insist
that they are our national dishes.
                    —Letter from home in *China Red*, by H. T. TSIANG

Chinatown is as American as chow mein.   —New York *Post*

THE RIVER TOWN might have been the Hannibal, Missouri, of
Mark Twain's time. But it was not. It was a Chinese river town
of the old West.

On the levee by the banks of the lazy river in the lowlands
of the Sacramento delta, the ranch hands had built a graceful
mirage. The old wooden houses that faced the river were con-
nected to the delta by catwalks and platforms that made it possible to walk from the river road onto the front porches where
the townspeople sat, shaded from the hot and humid sun of
the California valley, watching the riverboats as they moved
reluctantly down to the sea.

People said that the town looked exactly as it had when it
was built. The old-fashioned frame houses were unchanged. Lean-
ing this way and that, like old men, the houses were propped
up with tall trunks along their sides that kept them from falling.
On the old Main Street the second-story balconies and verandas
sagged wearily on their wooden posts, but they still overlooked
the town the way they had when the last stagecoach had stopped

here on its way to San Francisco. Though the town was not untouched by history, at first glance it seemed to be; it looked more like the set of a western movie than any set ever did.

On the fading, painted facades of its shops the usual signs were visible: GROCERIES. DRY GOODS. COLD CIGARS. The arcade of the empty, abandoned Star Theatre still beckoned visitors, though into a dark, blind alley.

The sons of its founders still sat on benches along Main Street, listening to the echoes of the past. And reminiscing. It is said that this town is one of the few authentic western towns left that is not a ghost town, for it still is lived in.

Founded in 1912 by one Tin Sin Chan, who built its first house, the town of Locke, California, boomed. By 1915 the population reached fifteen hundred residents, most of them ranch hands and shopkeepers from the Sacramento delta. And all of them Chinese. In those days it was an ordinary western town with its own doctors, schoolteachers, bakeries, grocery stores, shoemaker, restaurants, fish market, candy store and ice cream parlor, theater and saloon, clothing and dry-goods stores. The single "foreigner" in the town was the owner of the saloon, which was then, as now, named Al the Wop's Bar. No other foreigners were allowed, and life was peaceful.

One of the old-timers who has since died, a Mr. King, said of the town: "I've lived here all my life. There aren't so many opportunities for work here in Locke. But I would not live in a city. It's so peaceful here."

They were old-time ranch and rural people who built the town. It was the quiet and independent life of the West that they cherished. And, in their town, with the river at their front porch and surrounded by shaded pear orchards, they did live in peace. It was in many ways a typical western town, the kind of place that in retrospect seems idyllic as the American dream.

Still, the town was built entirely by Chinese men and women, for the Chinese people, and it was inhabited entirely by the Chinese. It was a wholly Chinese town. But it was never a China-town. Not then.

Nowadays the real estate developers and tourist guides have discovered that the town is a "unique center of cultural interest." Boutiques and antique shoppes are appearing on Main Street. The original house built by Tin Sin Chan has been converted into a "Chinese restaurant"—featuring "Great Pizza." And the white entrepreneurs who wish to "preserve the town's historical significance" have erected an "authentic Chinese phone booth," with fake oriental dragons and imitation gold paint, for the tour-ists. They are remaking the Chinese town so that it will soon be a Chinatown.

Originally, the town was owned by a local ranching family, the Lockes, for whom it was named. They sold it recently, and the pear orchards as well, to a Hong Kong developer, Ng Tor-Tai, who announced plans to turn the town into a new tourist attraction with a Chinese museum and floating restaurant. Sort of a Chinese Disneyland.

Sitting in the sun, the old men of the town must have thought of all this with bemusement and suspicion, as do old-time cowboys on seeing a Hollywood film company coming into town to "shoot a Western." They, after all, had never lived in a Chinatown.

On the early frontier there had been many Chinese towns. Those men who worked on the ranches and in the mines and built the railroads were independent-minded pioneers, self-made men who preferred living in towns of their own design and choosing rather than in the ghetto shacks of a ramshackle frontier town or on its outskirts amid the red light district. Whenever it was possible, and it was not always so, the men from China would build their own communities.

There was one of these Chinese towns near Reno, Nevada. It was built on the desert flat north of the Walker River by some adventurous gold prospectors. A small town, having no more than twelve houses and two stores, it was at the time as large as nearby Carson City; but unlike the eventual state capital, the town the Chinese built was unlisted in U.S. Army maps. It had no name that white men knew.

Even so, the Chinese town was well known. On the surrounding desert its farmers grew fresh vegetables that were rare as gold in that parched land. Its stores were crowded with white miners, who came to the Chinese town to buy food and went to Carson City to buy whiskey.

These towns were independent and self-sufficient. As well as they could, the people sought to take care of their own needs without depending on the neighboring white communities. It was not unusual for Chinese camps and towns on the remote frontiers of Idaho and Dakota to boast of a doctor, a pharmacist, a carpenter, a blacksmith, a barber, and an engineer among a population of a few dozen brave souls. So it was more likely for the white citizens to come to the Chinese town for help than for the Chinese to go to the white town.

In the style of their buildings and the designs of their architecture, these were typically western towns. They were frontier towns in setting and appearance. Not one fake dragon or temple roof was to be seen on their dusty Main Streets, nor was there any attempt to imitate Ming dynasty shrines in the building of dry-goods stores and horse stables and stagecoach depots.

The tourist rococco, pseudo-Ming dynasty architecture of Chinatowns was foreign to the Chinese towns. It had to be. For they were more likely the habitats of Chinese Wyatt Earps than of any Americanized Kung Fus.

Most of the pioneer towns that were built then have since

disappeared. The mobs who raged through the West in the late nineteenth century burned the Chinese towns to the ground. In the far mountains some of the town sites occasionally may be seen under the weeds, but there have been few attempts, so far, at archaeological discoveries. One thing that has made the town of Locke unique is that it has survived just as it was built, for fortunately it was founded after the anti-Chinese town burnings had ceased. And so it stands alone as a living memory not only of the differences between the Chinese towns of the frontier times and the Chinatowns of recent years, but as a memorial to the skill of the architects and construction workers of China who built so many of the famous towns of the West.

Frontiersmen from the eastern states were understandably annoyed at the Chinese who seemed so at ease in the West. They may have felt, as well, a certain sense of inferiority when confronted by the urbane "Celestials." Life in the cosmopolitan cities and raucous mining camps was in many ways more foreign to these Yankee farmers and Kentucky woodsmen than it was to the worldly Chinese, many of whom had worked overseas for generations in the mines of Borneo and Malaya, and the cities of Singapore and Manila. In the puritanical mind such experiences had to be devilish.

In rural America during the pre–Civil War years cities were thought of as demonic and evil. The "dark, Satanic mills" were seen as an urban curse, and America was envisioned as the idyllic land of independent farmers. Many of the men who had gone West had little or no knowledge of life in cities. The settlers from China were more sophisticated in these matters.

Of the earlier Chinese pioneers, many had come from Canton—one of the largest and most cosmopolitan ports in the world. For two thousand years the city and the fishing villages that surrounded the port had been a center for Chinese trade with the merchants of Arabia and Africa, Rome and India. Its peoples were accustomed to living with foreigners in their midst, and they were experienced in the ways of survival in distant and foreign cities.

When the Han dynasty, in 206 B.C., began uniting China, the emperor ordered the gathering of the people into fortified cities. In a few hundred years the seaports had become metropolises that harbored people of many nations behind their walls. By the time travelers from medieval Europe arrived in China in the thirteenth century, these coastal cities were said to have become the largest in the world, beyond anything the Europeans had ever seen in splendor and size.

And as wealth came to these cities from overseas, so their people went overseas in search of wealth. From the time of the Han dynasty and perhaps even before, the colonies of overseas Chinese were forming through much of the Asian and Pacific world. Wherever they went, the settlers founded cities. Even today in many of the cities of Southeast Asia a major group of the population is Chinese; it is especially true of Malaysia, where they are the urban majority. Still, they did not attempt to change the people of these lands into Chinese. Nor did they change their own ways. They built colonies, but they did not colonize.

"Centuries of contact and in more recent periods close contact with Chinese migrants made virtually no impact upon such matters as dress, furniture or ways of living. Neither did the Chinese modify their habits," noted C. P. Fitzgerald in *The Southern Expansion of the Chinese People;* ". . . the Chinese themselves, wherever they have settled, have brought with them their own culture. At first in simple forms suited to a mainly migrant population, but as the level of their wealth and standard of living rose they turned without hesitation to the more sophisticated art and literature of their ancestral land." It was a peculiarly

Chinese way of colonial life. And hundreds of years later, it was a way of life that was to be repeated in America.

So expert were the Chinese in applying their skill and industry in developing the nations where they settled, without being influenced by the nations' way of life, that King Rama VI of Thailand, in admiration and anger, called them "the Jews of the Far East." They remained Chinese, in their Chinese cities, all through the centuries.

And yet the cities they built in strange lands were not replicas of those they had left in China. They built them in a style and construction that fit in their new environment and climate. Except for religious temples and official buildings, these Chinese towns resembled the ordinary towns of the countries in which they were built. They were not Chinatowns.

Not until the Europeans arrived in China during the sixteenth century, inspired by the romantic dreams of the Renaissance, did the Chinese builders begin to create Chinatowns for the fantasies of foreigners. The traders from Portugal who had established a European enclave on Chinese land, in 1557, on the peninsula of Macao, near Canton, encouraged the building of a Chinese town that was dependent on their own. It was to have two purposes: one was to have a place of shops and restaurants for the Europeans, and the other was to house the native men and women whom the Europeans employed as servants. It became the first Chinatown. Perhaps it was, as well, the first place where Chinese people cooked the food, cleaned the houses, and washed the dirty clothes of Europeans.

In this way, the first Chinatown was created by Europeans. The irony of it was that this original Chinatown, an ancestor of all those to be built in foreign lands, was built on the soil of China.

In the Philippines, the Portuguese idea was adopted by the Spaniards. They needed skilled professionals to conduct trade and to build ships, and so recruited and hired thousands of Chinese, mostly from Canton. By 1586 there were said to be ten thousand Chinese in Manila alone. By 1600, after twelve thousand had been deported to China, it was said as many remained. And by 1747, the population of the city consisted of forty thousand Chinese and a few hundred Spaniards.

Men of Canton largely built the city of Manila, as they had so many cities in Southeast Asia. But even though they outnumbered the Spaniards by more than one hundred to one, it never became an overseas Chinese city. The Spaniards saw to that. Since the industrious emigrants from Canton soon dominated retail trade, farming, and manufacturing, the king of Spain, in 1628, decided that they were a "great peril to the Spanish population." And yet they were needed. So, rather than deport these Chinese people, they were confined to a barrio such as the conquistadores had set up for their native servants in the Americas. It became a colonial Chinatown.

The *Parián* was the name the Spaniards gave to this barrio: a place for the pariahs, the outcasts, and the caste of untouchables. In the beginning there were four houses, set aside down by the harbor for Chinese traders and seamen, that were fenced off from the city with fish nets—"nets so closely knit no one could escape through them," as a Chinese merchant described them in the history *Tung hsi yang K'ao*. And behind the wall of fish nets the Chinese lived, much like exotic fish.

In a few years, when the *Parián* grew, the Spaniards surrounded it with a high stockade. The residents were permitted to leave only to go to work and had to return by nightfall. Every man had to have a residence license, costing sixty-four reales, and a house license, which cost another five reales, a system that was later employed by the State of California, beginning with the Foreign Miner's Tax of 1850.

In the Philippines, as later in California, the system led to bureaucratic bribery that was self-defeating. Even the king of Spain complained that "because of greed" on the part of officials for tax money, the Chinese population was "allowed to increase."

Nonetheless, the licensing of people was an ingenious way of controlling them, and it has been effectively used by governments into this century. It assured that the Chinese, no matter how long they might be residents, would be treated as permanent immigrants. They were denied any legal status. They were vulnerable to deportation at any time if they lost their licenses. They were forever doomed to be sojourners and pariahs.

The need for a license to live became a restriction upon life that was to shape the nature of Chinatowns. In California the licensing of Chinese residents was required by a law passed in 1891, modeled on those of the old Spanish Empire. But this law was ruled unconstitutional. The Congress then passed the Geary Act of 1892, an immigration act that made licenses for Chinese residents a federal statute. Resistance to these licenses— called certificates of residence—was so strong that merely 13,242 of the 106,668 Chinese people known to be in the country registered. Still, the Immigration Act of 1892 established a system of registering resident aliens in this country that still persists and is as stringently enforced as it was in the days of the Spanish Empire.

Curious, too, are the similarities between the political regulations that the Spaniards instituted for the governing of Chinatowns and those that later developed in California. The Spaniards appointed an *alcalde*—mayor—from among leaders of Chinatown. And though the unelected mayor was called on to represent his community, he had no authority to govern the city as a whole nor to govern the non-Chinese in Chinatown. That, too, was to become a ceremonial custom in the Chinatowns of this country.

One drama of life that was characteristic of the old Chinatown in the Spanish Empire did not, however, develop in America. That was the revolt of the Chinese people against their subjugation and ghettoization. Beginning in the early 1600s, the population of the *Parián* in Manila launched repeated rebellions against the Spaniards. And several times they tore down the high stockade that surrounded Chinatown and burned large sections of the city. By 1769, Governor Anda bitterly complained that since the founding of the colony there had been fourteen insurrections by the Chinese, many of them armed revolutions. That came to a rebellion almost every fifteen years.

In America, there was no possibility of armed revolt. Even if they had wished to, the people who had journeyed to the Golden Mountain could not have done as their brothers did in the Philippines. They were soon not merely outnumbered but overwhelmed by the influx of white men. And they were too distant from their homeland to hope for any support from the coastal pirates and secret societies of patriots from China who often aided the rebels in Manila to escape to the mainland.

So the Chinatowns of the country turned inward, not outward. They did not burn the cities, but rather their cities were burned. And facing the pressure of mob violence and oppressive laws, the people withdrew more and more behind the invisible walls that the white society erected around their Chinatowns.

Those who dared to go beyond the walls risked abuse and beatings. In the late nineteenth and the early twentieth centuries, few people ventured out of the Chinatowns unless it was absolutely necessary for them to do so. And the society that had forced the people into the ghettos began to complain, "The Chinese keep to themselves."

One old man, Gim Chaung, remembered how he feared walking on the streets of downtown San Francisco: "Chinese were often attacked by thugs," he said. "All of us had to have a police whistle with us all the time. I was attacked there once on Sunday night. A big thug about six feet tall knocked me down. I remember I didn't know what to do to defend myself because usually the police didn't notice when we blew the whistle. But once we were inside Chinatown, the thugs didn't bother us."

And so Chinatown became not only a ghetto but a refuge. It was not secretive so much as it was self-protective; on its streets and in its houses, the people were safer than they were in the hostile city beyond. It was a familial compound of an entire urban community, protected by a paradox not of its own creation, but created by the city outside its gates. The fantasies and mysteries the white citizens attributed to Chinatown made them fear it. Few white men would go into Chinatown, except in mobs and large groups. And the very images of it that they created became another invisible wall that not only kept the Chinese people in but kept the whites out.

Ever since, the people have been confined to Chinatown. And they were barred by popular violence and local laws from earning a living in the city beyond except as servants. They were no longer able to work in those industries they had helped establish in the West: the mining and railroading, fishing and manufacturing trades that they had largely pioneered.

Of necessity they began to develop the "Chinese" trades that until then hadn't been thought of as exclusively or especially "Celestial." They became gardeners, laundrymen, cooks, restaurant owners, and "house boys"—servants to the white citizens. They had not much choice. Even that stalwart defender and admirer of the Chinese people the western historian H. H. Bancroft wrote with patronizing benevolence: "It is not true that the Chinese are filthy in their habits, inefficient in their work, or untrustworthy. As cooks, domestic servants, launderers, and for orchard and vegetable garden work, they have no superior. . . . The American and European are best for high grade work," said Bancroft; "the Chinaman is best for low grade labor."

In the old days when the people worked as miners in the mountains and ranch hands in the valleys the idea of the "insolent Chinaman" becoming a servant would have seemed absurd. The San Francisco newspaper *Alta California* expressed this view when it warned that the Chinese were "more clannish, therefore more dangerous than the negro, more cunning and deceitful," and so they were *"less fitted to become menials and servants."* But that was in 1853, before the Chinese had learned the melancholy of the Chinatown blues.

One of the mining camp stories of how these Chinese miners became laundrymen reflected the belief that the men from China were too proud and clever ever to be servants. The old tale was retold almost as a parable in *The Chinese in the Black Hills*, by Mildred Fiedler. "One wonders at the predominance of the laundrymen in those first early Chinese young men in town," she mused and then explained, ". . . it was said that the Chinese laundrymen collected gold dust washed from the miners' clothing and sometimes made more money that way than if they had washed the gold dust directly from the streams." It was an often told tale, so often that it became a folktale. And whether it was true or not, it did voice the incongruity the white miners sensed at the thought that the dignified men from China would willingly wash anyone's dirty clothes.

In 1903, Liang Ch'i ch'ao, the distinguished writer and leader of the Progressive Party of China, visited America and was somewhat bemused by the numbers of men he found working in laundries. Of the 79,000 people he listed by occupation in his book *Hsin ta-lu yu-chi chien-lu (Excerpts from a Travel Journal of the New Continent)*, about half—40,000—were laundrymen. And barely 1½ percent of the employed were even marginal professionals; it must have seemed very strange to Liang, coming from the intellectual circles of the court in Peking.

There was an old saying: *There were no "Chinese" laundries in China. There were only laundries for the Chinese.*

Be that as it may, there was not much gold to be found in washing clothes. It meant day-long and night labor for the rest of one's life. The lament of the poor laundrymen was to be heard in an old miner's ballad:

> So I set up a washing shop
> But how extremely funny,
> The miners all had dirty clothes,
> But not a cent of money.

If they wished to stay in the country, as many did, the people had to accept these new jobs as "menials and servants," there was no other way for them to live. Even when they dreamt of returning to China in their old age, as many did, America remained for them the country of their youthful dreams; it had become their country, as much as that of any other settlers of the West.

And as they were demeaned and debased by the land where their families had lived for generations, they turned their eyes not only inward to themselves, but backward to history. The buildings of Chinatown began to resemble their nostalgia. Year by year the facades grew more ornate with replicas of their past. Since they were denied real participation in the life of the West they helped shape, they reshaped the surroundings of their poor ghetto with exaggerated images of their memory. In those years it became easier to gather money and support for reforms in China than in America, as Dr. Sun Yat-sen, the "father of the

Chinese Republic," was to learn when he visited San Francisco in 1910.

When the white residents, whose envy and anger had confined the people to Chinatown, began to realize that they were no longer challenged for the power and wealth of the West, their images of Chinatown began to change. They had been triumphant over these once feared "hordes of coolies." And they had reduced the once proud people to the social servility of "menials and servants." In the same years, the white men proclaimed their defeat of the Indian nations. So the West was theirs.

In light of this, Chinatown was no longer seen as a threat. Rather than a reservoir of potential evil, it became a source of celebration. It was no longer merely a refuge and a ghetto, but an entertainment.

The facade of Chinatown began to change to fit its new image. It was adorned with a public opulence of design that was as ostentatious as it was exotic—more so, perhaps, to its residents than to its visitors. And yet not even this could quite hide the sorrows that generations of "menials and servants" had been reduced to. In the dark alleys behind the pomp of the newly ancient papier-mâché dragons, the people had fallen into the deepest poverty; it was an irony that embittered every Chinese town that had been transformed into a Chinatown.

Beyond the noises of the streets which went off like firecrackers, there was another Chinatown. It was as though there was a city within the city, a town within the town. One seemed muted by the other.

Of all the Chinatowns in the West, the most enduring was San Francisco's. But, in the beginning, it too was not a Chinatown at all. Its settlers were not restricted to a ghetto. They lived wherever they built houses, in different sections of the city, much as they wished. Since the excellence of the early

Chinese carpenters and architects was highly valued, they were in great demand for the construction of homes throughout the city and they built in such numbers that in some ways San Francisco might have been called, in large part, a "Chinese town." Bancroft, the historian, called it just that. The "Chinese houses" were so popular that prefabricated models were imported from China.

These early settlers had naturally settled in the very heart of the city. On the slope of Nob Hill, facing the bay, where the gentlest sea breezes cleansed the streets, they built their houses and shops in what was and is a choice location. As founding fathers, the Chinese emigrants had that choice.

So they settled around the gracious old Spanish plaza, where the Mexican Customs House once stood and where the first American flag had been raised. In that historic heart of the city was the heart of the Chinese town. And even now the trees of Portsmouth Square are the center of the modern Chinatown that has grown up around them.

Of these early Chinese settlers a contemporary observer enviously said: "The advance guard of the Mongolian army saw that the location was good and they advanced upon and captured it." They did so, he said, because the whites "instinctively" fled from their presence "with the same feeling of horror that the fair and innocent maiden would exhibit in shrinking from the proffered embrace of an unclean leper." The memory of history was somewhat different. If the Chinese settlers had settled in the heart of the city, it may have been because that was where they built their Chinese town; for they had come there first.

Though history may be changed, like energy it cannot be destroyed. And inside every Chinatown there still exists the Chinese town it once was.

XV

THE INSCRUTABLE TOURISTS

Our Father Which Art in Hollywood, Charlie Chan be Thy Name.
Amen. Everybody took to Charlie Chan, but saw him as the
real image of Chinaman, anyway.
—"Confessions of a Number One Son,"
by FRANK CHIN, *Ramparts* magazine

The gladiators will now
perform for you the Roman
battle to the death
If they stab each other
please dodge out of the way.

But your suit will be
laundered free
of blood stains.
—"Tourists in Paradise," by DAVID RAFAEL WANG

IN THE MORNING the old men come out of the dim doorways
of their tenements. They dignify the halting walk of their aged
legs by their solemnity, pushing their canes before them, with
skeptical eyes surveying the streets, as if to see that everything
is as it should be after the night of fireworks celebrating the
New Year—the Year of the Serpent.

Some of the old men know each other and nod to each other.
They talk in inaudible voices.

Yesterday they sat silently at festive dinners with their families.
The evening was long and tiring, with their children and grand-
children talking all at once in too loud English of baseball teams

and television shows. It made them feel proud and lonely. Somehow the traditional feast of New Year's was no longer the same; nothing was the same anymore.

Now, in the streets among their cronies, the old men seem to be more at peace. The morning fog has darkened the streets, but there is something orderly and familiar about this. On this day the illusion it gives of not being in America seems fitting and proper. So does the darkness.

In the fourth or fifth century, a poet of the Sung dynasty wrote that before the dawn of the New Year, it is good for there to be darkness. He wrote:

> Now, kill the crowing cock!
> Shoot the voice of dawn.
> Then there may be unending
> Darkness 'til New Year dawn.

The flower venders of yesterday are gone. Where they stood selling branches of plum blossoms and pots of red azaleas wrapped in red aluminum foil set out on the hoods of the parked cars along the gutters, there is no sign of any flowers, not even the fallen petals of plum blossoms. Instead, the gutters and sidewalks are covered with shreds of red paper, the remnants of the firecrackers that the little boys set off all night. The pieces of shredded paper blow in the morning winds like newly fallen red snow. Snows of the New Year. Snows of the Year of the Serpent. Snows of the Spring Festival. Snows of Chinatowns. The blood-red paper snows.

A small boy has set off a fresh string of firecrackers. Running into a doorway, he hides. The fireworks go off in a puff of smoke that becomes part of the fog that is coming in from San Francisco Bay.

Now the streets are silent. After the celebration of the New Year the silence is peculiarly pervasive.

The silence is gray as the fog. It does not descend on the city as fog is supposed to do in romantic novels, but falls with a sudden and myopic darkness on everything in sight; a fog is like a storm without wind, like a silent rain. And yet this, too, offers the old men an anonymity that is oddly comforting.

Now the morning wind has become as cold as night. It is wet on the skin and the sidewalk, the dampness clinging like moist clothing. In the early morning there is always a feeling of loneliness in leaving a warm, sweet-smelling apartment to go into the streets of the ghetto. But these old men have wrapped themselves in the fog like a familiar and worn old coat. They have learned to make adversity their friend. They are poor men.

In the fog the pungent and human odors of the nights will not rise. They creep along the street, hiding in the hallways and loitering in the alleyways. They have the smell of poverty. Even the morning cups of tea taste of the ghetto air. Nothing can escape the ghetto when there is no sky.

Now the ordinary people have returned to their ordinary lives. Once again the paper dragons of the New Year have been packed away until next year, and the real dragons of Chinatown have reemerged: the hidden poverty of people who live behind the grinning Buddhas in the gift shops and inhabit rooms that are seven times as overcrowded as the average for San Francisco, these people who are far poorer than the average ghetto resident of the city.

Will the Year of the Serpent be better than last year for them? Or worse? Probably both.

On the sidewalks the sound of children dragging their feet to school is heard. Some come running. In their echoes walk the older men and women, the garment workers and building janitors, carrying their lunches in paper bags. They seem tired even before they have become tired. And then come the office secretaries and shop clerks, late as always. Mostly young men and women, they are dressed in the chic fashions, looking like manikins in the store windows downtown.

The day has begun as it does in every ghetto—reluctantly.

Now it is eight o'clock. On the corner of Grant Avenue and Broadway, the first tourists have appeared. The old men smell them.

Coming from a topless nightclub are three men, a bit disheveled, squinting into the dim morning, unsure whether it is their eyes or the fog. From the opposite direction comes a bevy of excitedly chattering schoolteachers in prim freshly pressed dresses, squinting at the unsteady men and skirting them with expressions of disapproval as they go off in search of quieter adventure. In their own ways, both groups have come for the same reasons and, seeking to enliven their lives, will satisfy their expectations of Chinatown by the fantasy they bring with them. They barely notice the old men.

The old men frown imperceptibly at the tourists and disappear into the side streets. In their rooms, on single-burner stoves, they sit and heat water for a cup of tea and laugh to themselves.

So the day begins not once but twice in the ghetto of Chinatown. The tourists will soon crowd the streets. Before this day is over tens of thousands of these visitors will have come once again, perhaps outnumbering the residents, and in the end, though they will see mostly other tourists exactly like themselves, their imaginations will fulfill their fantasies. They have come, after all, to see an imaginary Chinatown. They have not come all the way from Des Moines to see a ghetto.

In the moment when the tourists first appear on the streets, everything and everyone changes its facade and face. The faces become masks. The facades become artifacts. The people become clothed in legends and myths that are as ancient as the European vision of a Cathay that never existed but for the dreams of Marco Polo and all those who have come after him on the guided tours of the contemporary pilgrims.

Even the grocery store on Grant Avenue, selling lettuce and cabbages, becomes a den of exotic vegetables. The buying of a bamboo back scratcher from Hong Kong or a soggy, oversteamed dish of sweet and sour pork becomes an esoteric experience. The mundane becomes transformed into the mysterious. In the fantastic atmosphere an aura of alluring evil, sensual and exciting, descends on the poor ghetto more opaquely than the fog.

They come day after day, seeking a world that does not exist and remaking the world that does. The fascination of the imaginary place that is the Chinatown of the tourists seems to grow in direct proportion to its unreality.

No matter. If the seekers after the exotic discover merely the prosaic, the images imbedded in their imaginations will supply what their eyes do not see. The fantasies of centuries crowd their memories with mysteries that are no less intriguing because no one has ever seen them; if anything, this makes them all the more alluring.

The seekers have come in search of more than excitement. It is the delicious titillation of vicarious evil, an "oriental mystique," that attracts them. Since the days of the earliest missionaries from New England who set forth to convert, in that wonderful phrase, these "Celestial heathen," the people of China have been portrayed, in the words of one exultant missionary, as "O Satan! True children of the Demon!" Not merely the unknown and the mysterious that is obvious in a culture that is strange to them, but the allure of evil that their own morality did not permit them to enjoy without damnation was always fascinating to the Puritans.

"Old Chinatown always had diverted San Francisco," Charles Dobie wrote half a century ago in his *San Francisco Chinatown*. "But it was its sinister aspects, its delinquent phases, which allured . . . Chinatown was a thing of bagnios; gun-men; underground windings; dark and desperate opium dens; filth; bubonic plague; leprosy. It was diverting." Dobie went on: "Although they would emphatically deny it they want the old days back, with the streets of Chinatown filled with lecherous gun-men, the *cul de sac* crowded with painted slave girls. . . ."

Sardonically Dobie commented: "There is no denying that a people's sins are much more thrilling than a people's virtues." That was especially so if the "sins" did not exist; for, as Dobie said, his own "quest" for these evils "always ended in futility" and he never met any "lecherous gun-men."

Remembering those early years of the thrill-seeking tourists, an old-time resident of Chinatown could recall few dens of erotic intrigue: "When I was a boy, you know, I used to follow the older boys everywhere and I knew all the dirty, secret places. When white people used to come to Chinatown looking for curiosities, I used to tag along behind the Chinese they took as guides. But I never saw an underground tunnel," sighed the old man. "Just mah-jongg rooms in basements."

Nonetheless, "Worthy citizens who would have been profoundly shocked at viewing depravity of their own kind," as Dobie said, "made tours of lascivious inspection, over and over again." In *The Europeans* had not Henry James remarked: ". . . nothing exceeds the license occasionally taken by the imagination of very rigid people."

The promise of evil that thrilled the puritan tourists had many faces. But whether it wore the mask of Chinese superstition, violence, infanticide, or paganism, all of which were attributed to the "Celestial heathens," beneath these masks "lurked," as was said, what was believed to be the pervasive and peculiarly Oriental obsession with erotic "licentiousness." And this may have been what attracted the imaginations of the voyeurs on their "lascivious tours of inspection," even more than the "barbaric" traits that repelled them.

It was the "perfect sensuous sensualism" of the Chinese that frightened the publicist of the West, Samuel Bowles. Not that their sophisticated eroticism was "coarsely filthy like [that of the] ignorant and besotted Irish," he wrote in *Our New West*, in 1870; it was worse, for Chinese sensuality was reflected in a "refined uncleanliness" and was therefore so much more devious and temptingly seductive. Even the hedonistic editor of the New York *Tribune*, Horace Greeley, who was given to evocations of frontier masculinity, seemed threatened by what he perceived as the "un-Christian" sensuality of Chinese men. "John Chinaman is thoroughly sensual," Greeley warned, and is "intent on the fullest gratification of his carnal appetite and nothing else."

So sensual were the Chinese said to be that "licentiousness, which taints [their] language with its leprosy, often decorates the walls of their inns with the foulest scenes called by them 'flowers' and lurks beneath the thin Chinese lacker [sic] as a deep dry rot in society," intoned the Protestant churches' American Board of Commissioners for Foreign Missions in 1878. These accusations of "sexual perversity and promiscuity" rested "firmly on the shoulders of the Protestant missionary," noted the historian Stuart Creighton Miller; for all their pretentions of ancient culture the Chinese were "disgustingly obscene."

Fascination with and fear of the "perfect sensuous sensualism" of the Chinese was spread throughout America by popular Bible tracts. The evils of sexual enjoyment became synonymous with the imagined eroticism of the "Celestial heathen," who, it was said, delighted in the erotic and decadent torturing of women in their hidden dens of Chinatown. Somehow eroticism and sadism became one in the popular imagination. On the West Coast it came to be commonly believed, as Oscar Handlin wrote in *The Americans,* that the "Orientals beguiled little girls to their launderies to commit crimes *too horrible to imagine.*"

There was little or no evidence in police files that such crimes were ever committed. So they were shrouded in mystery. An aura of a forbidden and illicit eroticism surrounded them. They were not manly and brutish acts of violence in the straightforward frontier tradition. They were cunning and secretive acts that the white man's imagination thought fitted the devious character of the men from China.

And the voyeurs were enthralled by their own fantasies, more so than if they had actually seen them with their own eyes. The imagined acts grew into images of orgies.

Newspapers and dime novels of the nineteenth century celebrated the Victorian images with ever more sensational and explicit stories. And yet those Victorians who projected and perpetuated these fantasies, in their own perversity, then performed a peculiar act: They reversed these sexual images that they had created.

Men of China, from the beginning, often had been portrayed as women. They had ladylike hands, they were small as young girls, and they indulged in feminine customs such as bathing and perfuming their bodies. On that rugged frontier, where these "little men" performed muscular feats of masculine strength in the mines and on the railroads, such feminine behavior was an intriguing anomaly that fascinated and frightened the frontiersmen of the West and the ideologues of the East. More and more they compared these Chinese men to women: "Were they not "quarrelsome" and "timid," "covetous" and "deceitful," "cunning" and "distrustful"? said the *Encyclopedia Britannica*. After all, they were no more than "beardless children," declared the *Anthropological Review* in 1868.

Railroad men from China handled "their tools like so many women," wrote J. D. Borthwick in *Three Years in California*. The "effeminate celestials" had "feminine hands," he explained. Even so, he "marveled at the strength of these little men," who, in spite of their ladylike physiques, had dug the tunnels and had laid the railroad tracks through the blizzards of the High Sierras and across the deserts by hand.

One chronicler of the California Gold Rush so completely reversed the images that he described the white frontiersman as a "fair and innocent maiden" whose moral virginity was threatened by the "embrace of an unclean leper." The Chinese were seducing the white maiden-men in their opium dens and their "hotbeds" of vice.

In England, at the time, the romantic essayist Charles Lamb pleasurably wrote that to him there was something feminine about China. He delighted in what he called the "feminine partiality" of Chinese customs. But this very trait had infuriated Samuel Johnson, who raged against the "eunuch" culture that he said surely would emasculate English manhood. On the male frontiers of the West, in that society of men, there appeared a similar ambivalence. And it bestowed an evil potency on the unsuspecting men of China, who accepted the paradoxes of life as naturally as they did the idea of yin and yang.

To the minds of the Yankees the paradoxes of yin and yang were doubly suspect. Either a person was virtuous or evil; to delve into those shadowy realms where human behavior was complex and mysterious, and good and evil coexisted, was too frightening to contemplate or accept. It had to be expurgated, as did the malignant culture of the Chinese "yellow devils."

And yet the forbidden was tempting. It seemed to be so plea-surable. Everything in the life of the "Celestial heathen," even their way of dress, suggested luxury and extravagance to the puritanical eyes of the Yankees; it reflected what one New En-gland observer termed a "delicious decadence" that any sensible Christian would seek to shun if he could. The immoralists' "wan-ton lewdness and public sexual orgies" had to be cleansed from the consciousness not only for their sake, but for that of the moralists.

As long ago as 1586, the conquistador Don Pedro de Rojas, in a memorial to King Philip II of Spain, righteously condemned the "effeminate" finery of the "Chinese eunuchs" that rendered men unfit for war and glory, and fit only for pleasure. "Effemi-nacy, vices, luxuries, fine clothes, wining and dining" of the Chinese was weakening the will of the empire, he said. In 1600, a Parisian play, *L'Île des Hermaphrodites*, proclaimed that these "fashions of China" were sweeping Europe. So they were. And England's Lord Shaftesbury enthused; "Effeminacy pleases me . . . the luscious colors and glossy paint [of Chinese fashions] gain my fancy." But he was rebuked by Daniel Defoe, who lamented these "effeminate fashions," which would bring about the downfall of the English male; while Samuel Pepys wondered if Parliament ought not to "forbid the wearing of silks" from China.

In America, the austere colonials and frontiersmen, whose way of life was frugal both of necessity and by philosophy, con-demned the luxuries of the Chinese as devilish, the temptations of Satan. The Chinese, under a veneer of "a very highly polished civilization [, were] morally a most wretched people," wrote the editor of the *Methodist Quarterly Review*. "Sin has spread its deadly venom throughout the whole body politic."

Mere closeness to a Chinese man might "poison" the soul,

as much as the embrace of a Chinese woman would "poison" the blood of a white man who loved her. So, too, the feast of a Chinese dinner, now savored, was believed to dilapidate the bodies of Westerners, and the "slow poisoning teas" of the Chinese were thought to dilute the manhood of white men.

The romantic fantasies were becoming bitter and terrifying. In the changing images of evil the older cultural fascinations had given way to irrational racial fears that were so ugly they no longer were at all tantalizing. For many decades at the end of the nineteenth and the beginning of the twentieth centuries the popular press depicted Chinatown as a place of bloody Tong wars, evil diseases, and sadistic crimes beyond belief.

So feared were the Chinese that the U.S. Commissioner of Immigration, testifying before a congressional committee in 1914, upheld the total banning of immigrants by declaring: "Asiatic immigration is a menace to the whole country, and particularly the West Coast. The danger is general. No part of the United States is immune." He was applauded. President Woodrow Wilson coldly echoed his fear of "Oriental coolieism." Expressing this popular view more crudely, Professor Robert DeC. Ward of Harvard University vulgarly declared: "We cannot make a well-bred dog out of a mongrel by teaching him tricks."

"Going to Chinatown" did not once more become a tourist amusement until after World War I. The end of the war brought a psychic sigh of relief to the country; it was the beginning of an era of frivolity and extravagance to the war-wealthy middle classes of America, a jazz age. One of its fads was to go "slumming" in Harlem and the black ghettos, a spectator sport that soon included Chinatown on its itinerary. And the coming of Prohibition enlivened these illicit excursions, for illegal liquor was to be found in the formerly forbidden dens of Chinese restaurateurs.

Still, the pilgrimages of the new tourists brought with them many of the old fantasies. They were merely modernized without dimming the aura of evils that may have seemed much less forbidding after the ghoulish World War. And though the fantasies of the past that clung to Chinatown retained their fear, they lost any resemblance to reality.

The narrow and dark alleys were no narrower and darker than those of other ghettos, nor were the tenements any more somber. But those of the other ghettos were not peopled with the fantasies, ogres, and demons who inhabited the poor streets of Chinatown in the imaginations of the tourists.

Even the physical bodies of the people were reshaped by the memory of the old fears. The mere fold of an eyelid became a sign of sinister mystery and cunning, concealing more than it revealed; the "slanty eyes" of Chinese merchants, schoolteachers, garment workers, and marine corps sergeants became symbols of their devious, inscrutable, secretive, and evil minds. Not that these "slanty eyes," especially in women, did not seem sultry and seductive to the tourists, but that made their allure all the more potentially evil.

Roman historian Marcellinus had bitterly complained of the deviousness of the eyes of the Chinese. He accused the traders on the ancient Silk Road of talking to each other "by their eyes alone." One thousand years later, Marco Polo was made uneasy by the "clever eyes" of the merchants he met; honest traders talked with their hands, not their eyes, in Italy. And not quite one thousand years after that, the French scholar Alain Payrefitte, in his recent study *The Chinese*, seemed no less leery of these eyes that were as mysterious to him as to those who came before him. In China, he wrote, "secrets and confidences seemed to pass from eye to eye," leaving outsiders in a darkness.

Curiously, these people whose every bodily characteristic was to become a symbol of their distinctiveness, became invisible.

The tourists, who scrutinized them so closely, did not see them at all.

On the streets the tourists and the people may have seemed to be walking side by side. But they were not. It was a strange phenomenon that a tourist once described by saying that to her the people of Chinatown were "just like papier-mâché dolls." They were not "people." In a documentary on Chinatown broadcast on educational television, it was explained that "For the tourist, they [the people] are anonymous." And that was merely another way of saying that they were not people, they were myths.

The "strangeness" of these people may have consisted of this. From the early days of the Gold Rush, there was the wondrous musing of a Yankee settler who said the Chinese "give a strange appearance to the city" though they are "laborious, quiet, and inoffensive." It was not what they were or who they were that made them "strange," but simply that they were Chinese.

"If the Chinese were white people," Senator Meade had perceptively told the U.S. Senate in the late nineteenth century, "being in all other respects what they are, I do not believe that the complaints and warfare made against them would have existed to any extent. The difference in their color, dress, manners, and religion have, in my judgment, more to do with this hostility than their alleged vices or any actual injury to the white people of California."

So, in the end, the evils attributed to the Chinese, once so seductive and mysterious, became no more attractive than any other racial myths. The dens of shadowy mystery and sensual intrigue became the Chinese laundries, contemptuously demeaned and a popular joke to whites—and sweatshops where people worked day and night for those who "owned" them. The Chinaman was becoming a Chinese man. He lost his power of evil over the tourists, even though they still sought out China-town. In his own way, he was beginning to shed the image that had been placed upon his head by history. And he was becoming, if not himself, at least no longer the Chinaman who, like Chinatown, had been created by white men for their pleasure and amusement.

And Chinatown itself seemed to be becoming "as American as chow mein," as a disenchanted reporter for the New York *Post* wrote one year. Its deepest mystery, to him, was the content of its egg rolls. The novelist Herbert Roth proclaimed in *The New York Times* that to most contemporary tourists Chinatown was "first of all, good cheap food. 'Let's eat Chink tonight.' " Charles Dobie had prophesied this denouement of the exotic fantasies years ago. "To enter the New Chinatown with your heart enthralled by the past is fatal," he had written. "You will find nothing that will beguile you. It will be empty."

He was wrong.

Though the image of the "Chinaman" has changed through the years, the image of Chinatown has retained its unreality. Some of the language used to describe it has been modified, in keeping with the objective and sterile language of the social sciences. But this is an artifice; it is not the language the tourists speak, or think in, or with which they create the worlds of their fantasies.

On Kearny Street, in the Chinatown of San Francisco, there is a gas station in the shape of a Buddhist temple. Its sacred architecture pays homage to nothing more than the distilled spirits of Standard Oil, but its pagoda form casts a solemn shadow upon these prosaic gases. The style of the gas station is a sort of Chinatown baroque that never existed in China, combining the refinements of the Sung dynasty and the opulence of the

Ch'ing dynasty with the garish mosaics of the chop suey Americanisms of Hollywood.

"Oh, the tourists dig it," said a young Chinese gas jockey with a shrug. "They think it's exotic. They expect a dragon in their tank."

Not far away, about one block up Kearny Street, is a newer and even more impressive tourist shrine. It rises far above Chinatown, like a great Han dynasty fortress built of vast blocks of cement, gray and awesome as the Chinese Wall, a massive structure that is entered over a brooding bridge adorned with plaques inscribed with ancient wisdom and by a flight of stone steps that lead to sliding glass doors which are opened by electric eyes.

This is, of course, the new Holiday Inn of Chinatown.

In the evenings, when the fog has returned to the Bay, the tourists come from such elegantly pseudo-Chinoiserie motels on their nightly tours of Chinatown. As they imagine it to be, so does it once more become for them.

Magically, at night, the ghetto recedes into the darkness. The Chinatown of fantasy reemerges in the lights that illuminate the gift shops and restaurants along Grant Avenue and Mott Street and the main thoroughfares of Chinatowns everywhere.

One guided tour of the Chinatown of San Francisco offers three and a half hours of "Adventure Conducted by Experienced Native Guides." Nightly for people "who want to see the *real* Chinatown" there are enticing excursions into the "Narrow Back Alleys." In these ancient dens of remembered evils and ever present mystery there are promised trips to exotic "fortune cookie factories," a "Buddhist temple," a "Kung Fu studio" and such secretive and enigmatic places as a "Chinese theater," an "herb shop," and a "jewelry store."

Most of the tours begin at 7:30 P.M., and most often they end by visiting the Chinese Wax Museum. There "all the splendor of ancient China is revealed" to the pilgrims.

In the Chinese Wax Museum there is indeed a pale wax figure of an elderly man, wearing a silk gown of rich brocade and gold thread, who is identified by a small sign that says: "There really was a Confucius." And there the master stands in wax, leering at the lovely effigy of a waxen queen.

"My, how gorgeous!" gasps a tourist. But her reverie is interrupted by a dark corridor lined with tableaus of wax figures in glass cages who depict the evils of Chinatown. The light is dim and ominous.

Once more, the tourist gasps.

On one wall there is a forbidding opium den, the waxen men dissipated in a grim and dingy room. There is a gambling hall. Some concubines. And the scene at a traditional wedding ceremony of a girl with bound feet. Nearby is a melodramatic panorama of a "Tong War." At the end of the dungeonlike corridor the executioner of a forgotten emperor is seen chopping off someone's head. The red paint flows all over the floor; it drips like blood from the wax hatchet of the wax executioner and the decapitated wax head.

The tourists shudder. The guide tells a joke.

Suddenly the tour has ended. A guide says: "This is the last time I see you. When you go back to the bus I never see you again. Not that I don't like you. But you go back to your suburbs and I go to the Convention of Chinese Chinatown Guides at the Hilton Hotel."

There is laughter. And the tension caused by the frightening wax figures is eased.

"Have you enjoyed the tour?" he asks. There is applause.

"We are happy. You are happy. Aren't these nice people in Chinatown?" There is applause.

Embarrassed by what he has to say and grinning to hide his discomfort, the guide briefly looks into the tourists' eyes. They are silenced. He looks away. "Now, you can go for a walk in Chinatown," he instructs them. "Very little crime. Oh, I don't say there is no crime, but there is less than elsewhere in the city."

"Streets very safe." He smiles. "Good night to you."

XVI

THE VISION OF

A CHINESE AMERICA

Created! Not born! No more born than heaven and earth. No more born than nylon and acrylic. For I am a Chinaman! A miracle synthetic!

—*The Chickencoop Chinaman*, by FRANK CHIN

Let here begin a Brotherhood of man,
Wherein the West shall freely meet the East,
And man greet man as man . . .

—Sonnet by HU SHIH, written
at Cornell University in 1915

ON HIS LONG HAIR the young man wore a cocky little cap of bright blue cloth with a small red star sewn on its center above the brim. He was wearing a cotton suit of the same blue cloth. It was one of the quilted outfits that was popular with cadres in China that year, the sort known as the "Mao suit." The suit and cap were perfectly clean, as though he had just bought them. And the young man seated himself gingerly on the New York subway, taking care not to dirty his proud new uniform.

The *Peking Review* was in his hand. He opened it ostentatiously, so everyone could see it.

No one seemed to notice him. At the Times Square station of the subway where the young man boarded the train he looked like an apparition. But none of the New Yorkers on that droning subway bothered to interrupt their staring at the dirty floor of the train to look up and acknowledge the young man's presence.

If they had, they might have seen that at that moment the world had changed before their downcast eyes.

But they did not see him. He was invisible.

At Chinatown the young man stood up and folded his *Peking Review* neatly, put it into the pocket of his Mao suit and got off the train. On his face there was the smallest sort of smile. He was pleased with himself.

Something remarkable had happened that day in 1972 on the subway from Times Square. If the young man in his Mao suit was not the first American of Chinese ancestry to wear his new identity in public, he was a symbol of the change that was coming.

On the streets, in ghetto gangs, and in the universities at their Asian-American Study seminars, the young people of his generation were beginning to insist that they be recognized. They had begun to demand their constitutional and historical rights as American-born citizens. And they often did so by clothing themselves in the newer symbols of an ancestral land that they had never been to, and whose languages many of them could hardly speak at all. The young man on the subway had, after all, been reading his copy of the *Peking Review* in English.

"Red Guards" who appeared on the streets of San Francisco and New York were almost all born in America. They had been inspired, in the beginning, by the Black Panthers. One of the organizers recalled that "the Black Panthers helped us get organized and gave us political education classes." But the "new militancy" of the "Chinatown militants," as newspapers described the youth, soon became adapted to the ways and needs of their own American communities, even as they clothed themselves in their Chinese heritage. That year, in 1972, when a celebration to honor the Chinese Revolution was held in San Francisco, it met in the Masonic Auditorium on fashionable

Nob Hill. And one of the featured speakers was a computer engineer, William Hu, who worked for IBM. Though the *Saturday Review* headlined its story of the occasion RED STAR OVER SAN FRANCISCO, Hu spoke less of China's successes than America's failures.

"This is the day we stand up," Hu said, "as Chinese *and* as Americans."

Strangely, in the eyes of their parents the behavior of the new generation often appeared "un-Chinese." Even as the young people sought to dress and to act with obvious pride in their newfound sense of "Chineseness," their elders chided them for becoming too vulgarly and blatantly American.

It was not proper to behave in this way. Nor was it wise. To attract attention to oneself was to offer oneself as a target for insult and abuse; it was to invite trouble.

Besides there was an old saying: *Chu chu wa ya yi pan hei*—"A blackbird is a blackbird everywhere."

The wiser and safer ways of behavior were to be as quiet and inconspicuous as possible. For generations the people had "often promoted this image of themselves—with good reason," the magazine of the new generation, the *Bridge*, commented; for they "felt insecure of their acceptance by the majority," and they knew "a minority which raises its voice invites the raised club to quiet it." And so, for them, it seemed "the only game was the quiet game." They worked silently and they talked quietly and they were as inconspicuous and invisible as possible.

On the pioneer frontiers of the hostile West they had learned that invisibility was the better part of valor. The murders and angers that characterized the behavior of white Americans during the anti-Chinese riots that tormented the latter years of the nineteenth century had understandably intimidated the older generations of emigrants. It was safer to withdraw quietly behind the walls of Chinatown.

Emigrants from Kwangtung surely found it hard to assume this disguise of humility and silence. They were the bold, adventurous people who had crossed a vast ocean under the harshest of conditions to become pioneers and explorers in a strange land. More than that, they were by tradition a boisterous and vigorous people who enjoyed living with a buoyant gusto, who talked in expressive and volatile dialects, and who were known for the unique *joi de vivre* peculiar to South China. And their early years in America, in the roaring gold mining camps or as the roughnecks who built the railroads or the farmers and fishermen who pioneered so many of the crops and fishing industries of the West, did not prepare them for servility. They were as boastful as any raucous and exuberant settlers on the frontiers.

"There is a spirit of adventure which is uniquely Chinese-American and which smacks of legend," as Frank Chin has said of these pioneers; they are as "deeply rooted in American folklore as Paul Bunyan and Johnny Appleseed." Though their voices were stilled, the echoes resound still, however muted.

Silence was not natural to them, and humility was unnatural. It was forced upon them. The choice, in any event, was not theirs to make. Even if the people of the ghetto had not decided to become invisible, they would have been. They were forgotten by the country. By the end of the nineteenth century the pioneers of the West who had come from the Far East and who had been so essential in the settlement and growth of the nation had been all but expurgated from the nation's history if not its memory.

In the 1890s when Frederick Jackson Turner envisioned his epochal history *The Significance of the Frontier*, his vision apparently did not enable him to see the presence of the pioneers from China. He made no mention of them. Nor did his distinguished disciple, Ray Allen Billington, who compiled the many-volumed *Histories of the American Frontier* during the 1960s.

By then the lusty pioneers from China had been reduced to shadowy footnotes or esoteric references.

The influence of these Americans from China on their new native land was "obscure," the anthropologist Stephen Powers recently wrote; for "virtually no information was available about them." He thought that at best they left behind a few "new genetic materials" in railroad whorehouses. And to this, the English historian C. P. Fitzgerald emphatically said of the overseas Chinese in general, "They have not deeply influenced the peoples among whom they settled," so their "cultural influence was negligible." Indeed, they had become almost invisible.

In the earlier years of the Gold Rush, the California *Post* had prophesied: "The silence of the grave would be all that would tell of the Chinaman's existence here." They had been only partially wrong.

No wonder that the Chinese Historical Society of America has lamented: "The history of the Chinese in America is buried under a 'shield' of anti-Chinese hostility which persisted even through World War II. A search of the literature of the history of California and the American West from the 1880s until the present time will reveal that the word 'Chinese' is rarely to be found in such indices." This plaint was issued at a conference on "The Life, Influence and Role of the Chinese in the United States: 1776–1960" that was held as an "American Revolution Bicentennial Observance" to proclaim the "enormous stake [of the Chinese] in the building of the United States."

For generations the white Americans had viewed the Chinese Americans as foreigners and strangers. It was easier to accept the pioneers from China as invisible and passive "sojourners" than to acknowledge them as founding fathers of the country some of whose ancestors may have come to America on Spanish galleons of the Manila trade long before the *Mayflower* had set forth from England. That may have been why so many historians have found it preferable to depict the early Chinese settlers as "sojourners" and wanderers, rather than as explorers and frontiersmen. Even after several generations, some were still described as "sojourners," a phrase not used to describe the English, French, Russian, and Australian settlers, so many of whom gathered up their American-made fortunes and promptly returned home. And yet the majority of the emigrants from China, in spite of persecution and discrimination, stayed in America. They became Americans even before they could become citizens.

Some went back to China as soon as they had enough money for a triumphant return. Some fled in fear. But many, from the beginning, had chosen this land as their own. One of the first, if not the very first, proclamations of principle was issued by the Chinese settlers meeting in the Canton Restaurant in San Francisco in 1849 who spoke of America as "our adopted land." In an appeal to their fellow citizens, the Chinese had pleaded for friendship and forbearance with the words: ". . . strangers as we are in a strange land, unacquainted with the language and customs of this, our adopted land. . . ."

Not that these Chinese settlers were less Chinese for becoming Americans than Irish settlers were less Irish. Both were equally American. Both created America out of their very Chineseness and Irishness. And their history, in America, was American history.

"Because our American history and culture aren't well known to whites," as Frank Chin has said, "doesn't mean they are foreign to America." It merely means "that whites are culturally deprived" of their own history, Chin says; they suffer from a "mythological" belief that is "schizophrenic" and untrue.

"The white lie of yellow dual identity" does not exist in reality, Chin believes. Since the life and work of the Chinese in America was the source of so much American history, there was no contradiction in being Chinese and American, or an American Chinese. The paradox arose when that shared heritage was denied to either group of the people. And since to recognize the extent to which the heritage of the American West had been the heritage of the Chinese in the West meant that white Americans might have to recognize the extent to which their identity was Chinese, there was something of a problem. It was the white Americans, not the Chinese, who had the "identity crisis," said Chin.

For Chinese Americans were uniquely American. They did not exist anywhere else in the world.

So, too, the Chinatowns of America were a phenomenon peculiar to this nation and no other. They were not like rural villages or urban communities in China. As the cities that they helped found began to grow around them, these settlements of Chinese Americans changed with them; they could not be immune to the successes and failures of the society that completely surrounded them. It was a myth that the Chinatowns of the American West were mysterious and foreign, as if they existed on the far side of the moon. Most of them were downtown.

When the people had hidden within the walls of the Chinatowns, their history was hidden with them. It was beyond the vision of most observers in the outside world. But it existed. The walls of Chinatown offered both a refuge and an archive that guarded the people and their history from the contempt and humiliation that both suffered in the world outside.

Of the hidden history of the Chinese town of Locke, on the delta of the Sacramento River, Mrs. King, a granddaughter of one of the town's founders, said: "No real history of this town is written down. No book. No scholarly studies. No pamphlet. No, there is nothing like that. But the history of the town is all here. It is in the town itself."

That was true everywhere in the American West. For history, like light, did not vanish because it was not visible; it was merely buried beneath the darkened earth. Like a memory. Like a bone. Like a jade stone that possessed its own inner light, preserved in the luminous darkness.

One by one the old walls of the ghetto that were the womb of the Chinatowns of the West began to open up. And the "Chinaman," resplendent in the imagery of the American dream, reemerged. In the decades of civil rights legislation and the re-awakening recognition of the so-called ethnic people by the rest of the nation, Chinese Americans began to reclaim their American history and proclaim their American heritage.

Not at once, but in their own way and time, the sons and daughters of Wah Q, the overseas Chinese, and of ABC, the American Born Chinese, rediscovered the roots of their ancestors—in America. Some who did not remember the past may have thought of themselves as pioneers. But they were not. They were following in the footsteps of those ancestors who had pioneered, so long ago, in the American West. And it was no easier now than one hundred years ago.

Still, to the young the world is forever new. They boldly challenged not only the old stereotypes of the whites, but the old fears of their parents. The ideas of the older leaders of the Chinatowns were "obsolete," declared Kin Wah Chin of the Asian Americans for Equal Employment.

"Our generation will no longer accept the old and still prevalent Confucian doctrine of success coming only through hard work and humility," said Mason Wong, a student at San Franciso State, who was president of the Intercollegiate Chinese for Social Action. In New York's Chinatown, Lee Chong of the Asian Americans for Equal Employment said, "We have a saying: 'You can call me a Chink, or a Chinaman and get away with it.

But if you step on my toes, I'll hit you back.' And that's what's happening.

"We are not going to be invisible like our fathers and suffer in silence," Lee Chong said.

The resurgence of the new China intensified the rediscovery of their American heritage by the younger Chinese Americans; it exhilarated them. It affected Chinese everywhere, no matter how distant they were in time and culture from their ancestral homeland. Nor did it matter whether they welcomed or opposed the political changes taking place in China. The non-Chinese around them no longer looked at them in the same belittling way. And so they could no longer see themselves in the same way; the image that others had of them had changed, and so the image they had of themselves changed too.

Sardonically, one young writer with the unlikely name of Maryland Wong Lincoln wrote of this metamorphosis in her self-portrait entitled: "I'm Very Sorry, But I Don't Know Charlie Chan." Her journey of American self-discovery was like so many—universal and personal, humorous and poignant.

"As a child growing up I was usually the only kid of Chinese origin in the neighborhood," she said. "Indeed, in the whole school."

She remembered that people looked at her and knew at once that she was a Vietnamese war orphan. Or a Japanese war bride. Or a Korean exchange student. Or, at the very least, a tourist from Hawaii. "I was never mistaken for an American," she said. They knew she was foreign. When people asked her where she had been born she "disappointed hundreds by telling them the truth," she said. "I was born in Portland, Maine." She was a Chinese Yankee.

In elevators strange men whom she did not know always smiled at her and asked: "How do you like this country?" And the director of a play she was acting in sought to compliment her by congratulating her on how "Americanized" she seemed to him to be.

Children, little children, knew better. They would look up at her face in wonder and whisper expectantly: "Do you know Charlie Chan?"

Then, the crowning blow to her ego descended upon her after the President, Richard Nixon, visited China. "Suddenly all America was learning to cook with a wok," as she remembered it. Zen, once an esoteric religion in Greenwich Village, became a learning experience taught in Young Men's Christian Associations. So did yoga, while Kung Fu, on television, and Tai Chi, in the suburbs, became popular entertainments.

Women's clubs asked her for her recipes for sweet and sour pork and egg rolls, neither of which she had ever cooked. So, to "save face," she learned to cook sweet and sour pork and egg rolls. One of her recipes won a Boston newspaper award and she wrote an article for a national women's magazine—on her Chinese cookery.

And yet she felt, "I lack authenticity." She could not "speak the language." When non-Chinese who were studying Chinese talked to her she had to answer in English. It was embarrassing. So she enrolled in "Chinese language classes," and began to save her money to go "over there," as she said.

That was the American Way. "As I grow older, I hate to disappoint anyone," she said, "and like most Americans, I feel I must keep up the image."

She voiced, as did so many of her contemporaries, a vibrant and distinctive sort of Americanism. It was an expression of the Chinese-American experience that had found a force and style of its own. But to the older generation it was strange and threatening.

The old conflict between generations, between fathers and sons, between mothers and daughters, was as painful as ever. And yet something quite different from the clash of cultures that traditionally scared the families of emigrants was taking place. By proclaiming their American heritage, the Chinese-American youth were not denying their father's heritage but were reaffirming it. For they were "part of a culture discovering itself," as the poet David Oyama had said. It was a vision "rich in life, rich in culture and talent, rich in opportunities to create life that is both unique and universal, American, and yet itself."

In sublime irony and exultation Frank Chin celebrated the re-creation, or perhaps self-creation, of that very old and very new American, the rebirth of the "Chinaman" as an American. Chin wrote of this transformation: "Created! Not born! No more born than heaven and earth. No more born than nylon and acrylic. For I am a Chinaman! A miracle synthetic! Drip dry and machine washable. For now, in one point in time and space, as never before and never after, in this one instant of eternity was focused that terrific, that awesome power of the universe that marks a divine moment. . . ."

And that moment was the rebirth of the memory and the vision of a Chinese America.

XVII

GOING BACK AND COMING HOME

There were always the basic questions about the land, temperature, and of course, the crops (in America). *Does it rain there?* (in America). *The sun comes up and sets at the same time, doesn't it?* (in America).   —"Going Back," by JEANNE QUAN

The Master had said on the river bank:
"Thus do all things flow away."
    —*On Swimming the Yangtze*, by MAO TSE-TUNG

ON A BOLD VOYAGE in the twentieth century, eleven young adventurers set forth on a journey through the sky above the Pacific Ocean to seek their ancestral homeland, which only one of them had ever seen. They were going to China. Surely a fantasy trip— but the best kind of fantasy. A real one. One of the young adventurers said she felt like Marco Polo in reverse, going to the mythical land of Cathay in the hope of discovering her living "roots" in the earth of her ancestors.

And so they set off, not knowing what they might find. For years their parents and grandparents had told them tales of a wonderful and terrible land of their forebears, a land of sublime civilization and inhuman misery. But these stories seemed as distant as the nostalgia of childhood.

Most likely there was a sign on the border that said YOU ARE NOW ENTERING THE PEOPLE'S REPUBLIC OF CHINA. But if there was, these young sojourners were looking beyond it. The sense of wonder they may have felt was expressed by a student,

Warner Lee, who came later: "In the Occidental imagination, China was always a place of fascination, symbolizing the exotic and the mysterious. How much more so for those of us of Chinese ancestry who have never been to China," he said.

On crossing the border into the memories of his parents, Lee experienced a "cultural shock." It was the "climactic moment" of his life when he crossed the Shumchun Bridge on foot "to enter a world closed to the outside for so long."

In the simmering heat and humidity of a summer day in 1972 when those college students from California finally came to the land of their ancestors, there was something dreamlike in their journey. Somehow it was like awakening from a dream only to discover that one had not been sleeping.

"Full-sailed junks seemed to magically glide over mountains and villages, mirrored in the smooth waters," said Jeanne Quan, a student from the University of California at Berkeley. "It was like an ancient scroll." And the landscape of the new China superimposed upon that of old China, where the "electric lines stretched over rice paddies," did not add to her sense of reality.

Gentle breezes rising from the bamboo groves all day bathed them in pleasant surprise. They had not imagined that southern China was quite so tropical. In the moist air of the bamboo grooves and the mangrove swamps and fields of sugarcane there was a sensual warmth that embraced them. She had not expected "the lush tropical vegetation, humid climate and buffalo boys perched on the backs of water buffalo," said Jeanne Quan in delight. It was so wonderfully strange.

And yet the strangest thing was that it was not strange at all. "On the contrary, I felt something akin to a homing instinct," said Candy Chin.

In the small peasant villages there were bamboo tea stalls and roadside stands laden with tropical fruit of every sort—the luscious and juicy "dragon eyes," lichee nuts and pineapples, sweet oranges and small fat bananas, ripened guavas and succulent little plums. "So refreshing in the humid heat," said one sojourner.

All of their lives they had been told of the wonderful fruits of China. "These peaches are very good," Jeanne Quan's mother would tell her, "but not as sweet as those at home." It was a forgivable nostalgia. The fruits of childhood memory always seem to taste sweeter. But it was true.

Nonetheless these villages were no pastoral paradise. They were poor. The middle-class young people from the shopping-center culture of California had been prepared for this. Said one: "I bid farewell to white sheets, private baths, running water, and flush toilets." Laughed another: "What—no flush toilets? How can man survive?" But they were not prepared for the ease and comforts of village life.

"The village was not as poor as I had imagined," mused Barbara Jung. No running water, outdoor toilets, houses of mud and floors of dirt, with pigs and chickens everywhere—"all of this was as expected," she said. "However, I did not expect the homes to be so large, nor so well cared for." Nor that so many things could be "made by hand."

Rural life, the way of life for most of China, was what seemed to intrigue them most. The people lived so close to the earth. And "this was no romantic back-to-nature movement," said one girl. Everyone asked her, "Hadn't I ever seen rice grown? How do you grow rice in America, anyway?" She lamented: "My ignorance stunned them." And so she began to learn from the peasants, as did all the rest. The roots they were searching for were literally in the earth. As university students that was something they knew very little about.

One girl said: "I've never seen so many peasants in my life."

Said another, even the English word "country" did not seem right in describing the Chinese countryside; it was too "folksy" for a land where rural life is the way of life for ninety percent of the people, as it has always been.

In America, their great-grandparents and great-great-grandparents once had lived close to the earth. One hundred years ago they had shaped the soil, dug mines in the mountains, sculpted the beds of railroads out of the deserts, and sown the seeds of the West. But to these young people that was history they knew as little about as they did about their own earth. Some had never held the earth of a farm in their hands until they came to China. If they had, they might have known better where to search for their heritage.

In the village of her grandfather one girl searched for the house of her grandfather's father's father's father. She had been told it was made of seashells and mud. And she found it. The roof was gone, but "the seashell and mud walls are still standing," she said. "Although weathered by wind and rain and time, they are still standing—strong and thick and rich." The seashell house was more than an old ruin. For "young Chinese Americans searching for an identity and waiting to find and go back to their roots," said Marcia Chin, "this was my history. These were my roots."

Some of these villages of their ancestors had suffered from the ravages of wars and invasions. Some seemed to be much as they had been when their ancestors had left them generations ago to become Wah Q, the people who were simply known as "overseas Chinese."

These villages were labyrinths of dark and narrow winding alleys. It was as if they were built to bewilder any outsiders who wandered into them. Even a stranger from a nearby village would be hopelessly lost, much less visiting college students from

America. "We were led on a cobblestone path, through a maze of crooked alleys," said Barbara Jung. "The village did not seem to have any straight passages." It was an odd thing. One of the girls had asked her parents about these crooked paths. It was explained to her that the reasons for them were quite practical; if the paths and alleyways were straight, the *fung shui*, the good spirits, would pour out of the villages and might be lost. The crooked paths were ecological planning to keep these good spirits within the villages.

Such old superstitions had been discredited long ago, the girl thought. But the village paths were nonetheless still crooked as they led down to the paved modern roads.

If the old ways of rural living were changing to fit within the newer ways of life, they had not disappeared. There were schools and medical clinics in the villages. Some had light industry. "But, basically, the villagers' lives are bound to the land around which all else revolves," said Candy Chin. "Life is dictated by the growth cycle." Nature is still respected; and even with electricity and industry, "The atmosphere is strictly rural, so quiet that you can hear the insects buzz around."

The villages had gone from feudalism to socialism in one generation, but if their ancestors returned they would know their way around. One girl said the "feeling of continuity" was surprising to her. It made her understand the "little things" in Chinese customs in America that were "so exasperating, so comforting." And perhaps it offered some small insight into the survival and endurance of the Chinese character.

Still, living in a peasant village in a mud and stone house was not all that easy. One of the village grandmothers said the visitors were "like new brides on display."

Many of the villagers had found it difficult to believe that the young people came from the rich land of the Golden Mountain. They wore blue jeans and ordinary shirts. One girl remembered this conversation:

"Do you really think she's from the Golden Mountain? She's dressed so plainly, Hong Kong people look fancier than her."

"What's she doing here by herself, anyhow?"

"Maybe she left as a child. Do you think they speak Chinese in America?"

"America's full of foreign devils, of course, they speak foreign devil language."

"Do you think the Chinese there speak foreign devil language?"

"Are you crazy? Chinese always speak Chinese!"

Nonetheless, the young wanderers were welcomed warmly. Some of the villagers decided that their parents "must really love Chairman Mao" to let their children come so far by themselves. Oh, you have come such a long way, they said. Besides, "Chairman Mao tells us to serve the people," they explained. When one of the girls protested, "I am not the people," they just smiled broadly.

In the villages near Canton the people grew accustomed to unusual visitors. Forever, so it seemed, the Chinese were returning to China. If they could not come when they were alive, they came after they were dead. Shelley Wong said: "My mother died abroad and wanted her bones to be buried in China. She was a peasant woman and you know how the Chinese are. All Chinese, no matter how far they are from China, want to be buried back home."

An old man who had returned from a lifetime in New Zealand told the students from America, "We are all like homing pigeons."

Some of the villages had as many as one of every three families with relatives overseas. Their old houses were boarded up, their furniture guarded, waiting for the day when the Wah Q, the wandering overseas Chinese, returned.

But these young sojourners had not come in search of their families' furniture, nor their wealth. Nor were they seeking the peace of their grave to rest their bones. They were searching for their identity in the faces of their families.

On coming back to America they tried to understand why they had gone on so great a journey. And they wrote: "For those of us who are third, fourth, fifth generation born in America, living in white middle-class neighborhoods, our acculturation into white society has been gradual and continual"; but "we are in a marginal position, not fully part of white society because of our race, and no longer part of Chinatown." And so they journeyed to China, "to return to the home of our ancestors, to learn about our history, and to see how old China has changed." More than anything else they sought to find themselves, "to realize a new position in ourselves and our people in American society," they said. And "we have learned more about ourselves." Some found what they were looking for. And some found more than they were looking for.

Said Barbara Jung: "A young Asian American said to me, 'Guess why I applied to come to China. I can't even talk to my eighty-one-year-old grandmother. All my friends are white. You know, I'm here for all the wrong reasons. I've sure got a lot to learn.'"

Said Candy Chin: "I had gone back to look at the roots of history. When I left, I left feeling a member of the larger Chinese family, richer in knowledge about New China and the people, my people."

Said Jeanne Quan: "It is a time for many more family reunions. . . . Our villages welcome us back."

Once, before their pilgrimage, she was a *jook sing*, a "hollow bamboo," said Jeanne Quan. She was "fated, it seemed, to never grasp either culture, Chinese or American." Now she was no longer a *jook sing*. She was no longer the "hollow bamboo" she had been. In the earth of her ancestors in China she had discovered the sources of her roots in America.

EPILOGUE

ONCE THERE WAS a young man who went to sea. He sailed far away on a daring voyage into an unknown ocean. While he was sailing, a fearful storm arose and the waves smashed his boat against a mountain island. He was shipwrecked. In despair the young man believed he would be alone on the lost island forever. But he was not alone. There was a female bear living there who was beautiful and strong, but who had never had a mate. She was desperately lonely.

The Bear Woman lived high upon the mountain in a cave. One day she came down to the seashore and there she saw the poor young man. She fell in love with him.

She cradled him fondly in her arms and carried him up the mountain to her cave. There she held him captive. He tried to escape, but he could not because the Bear Woman was stronger than he. Besides, there was nowhere to escape to on the island. And so he accepted his fate. In her cave the Bear Woman made love to the young man. So they became husband and wife. And as the years passed, the Bear Woman gave birth to two children of her captive lover, whose name, it was said, was Wang p'ing.

As a wise bear, the Bear Woman knew that she could not trust a love that was held captive. When she left the cave to go hunting for food, she would close the entrance with great rocks. But even though she did not trust the young man, she did love him. And when she returned with the food she had found, she always offered the young man the first choice. In this way the Bear Woman treated the young man as her wife, and he treated her as his husband.

One day, while the Bear Woman was hunting, the young man found a way to escape from the cave with his children. He fled to the seashore. There he came upon a ship of Chinese seamen, and he begged them to rescue him and take him home to China. They agreed.

But as the ship set sail, the Bear Woman spied it. She jumped into the water and swam after it. In fear that he might be captured once again, the young man prayed to the goddess of the sea, T'ien hou, offering to build a beautiful temple in her honor if she would bring forth a strong wind that would blow the ship beyond the loving arms of the Bear Woman. And this happened. The goddess of the sea brought forth a strong wind, and the ship sailed safely away.

That is why near the village of Huimin there is a beautiful temple to the goddess of the sea. For Wang p'ing did as he promised. He was very grateful to be home. Not many young men who are captured by a Bear Woman ever come home again.

BIBLIOGRAPHY

The Assay of Sources

Even as I write this, my sense of history tells me that it is somewhat absurd to compile a list of books about a people who all but invented books. That seems to me as foolhardy as attempting to count the stars in heaven.

And so, why attempt it?

In our time we have become fascinated by lists. Have we not? They give us a sense of an ordered and knowable world, where everything is in place, neatly arranged and easily accessible, even though we know it is not.

So popular have lists become that several recent best sellers have consisted of nothing but lists. They are like a book of footnotes. In these compilations the matters listed become less important than the lists themselves; for ours is a age where knowledge is thought to be computed in a computer, and is institutionalized by the list of books in the bibliography at the end of a book.

It reminds me of the mischievous words of Ko-Ko, the Lord High Executioner in *The Mikado*, whose solution to all human problems was to merely compile a catalogue of them in his "little list":

> The task of filling up the blanks
> I'd rather leave to you.
> But it really doesn't matter
> whom you put upon the list,
> For they'd none of 'em be missed,
> they'd none of 'em be missed.

And yet, the list of books at the end of a book does serve a useful purpose; it is the writer's way of telling the reader how learned and erudite the writer is, how many more books the writer has read than the reader and therefore how scholarly the writer is, and more importantly how worldly and therefore truthful. The boasting that is inherent in a bibliography can be done ever so modestly. No word need be said; the list says it all.

In the empirical halls of academia the writer who is personal and subjective is considered suspect or, at the very least, unscientific. The writer can escape this stigma by compiling a bibliography that seems impersonal and wholly objective. By doing so the writer is in effect saying, Now, don't blame me entirely for whatever you may think foolish; I am merely quoting someone else. And this lends authority to whatever the writer has written, while absolving the writer from some of the responsibility for having written it. For it comfortably places the book among the list of books, one of many, within a tradition that is larger than itself, a part of a body of literature, like William Blake's eulogy for death itself as "a peece of the Continent, a part of the Maine."

So doing, the list of books that appears at the end of a book does wonders for a writer's psyche. It makes it feel less lonely and more secure. And, the writer may wrap the bibliography around the book like the toga of a learned Greek who, hiding his nakedness from the audience, dons a mantle of wisdom to clothe his human frailties and protect his vulnerability; even though everyone knows it is but the thinnest of all disguises, that it covers the body of a work with the fabric of history.

Who, after all, wishes to see the writer naked? Not the writer, surely.

And so, understandably, the list of books at the end of a book may be popular not only with readers and editors, teachers and students, but with the writer. In saying that, may I offer this list of books for what it's worth. Not too much, I would think.

It seems to me that the voices in this book speak clearly enough. But who am I to defy the scholarly fashion of our time. Here, then, is a "little list."

BOOK ONE: *The Chinese Who Discovered America*

In going far, far back into the past of the people and the land, what I sought was the sources of their spirit of adventure. What was it that inspired them to set forth across the oceans, to navigate into the unknown, to boldly go beyond the borders of their culture, to explore and settle strange lands and to become the seamen and merchants for half the world. No people in history have shown more daring in these things than the Chinese. But why?

Believing, as I do, that history is like energy and is difficult to destroy, that it merely takes new forms, I began as far back in time as I could reach. The origins of the Chinese spirit are ancient indeed.

The guides I chose were *The Archaeology of Ancient China* by Kwang-chih Chang (Yale University, 1968) and P. K. Cheng's *Prehistoric China* (Cambridge University, 1959 and 1966). Enlightening, as well, were the *Prehistory of China* by Judith Treistman (American Museum of Natural History, 1972) and *Ancient China: The Discoveries of the Post Liberation Archaeology* by William Watson (New York Graphic Society, 1974), which is most notable for its illustrations. Besides these there is the series published by the Foreign

Languages Press of Peking, which includes *New Archaeological Finds in China* (1974) and *The Cave Home of Peking Man* (1975).

And, of course, the personal and delightful musings in *Children of the Yellow Earth: Studies in Prehistoric China* by J. Gunnar Andersson (London, 1934; MIT Press, 1973). As the Swedish geologist of wide learning whose wandering curiosity helped lead to the discovery of Peking Man, Andersson offers the inspired insights of an amateur archaeologist.

In these books of bones I sought the neolithic origins of sailing and of seamanship. Riverbeds and coastal shores offered fertile waters for such development in China. But these waters have been little explored by modern scholars. Some clue to the ancient mariners may be found, however, in *Sail and Sweep in China* by G. R. Worcester (London, 1966) and in that lovely slender book on maritime adventure, *China and Britain* by Sir John T. Pratt (London, no date).

For a wider view of the seas and the explorers who sailed them one has to turn to *The Traditional Trade of Asia* by C. G. F. Simkin (Oxford University, 1968) and *The Southern Expansion of the Chinese People* by C. P. Fitzgerald (Praeger, 1972), as well as his companion volumes: *China: A Short Cultural History* (London, 1961) and *Hu-ch'uang, or Barbarian Beds* (London, 1964). Though to these books by Fitzgerald I must add a cautionary note: his English conceits at times equal his scholarship; a tendency to pontificate does cast a shadow upon the texts.

On the long journey thus begun I would suggest the reader travel further back to the *Sources of Chinese Tradition* edited by William T. De Bary, Wing-tsit Chan and Burton Watson (Columbia University, 1960), a two-volume encyclopedia of original texts from antiquity to the modern Marxists. So prepared, one may go, as I did, to *Folktales of China* edited by Wolfram Eberhard (University of Chicago, 1973), *Religion in Chinese Life* by C. K. Yang (University of California, 1970) and *Buddhism in China* by Kenneth Ch'en (Princeton University, 1964). To these, one of any number of the translations of Confucius may be added. Be it the James Legge translations of the *Confucian Analects, The Great Learning* and *The Doctrine of the Mean* (Oxford, 1893; Dover, 1971) or the very much gentler Lin Yutang translation for the Modern Library edition, *The Wisdom of Confucius* (Random House, 1938). If the Master is a bit too subtle for the reader to grasp, that modestly brief but wise essay *A Confucian Notebook* by Edward Herbert (Grove, 1960) may or may not help.

Of all the books on China, though, those of the Cambridge historian Joseph Needham all but stand alone. The many-volumed *Science and Civilisation in China* (Cambridge University, 1964–) is surely one of the great scholarly works of our century. If any work may be placed beside this, it would have to be *The Cambridge History of China* edited by John K. Fairbank and D. Twitchett (Cambridge University, in preparation), to be published in fourteen volumes and composed of the work of dozens of scholars.

Most valuable to me, as always, have been the histories written by the people themselves. Of these, *The Travels of Fa-hsien* (Cambridge University, 1923) translated by H. A. Giles was a good beginning. The expeditions of the Ming dynasty ships were celebrated by the equally famous *Ma Huan Ying-yai Sheng-lan*, translated as *The Overall Survey of the Oceans' Shores, 1433* by J. V. G. Mills (Cambridge University, for the Hakluyt Society, 1970), and commented upon in *Studies in the Social History of China and Southeast Asia* edited by Jerome Ch'en (Cambridge University, 1970). *Trade and Expansion in Han China* (206 B.C. to 200 A.D.) by Ying-shih Yu (University of California, 1967) set the stage for those later maritime histories.

Europeans at first viewed the early explorers from China somewhat egocentrically and obliquely. They wrote with a mixture of romanticism and superstition. Nonetheless, the accounts in the work of the Greek historian Herodotus do have a strange fascination. So do the accounts in the *Natural History* of Pliny the elder and in Ptolemy's *Geography* and Apuleius' *Golden Ass*. There is a detailed analysis of these texts in *Europe and China* by G. F. Hudson (London, 1931); and some of the texts are presented with refreshing commentaries in *Silks, Spices and Empire* by Owen and Eleanor Lattimore (Delacorte, 1968).

No less romantic were the visions of Cathay in the journals of the Europeans who traveled to the East. The numerous editions of the *Travels of Marco Polo*, *The Journey of William of Rubruck* (1255), *The Merchants' Handbook* (1340) and *The Travels of Sir John Mandeville* have been rendered in the framework of the history of the time. Nigel Cameron's magnificently rich account, *Barbarians and Mandarins: Thirteen Centuries of Western Travelers in China* (Walker, 1970), is a book valuable not only in itself but for its comprehensive bibliography, second only to that in Ying-shih Yu. Equally interesting are *Cathay and the Way Thither* edited by Sir Henry Yule (London, 1915) and *To Change China: Western Advisers in China: 1620–1960* by Jonathan Spence (Little, Brown, 1969).

The influence of the romance and reality of China on Western thought and culture is sumptuously chronicled, with gorgeous plates, in *Chinoiserie: The Vision of Cathay* by Hugh Honour (London, 1961; reprinted in USA, 1973). Mostly concerned with the arts and architecture, with forays into the realms of science and literature, this is one of the few full-length studies of the subject; there is a need for many more. A beginning has been made in *Asia in the Making of Europe* by D. Lach (University of Chicago, 1965) and *China and the West* edited by A. Dyson and B. Towers (Humanities

Press, 1970). John Fairbank touches briefly on the mutual effect of the East and West upon one another in the chapter "The Western Impact" in *The United States and China* (Viking, 1948), a theme he returns to in *China Perceived: Images and Policies of Chinese-American Relations* (Random House/ Vintage, 1976).

Even less has been written of the physical explorations of the Americas by the Chinese. There is the meagerest of hints in *From New Spain by Sea to the Californias* by Maurice Holmes (Arthur Clark, 1963) in the chapter "First Aliens in California," and in George Chapman's chapter "The Chinese along the Pacific Coast in Ancient Times" in his *History of California* (Macmillan, 1951). Further evidence of possible Chinese explorations appears in *Mexico South* by Miguel Covarrubias (Knopf, 1946) and in the somewhat sketchy *Pale Ink* by Henriette Mertz (Swallow, 1972), as well as in *Trans-Pacific Relations of Latin America* by Anita Bradley (Institute of Pacific Relations, 1942) and "Possible Transpacific Contact of the Coast of Ecuador" by E. Estrada, B. Meggers and C. Evans *(Science*, February, 1962).

None of these works are as challenging as the flamboyant *Inglorious Columbus: or, Evidence that Hwui Shan and a Party of Buddhist Monks from Afghanistan Discovered America* by Edward P. Vining (Appleton, 1885). Vining's controversial work was buttressed by two essay speeches given by Charles Walcott Brooks to the California Historical Society: "Origins of the Chinese Race, with an Inquiry into the Evidence of their American Origin," in 1876, and "Japanese Wrecks Stranded and Picked up Adrift in the North Pacific Ocean, Ethnologically Considered." Few modern scholars have taken up the works of Vining, and Brooks, except to cast doubt upon them. But few nowadays indulge in the intellectual adventurism of the nineteenth century.

There is a larger literature in the West of the West's exploration of China. In modern times one may reasonably begin with *The Political History of China, 1840–1928* by Li Chien-nung (Van Nostrand, 1956) and supplement it with *China: From the Opium Wars to the 1911 Revolution* by Chesneaux, Bastid and Bergere (Pantheon, 1976), if, that is, one makes allowance for a certain Gallic impressionism. A fine balance may be attained by reading *The Opium War through Chinese Eyes* by Arthur Waley (Stanford University, 1958) and *Strangers at the Gate* by Frederick Wakeman, Jr. (University of California, 1966). To these may be added *The China Reader* edited by Franz Schurmann and Orville Schell (Penquin Books, 1967), especially the volume on "Imperial China," as well as the series from the Foreign Languages Press in Peking: *The Opium War* and *The Taiping Revolution* (1976). A fuller history of the latter appeared in *The Taiping Revolutionary Movement* by Jen Yu-wen (Yale University, 1973), a study whose insights into the people of Kwangtung, even more than its historical information, I found most valuable.

And now some words should be said by way of summing up what cannot be summed up concerning books on Chinese life and culture.

There are many thousands of such books. Some that I would arbitrarily recommend for reasons of my own tastes and enjoyments might begin with the epic *The Dream of the Red Chamber (Hung Lou Meng)* by Tsao Hsueh-chin and Kao Ngoh, a novel I would place in the pantheon of literature beside *War and Peace, Don Quixote, Moby Dick* and the *Chilam Balam;* for without it no one can begin to understand modern China. I prefer the McHugh translation (Pantheon Books, 1958), but that is a most personal choice. To put *The Dream* in its proper historical perspective there are the brilliant *Brief History of Chinese Fiction* by Lu Hsun (Foreign Languages Press, Peking, 1964) and the poetically conceived *History of Chinese Literature* by Herbert A. Giles (Appleton, 1923; Grove Press, no date).

In the end it is the poets who may perhaps best illuminate what others have merely stated. And so I would recommend *Sunflower Splendor: Three Thousand Years of Chinese Poetry* edited by Wu-chi Liu and Irving Yucheng (Doubleday/Anchor, 1975), a massive and unwieldy but certainly an impressive book, the greatest collection of Chinese poetry in English in any single volume. Though, to be honest, I personally feel more at ease with intimate and slim books like *More Translations from the Chinese* by Arthur Waley (Knopf, 1937) and *One Hundred Poems from the Chinese* by Kenneth Rexroth (New Directions, 1971), if only because they fit, like flower petals, so perfectly in the palm of one's hand.

Book Two: *The Chinese Who Built America*

No one to my knowledge has written anything that comes within a shadow of portraying the epic feat of the Chinese in the building of the West. Perhaps it is still too soon after the event to expect anything but shallow journalism and narrow scholarship. After all, so often the greatest literature of an era is not written until years, decades and sometimes centuries later.

In any event, few of the books I here recommend do justice to the nobility of their theme. They are all merely beginnings.

The sweeping drama of the Chinese endeavors in America has been most enthusiastically and heroically portrayed in two books that are not really books at all. One is the tersely and factually written outline, *History of the Chinese in America* by H. M. Lai and P. P. Choy (Chinese American Studies Planning Group, San Francisco, 1973), and the second is *A History of the Chinese in California: A Syllabus* edited by Thomas Chinn, H. M. Lai and P. P. Choy (Chinese Historical Society of America, 1969). Although the first covers a greater span of history, the second is written in greater detail.

Some of the histories hinted at by these outlines are elaborated in *The Life: Influence and Role of the Chinese in the United States, 1776–1960* (Chinese Historical Society of America, 1976). These essays are taken from the proceedings of the Society's national conference held as a part of the Bicentennial celebration at the University of San Francisco.

The modern history of the Chinese in America begins with the Spanish conquest. Merchants and traders from China began arriving in the Americas in large numbers during the sixteenth and seventeenth centuries on the Spanish ships that crossed the Pacific, ships which the Chinese built. These voyages are described in *The Manila Galleons* by W. L. Schurz (Dutton, 1939). And further documentation is to be found in "The Chinese in Mexico City in 1635" by H. Dubs and R. S. Smith (*Far Eastern Quarterly*, Vol. I, 1941) and in "Notes on Chinese Abroad in the Late Ming and Early Manchu Periods" by C. R. Boxer (*T'ien Hsia Monthly*, Vol. 9, Aug.–Dec., 1939). The previously mentioned *Europe and China* by G. F. Hudson also discusses the voyages of these early traders.

Once the crossings of the oceans became common, the explorations in both directions became common too. These are noted in the *History of California* by H. H. Bancroft, Vol. VII (San Francisco, 1890). The "opening" of the Pacific Northwest by the Chinese frontiersmen and settlers is described in the *Voyages Made in the Years 1788 and 1789 from China to the North West Coast of America* by (Captain) John Meares (London, 1790). The story of the trade routes is expanded in *The Old China Trade* by Foster Rhea Dulles (New York, 1931), *Adventures to China: Americans in the Southern Seas* by James Kirker (Oxford, 1970), *The Rise of American Civilization* by Charles A. Beard and Mary R. Beard (Macmillan, 1927) and *Culture Contacts of the United States and China: 1784–1844* by George Danton (Columbia University, 1931).

The spirit of the people who later came from China to California is described judiciously by Mary Roberts Coolidge in *Chinese Immigration* (Holt, 1909; Arno, 1969). After all these years it is still to me the pre-eminent book on this subject, for it depicts the Chinese as integral to American history.

Fittingly, the history of the Chinese in America is to be found for the most part not in books about the Chinese as a minority but in books about American history. H. H. Bancroft's vast histories of the West are a good place to start the search, or one may begin with the chapter on "Asia and Africa in America" in the great historian's *Retrospection* (Bancroft, 1913). From there one may go to *Mining Camps: A Study in American Frontier Government* by C. Shinn (Scribners, 1884; Harper & Row, 1965), *The Mining Frontier* edited by M. Lewis (University of Oklahoma, 1967), *The Songs of the Gold Rush* edited by R. Dwyer and Richard E. Lingenfelter (University of California, 1965), *Pigtails and Gold Dust* by A. McLeod (Caxton, 1948), *Three Years in California* by J. D. Borthwick (Oakland, 1948), *Mining Frontier of the Far West* by R. W. Rodman (New York, 1963), *The Hard Rock Miners* by R. E. Lingenfelter (University of California, 1974) and many more.

And then there are the travelogues and accounts of personal journeys to the West, which often contain glimpses of the Chinese pioneers: *A California Tramp* by T. S. Kenderdine (Globe Printing House, Philadelphia, no date), *Across the Continent* by S. Bowles (Hurd and Houghton, 1866), *Across the Rocky Mountains* by L. Boyer (Wells-Sackett, 1878), *Beyond the Mississippi* by A. D. Richardson (Bliss, 1867), *California and the West* by L. V. Briggs (Wright and Potter, no date), *California* by M. P. Wilder (Wright and Potter, 1871) . . . The list goes on and on. It was my good fortune to discover many of these books, and many more, in the bibliography of Charles Dobie's *San Francisco Chinatown* (Appleton, 1936).

And for books on the Chinese railroadmen there are *The Great Iron Rail* by R. W. Howard (Putnam, 1962), *A Work of Giants: Building the First Transcontinental Railroad* by W. G. Griswold (McGraw-Hill, 1962), *The Chinese Role in Building the Central Pacific* (Southern Pacific, 1966), *The Big Four* by Oscar Lewis (New York, 1938) and *A World on Wheels* by B. H. Taylor (S. C. Griggs, 1874).

And for the agricultural endeavor of the Chinese there are *California: A Book for Travellers and Settlers* by C. Nordhoff (New York, 1873) and *Factories in the Field* by Carey McWilliams (Boston, 1959).

Though it deals only with California, by far the widest-ranging book on the subject of these pioneers of the West is *Chinese Labor in California* by Ping Chiu (University of Wisconsin, 1967). It is a singular book. Nothing equals it except perhaps the collection of historical reprints and comments contained in that thin *Bulletin* of the Chinese Historical Society of America, under the direction and editorship of Thomas Chinn, the dean of all Chinese American historians.

One valuable and interesting addition to this sparse literature is the California Historical Society's quarterly for Spring 1978. They compiled a special edition on "The Chinese in California," featuring an overview by Thomas Chinn and some worthwhile articles, including "Chinese Sailors" by Robert Schwendinger and the "Diplomacy of Discrimination" by David Anderson.

But for the most part, as I have said, the history of the Chinese pioneers and builders of the West is still hidden in an occasional sentence and obscure paragraph in the dusty and forgotten old books of the last century. These bits of the past can be found only by an endless search through these lost books. Having searched through hundreds, perhaps thousands, I know.

Sometimes I dream that the whole story is told in books hidden in an archive in China. It is a comforting and recurring dream.

Most recently there has been a renewed stream, small but steady, of books on the problems the Chinese pioneers to the West faced once they arrived—and on the attempt to eliminate them from American history. For reasons that would make an interesting book in itself many of these books portray not the achievement of the Chinese but the persecution they suffered, and many of them are written not from the point of view of the Chinese but from that of their persecutors.

Of these books, within the limitations of their approach, I was deeply impressed by *The Indispensable Enemy: Labor and the Anti-Chinese Movement in California* by Alexander Saxton (University of California, 1971), a sympathetic study of the human ironies involved in so inhuman a struggle. *The Unwelcome Immigrant: The American Image of the Chinese, 1785–1882* by Stuart Creighton Miller (University of California, 1969) is another excellent study, not of the Chinese pioneers but of their opponents. Less satisfying, to me, was *The Anti-Chinese Movement in California* by Elmer C. Sandmeyer (University of Illinois, 1973), its most striking feature being a magnificent bibliography. The *Chinese Americans* by Stanford M. Lyman (Random House, 1974) seems to be written in a social science shorthand. Most disturbing to me, however, was *The Bitter Struggle* by Gunther Barth (Harvard University, 1964), a work I found wanting in both the author's attitudes and research, with a too easy acceptance of historical stereotypes.

And speaking of stereotypes, there is a wonderful conglomeration of these in Reverend Arthur Smith's nineteenth-century tome *Chinese Characteristics* (reprinted by Kennikat Press, 1970). The good reverend's naïve racism may either amuse or anger, but in any case it is instructive. Perhaps as an antidote one may read the summary of prejudice and discrimination suffered by the Chinese in *Chink!* edited by Cheng-Tsu (World, 1972).

Naturally, the best histories will be those told by the people themselves. But they have just begun to tell them. One of these beginnings is *Longtime Californ'* by Victor G. and Betty de Barry Nee (Houghton Mifflin, 1974), a fine collection of first-person reminiscences and commentaries. Then there are local and regional collections, such as *Chinese Argonauts: An Anthology of Chinese Contributions to the Historical Development of Santa Clara County* edited by Gloria Sun Hom (Foothill Community College, 1971) and *Chinese American Workers: Past and Present* by the Getting Together Group of I Wor Kuen (San Francisco, no date). And those old photographs and prints in the *Chinese Working People in America* by the Wei Min She Labor Committee (United Front Press, San Francisco, no date) give a dramatic, if opinionated, panorama of the Chinese builders of the West.

Still, I feel, these books are but the barest of beginnings.

To me the story of the Chinese in the West is the proper subject for great novels, heroic dramas, epic poems and grandiose operas. As far as I know, these have not yet been written.

Book Three: *The Chinese Who Became America*

Many aspects of the life of the Chinese Americans have not been touched upon in this book. This is not an oversight. I feel that people have a right to privacy in their personal, intimate and familial affairs. And no one has a right to probe, examine, dissect, study, violate and expose in public what people do in private, unless the people, for reasons of their own, wish to make such things public; these things are sacred and inviolate; they are not "data" for social scientists and journalists.

And so there are many things I have not written about. In my travels in the Chinese communities I sensed a hesitancy and reticence among the people when it came to talking about their personal lives. They were polite but uncomfortable. So I decided early in the writing of this book not to try to pressure people by asking unwanted questions and receiving unwilling answers; for, long ago, I learned that when people talk reluctantly about themselves they disguise their thoughts with their words and often tell a stranger whatever they think he may wish to hear. It is a pantomime of illusions, which may create good poetry but makes for poor mythology.

There is little or nothing, therefore, said in this book about the intimacies of childhood fantasies and dreams of puberty, courtship and marriage, birth and death. Nor is much said of the soul and the psyche, of religion and rituals. Those who wish the titillations of these matters will have to seek elsewhere. And there are many, many books by others to quiet their curiosity. One of the best-known is *My Country and My People* by Lin Yutang (John Day, 1935). There are also *The Silent Traveler in San Francisco* by Chiang Lee (Norton, 1964), *Americans and Chinese* by Francis L. K. Hsu (Doubleday, 1970), *The Challenge to the American Dream: The Chinese in the United States,* also by Francis L. K. Hsu (Wadsworth, 1970), and *Mountain of Gold* by Betty Lee Sung (Macmillan, 1967). One of the books of this genre that gave me a quiet pleasure is *Ting: The Caldron, Chinese Art and Identity in San Francisco* edited by Nick Harvey, Loni Ding, Robert Johnson and Ling-chi Wang (Glide Urban Center Publications, 1970). It is one of the few Chinese American books that seem artistically original in design. While I have quite mixed feelings about it, I must certainly mention the brilliant and painful *The Woman Warrior: Memoirs of a Girlhood among the Ghosts* by Maxine Hong Kingston (Knopf, 1975).

Some of the most knowledgeable accounts of life in the Chinese towns and Chinatowns of America are not easily available to the general reader. These are the unpublished theses in university libraries. A few that I found of interest were these: *The Chinese Community in New York* by Chen Wen-Hsien (American University, 1941); *A History of the Chinese in Nevada* by Gary BeDunnah (University of Nevada, 1966); *Chinese Residents of Chicago* by Fan Ting-Chiu (University of Chicago, 1926); *The Growth and Decline of Chinese Communities in the Rocky Mountain Region* by Rose Hum Lee (University of Chicago, 1947); *The Detroit Chinese* by Emiko Ohnuke (University of Wisconsin, 1964); *The Chinese in Colorado* by Gerald Rudolph (University of Denver, 1964); *The Future of Chinatowns in the United States* by Chou Shao-Hwa (Columbia University, 1968).

And then there is the university thesis that became a book, *The Mississippi Chinese* by James Loewen (Harvard University, 1971).

Books about the Chinese communities abound. Most of those that have been written in a popular vein for a popular audience tend to be romantic quests in search of the "exotic" and vicarious; they should be read for what they are.

Of these books, my personal favorites are those that are unashamedly romantic, to a point of being parodies of themselves, such as *San Francisco Chinatown* by Charles Caldwell Dobie (Appleton-Century, 1936) and *Old Chinatown* by Arnold Genthe and Will Irwin, a nostalgic relic of lost myths (Mitchell Kennedy, 1913). No one will ever write books like these again. So, in their own way, they have become historic documents that reveal little about the Chinese Americans but reveal a great deal about how non-Chinese Americans viewed these, their pioneer ancestors from China. It is interesting to look at the dark side of the moon.

Day-to-day news of life in modern Chinese communities is not easy to obtain in English. But it is more and more available. In San Francisco there is the weekly *San Francisco Journal*, a "third world" publication of the young activists, and in New York there is the older *China News*. There have also been a number of stimulating and informative magazines published by the younger generation in recent years: the *Asian American Review* (Department of Ethnic Studies, University of California, Berkeley), the *Amerasia Journal* (Asian American Studies Center, University of California, Los Angeles) and the handsome and creative, but unfortunately defunct, *Bridge* (Basement Workshop, New York), copies of which can still be found in some Chinese American bookstores.

For myself, in seeking a human and passionate understanding of these founding fathers and mothers of the American spirit, I prefer to turn to the poets, to the dramatists, to the writers of legends. There have been, fortunately, a number of books by what are now called "Asian American" authors: *The*

Asian American Heritage: An Anthology of Prose and Poetry edited by David Hsin-Fu Wand (Washington Square Press, 1974), which has a collection of the works of Diana Chang, David Rafael Wang, Wing Tee Lum, among others; *The Asian American* edited by Norris Huntley, Jr. (Pacific Coast Branch, American Historical Association, 1976); *Asian American Authors* edited by Kai-yu Hsu and Helen Palubinakas (Houghton Mifflin, 1972), which features excerpts from Frank Chin's "Food for All His Dead" and Diana Chang's "Frontiers of Love"; *Aiiieeeee!: An Anthology of Asian American Writers* edited by Frank Chin, Jeffrey Paul Chan, Lawson Fusao Inada, Shawn Hsu Wong (Doubleday, 1975), notable for its publication of an excerpt of Frank Chin's "The Chickencoop Chinaman"; *Roots: An Asian American Reader* edited by Franklin Odo, Amy Tachiki, Eddie Wong and Buck Wong (Asian American Studies Center, University of California, Los Angeles, 1971); and the poetic and poignant tribute by the young to the old men of San Francisco's Chinatown, *We Won't Move* (Asian American Writers Workshop, San Francisco, no date), a modest but moving volume of photographs and poetry.

That there are no serious collections of the works of writers like Frank Chin may indicate a certain faddishness in these publications. And that, in turn, may be a result of the continuing failure to recognize these writers as important contributors to our literature.

Nonetheless, to me the deepest insights into the joys and pains of Chinese American life are to be found in these writers. Though I hope it goes beyond my personal favorites, my list of books is of course a personal one; it can be no other. And, yet, to the reader who is unfamiliar with the depth and breadth of Chinese American literature, the list may open his or her closed eyes a little.

These, then, are a few of the books I would suggest: *Number One Son* by Monfoon Leong (East/West Publishing Company, 1975), most of all his story of "Precious Jade"; *Father and Glorious Descendant* by Pardee Lowe (Little, Brown, 1943); *Fifth Chinese Daughter* by Jade Snow Wong (Harper & Row, 1945); *Eat a Bowl of Tea* by Louis Chu (Lyle Stuart, 1961); *Frontiers of Love* by Diana Chang (Random House, 1956); and Chang's other novels— *A Woman of Thirty, A Passion for Life* and *The Only Game in Town*. And there is that remarkable novel *China Red* by H. T. Tsiang (Liberal Press, 1931), which at the time of its publication was undoubtedly praised and condemned as little more than another "proletarian" novel, but which in retrospect seems a visionary exultation of those daring and bold spirits that shaped the psyches of both the old and new pioneers who came from China and helped shape America in their own image. For in his book Tsiang created one of the first Chinese American heroes in modern literature.

And so we come in the end to the beginning, and to the rites of passage toward a rediscovery and a renewal of their psyches, like the Chinese Americans described in *Going Back*, a privately printed account of the voyage of some young Californians of Chinese ancestry who a few years ago "returned" across the sea to the land of their forebears, a land they had never known.

Going Back was the basis for the last chapter of this book. It seemed to me to be somehow right that this little book had no publication date and had no address, in America.

Nothing but a blank page.

INDEX